Authors Lesley Reynolds (left) and Liesbeth Leatherbarrow (right). Photo Robin Rice.

❧

Liesbeth Leatherbarrow and Lesley Reynolds are freelance writers and enthusiastic gardeners with many years of experience coaxing plants to grow in the challenging prairie climate. Their gardening philosophy includes more than a love of plants, encompassing also a great passion for nature and deep respect for the prairie environment. Based in Calgary, Alberta, they are regular contributors to several publications, including *Calgary Gardening*, *The Gardener for the Prairies*, and the *Calgary Herald*, and have also written for *Gardens West*. In addition, they are contributors to *The Calgary Gardener* and co-authors of *The Calgary Gardener, Volume Two: Beyond the Basics.*

101
BEST PLANTS
FOR THE PRAIRIES

Liesbeth Leatherbarrow
and Lesley Reynolds

FIFTH
HOUSE
PUBLISHERS

Front cover image by John Luckhurst / GDL
Cover and interior design by John Luckhurst / GDL
Illustrations courtesy the Perennial Plant Association

The publisher gratefully acknowledges the support of The Canada
Council for the Arts and the Department of Canadian Heritage.

THE CANADA COUNCIL | LE CONSEIL DES ARTS
FOR THE ARTS | DU CANADA
SINCE 1957 | DEPUIS 1957

We acknowledge the financial support of the Government of Canada
through the Book Publishing Industry Development Program for our
publishing activities.

Printed in Canada.

01 02 03 / 5 4 3

Canadian Cataloguing in Publication Data
Leatherbarrow, Liesbeth.
101 best plants for the prairies

Includes bibliographical references and index.
ISBN 1-894004-30-2

1. Gardening—Prairie Provinces. 2. Gardening—
Great Plains. I. Reynolds, Lesley. II. Title.
III. Title: One hundred and one best plants for the prairies.
SB453.3.C2L42 1999 635.9'09712 C99-911056-X

Published in Canada by
Fifth House Ltd.
1511 - 1800 - 4th Street S.W.
Calgary, Alberta, Canada
T2S 2S5

Published in the U.S. by Fitzhenry & Whiteside
121 Harvard Ave.
Suite 2
Allston, Massachusetts
02134

Table of Contents

Foreword

All gardeners need a good guide to which plants grow best in their region, and this one fits the bill perfectly. Authors Liesbeth Leatherbarrow and Lesley Reynolds are both accomplished gardeners, something I can vouch for, having seen their gardens in full glory. In my experience, I've found it's very important to take advice from people who do, not just from people who do good research.

This book is a wonderful mix of annuals, perennials, and woody plants that are hardy, not just to the prairies but anywhere the temperatures are extreme and the gardener's imagination needs a little jolt. The authors not only tell you about their favorite plants, but also how to maintain them and what to put them with.

I love reading about the lore and history of plants and there's plenty of that here. Somehow, knowing where a plant comes from, who discovered it, and who brought it into the garden adds another layer of texture to any landscape.

My favorite part of this book is the Collectors' Choice section for each plant. It stretches the palette and choices beyond the good solid selections in the main plant list. A novice gardener could do no better than to take this book to the nursery and start shopping. The lively mix suggested here would look well in a small city garden or in a large suburban one.

I will use this book with pleasure, not only for its no-nonsense, straightforward writing style, but even more for the great good sense and information that come from both the heart and the garden.

Marjorie Harris
July 1999

Acknowledgements

The writing of this book about great plants for prairie gardens was, for both of us, a wonderful and satisfying experience this past winter. While prairie winds howled and blizzards raged, we indulged in the luxury of dreaming and writing about the many marvelous annuals, perennials, shrubs, and trees that form the backbone of prairie gardens.

We'd like to take this opportunity to acknowledge the thoughtful responses that we received from the prairie gardeners who completed our initial survey about which plants are reliable performers in their gardens. Their input, based on personal experience, was invaluable when it came to drawing up the list of plants to feature in this book. We also appreciated the many friendly letters that accompanied the surveys; they were always encouraging and confirmed that our project was, indeed, a worthwhile undertaking.

The same generosity of spirit was demonstrated by the gardeners who kindly shared with us their insights on the joys of growing specific plants. Their words of wisdom have become the quotes that appear with each entry in the book. What better way to reach out to gardeners than with the thoughts, knowledge, and enthusiasm of fellow gardeners?

We would like to extend our heartfelt thanks to the following gardening experts who took time from busy lives to answer our questions, read our manuscript, and make helpful, technical suggestions. Without a doubt, the book is much improved as a result of their efforts. Their moral support was also exceptional, and for this we are grateful.

Chris Biesheuvel (Horticultural Development Manager, A. E. McKenzie Co. Inc., Brandon), Rick Durand (Jeffries Nurseries, Portage la Prairie), Ken Girard (Greenhouse Manager, Department of Biological Sciences, University of Calgary, Calgary), Paul Hamer (The Saskatoon Farm, DeWinton), Dr. Dale Herman (North Dakota State University, Fargo), Olivia Johns (Horticulturist, Calgary Zoo and Botanical Gardens, Calgary), Michael Hickman (Associate Director, The University of Alberta Devonian Botanical Gardens, Devon), Kevin Lee (KRL Tree Services, Calgary), Ruth Staal (Golden Acre Garden Sentre, Calgary), Edzard Teubert (Fuzei Gardens, Calgary), Anne Vale (Vale's Greenhouse, Black Diamond).

As always, it has been a pleasure to work with the folks at Fifth House. Thanks are due to Fraser Seely, Charlene Dobmeier, Angela Bond, and Catherine Radimer for their patience, sound advice, reliable support, and flexible deadlines. Geri Rowlatt, copy editor extraordinaire, also worked her usual magic on our manuscript. Thanks, Geri.

Last, but definitely not least, we thank Camille, Kate, Vic, and Bob for their enduring patience and support. Our families seem to realize even better than we do that any planned task takes at least twice as long as we bargained for and that a "more relaxing next week" is as unlikely as predictable weather on the prairies. For this depth of understanding, we give them our love and gratitude.

Introduction

A Prairie Plant List

Prairie gardeners are a tough and determined group renowned for creating splendid gardens in a region infamous for its formidable climate. The challenges of the northern temperate prairies of Canada and the United States relate to both climate and soils. It is a land of extremes: winter temperatures may dip below -40° C (-40° F), and scorching summers devoid of moisture are not unusual. Even when temperatures are moderate, the wind can be an unrelenting adversary in these open lands.

Over the years these gardeners have discovered that peonies and petunias, potentilla and poplars, and a host of other old standbys are steadfast friends. Fortunately, the list of suitable prairie plants is ever expanding, and it is the goal of this book to offer beautiful and reliable choices to new prairie gardeners as well as to those with many years of experience who would like a more varied garden palette.

If you look at the people around you at your local garden center, you'll notice that there are as many plant-shopping styles as there are gardening styles. At one end of the continuum are the gardeners who have it figured out—they know exactly what they want and what will do well for them. They arrive with list in hand and stick to it, leaving with no more but no less than they had planned. At the other end of the spectrum are those who arrive completely unprepared—they shop with gay abandon, loading up their carts to overflowing with familiar and unfamiliar plants, not even

sure whether or not everything will fit into existing flower beds. But still, they leave well satisfied, not bothered by uncertainty and knowing that everything always works out in the end.

Somewhere between these two extremes is a large group of gardeners, often beginners, who are still somewhat confused by the plant shopping experience. For them, making choices in garden centers with seemingly never-ending aisles of mysterious plants can be overwhelming. They know that some plants work better than others in our difficult environment, but are not yet sure which. Many of these gardeners admit that a shopping list prepared by someone else would take the guesswork out of choosing, give them confidence that they are on the right track, and assist them in making their own choices in the future. This book is just such a shopping list, relying heavily on input

from experienced gardeners across the prairies. The list includes annuals, perennials, bulbs, vines, groundcovers, shrubs, and trees—all of the ingredients for a lovely garden.

For each plant on our list we have provided very specific cultivar recommendations. For example, rather than just suggesting garden phlox, *Phlox paniculata*, as a good choice for the garden, we recommend the cultivar 'David', a white phlox that is particularly mildew resistant. Each plant is described in detail, followed by growing tips, suggestions on plant placement, and a list of suitable companion plants.

Each entry in the book also includes a section called Collectors' Choice, an "If you liked this, then why not try these?" kind of a list. So, using phlox as an exam-

Plant Propagation

Several methods of plant propagation are mentioned in plant entries. Annuals are easily grown from seed, but many perennials are more difficult, having evolved complicated germination strategies to help ensure that new seedlings will have the best chance of survival. Gardeners should consult a seed-starting manual for specific directions for growing individual perennials from seed.

Dividing perennials: Split plants into several sections, each with vigorous young growing points; discard older and less-productive portions. A few bulbous plants, such as lilies and species tulips, increase by small bulblets that may be dug up and replanted in late summer. As a general rule of thumb, divide spring-blooming plants in summer when flowering has finished, and late summer-blooming plants in the spring. This ensures that you will not miss a season of bloom.

Layering: Some perennials have self-rooting runners along which small plantlets grow. Make a slight cut in the stem between the new plant and the parent plant, anchor it to the ground, and then cover it with a small amount of soil.

Stem tip cuttings: Cut off the top of a stem with at least three sets of leaves, cutting just below a leaf node. Trim the leaves from the bottom half of the cutting and dip the cut end in rooting hormone powder. Insert it into a sterile growing medium, water, and cover with a plastic bag. Keep cuttings moist; when they show new growth they have started to root, and the plastic may be removed for longer periods each day to accustom them to lower humidity.

Basal cuttings are shoots that include a small portion of the crown of the plant and are taken from the base of the plant in spring.

Root cuttings are obtained by digging a hole next to the plant you wish to propagate, or by digging up the entire plant if it needs to be moved or divided. Sever a 5- to 8-cm (2- to 3- in.) portion of a large root, cutting it straight across at the top, and diagonally at the bottom. Place the cuttings in a growing medium slanted end down with the tops level with or just below the surface. Water well and keep moist.

ple again, after describing all you need to know about *Phlox paniculata* 'David', in Collectors' Choice we give brief descriptions of moss phlox and woodland phlox, two other phloxes that do well in prairie gardens. We also describe a plant that looks like phlox but blooms much earlier in the season—sweet rocket or *Hesperis matronalis*. Collectors' Choice will appeal to the more experienced gardener; in effect, it actually expands the list of 101 best plants into a list of several hundred.

Climate Zones

The plants we recommend are hardy across the prairies, where climate zones range from Zone 2 to Zone 4. However, gardeners should never regard zone ratings as absolutes. Much is dependent upon garden microclimates, that is, the specific growing conditions of your little piece of paradise. Elevation, buildings and other structures, and mature trees all serve to alter, and often moderate, the climate within a garden.

Different growers or plant retailers rate plants differently and, given the conditions they prefer, many plants will thrive at least one zone below their recommended level. For this reason some Zone 4 plants that have been successfully grown in many prairie locations are included in Collectors' Choice to tempt adventurous gardeners.

Botanical Names

In this book, plants are listed by botanical and common names. Although common names vary from country to country, or even from region to region within a country, botanical names are a universal means of plant identification, and are the best guarantee that you are getting the plant you want. Botanical names consist of a genus, a grouping of closely related but distinct species (spp.), and a species, a particular member of a genus that will breed true with others of its kind. Species are sometimes, but not always, sub-classified into subspecies (subsp.) and varieties (var.)—plants with naturally occurring distinctive features, such as color, that are not sufficiently distinct to be classified as a separate species. Cultivars refer to cultivated varieties bred from superior plants. Genus names are italicized and capitalized; species and variety names are written in lower case italics. Cultivar names are capitalized, but never italicized, and appear in single quotation marks. For example, the Oriental poppy cultivar 'Prince of Orange' is named *Papaver orientale* 'Prince of Orange'; *Papaver somniferum paeoniflorum* is a peony-flowered variety of the opium poppy.

Hybrids, indicated by an x sign, as in *Geranium* x *magnificum*, are crosses between two or more species or even between genera of plants. They seldom come true from seed and many are sterile. First generation (F_1) hybrids are consistent in size, color, and vigor; second generation (F_2) hybrids are extremely variable and seldom as vigorous as their parents.

Tips to Make the Most of the 101 Best Plants

Each plant featured in this book offers unique qualities that are sure to please even the most discriminating prairie gardeners. But before making your choices from the following pages, here are a few fundamental principles to keep in mind.

§ Design your garden on paper before you plant, considering carefully the mature size of trees and shrubs, light and shade patterns, and garden micro-climates.

§ Group plants with similar soil, water, and light requirements. Plant low-maintenance, drought-tolerant plants together in an area that you can ignore while you tend to those that need more regular watering or fertilizing.

§ A successful garden will appeal to all the senses. Color and texture are the tools gardeners most often use to create lovely garden compositions, but gardens can be much more than pretty pictures. Indulge yourself with fragrant blossoms, herbs or fruit for the palate, the tactile pleasures offered by smooth bark and silky seed heads, the whisper of leaves, and the rustle of grasses.

§ Choose plants with varying bloom times to ensure that there is something happening in your garden from spring to fall. Recording bloom times and studying pictures taken at one- or two-week intervals throughout the growing season will help you to eliminate any gaps in flowering succession.

§ Include trees and shrubs that offer all-season interest. Evergreens are, of course, essential to the winter garden, but many other woody ornamentals recommended in this book are also

Growing Spring-Flowering Bulbs

Plant spring-flowering bulbs in groups or even in lavish drifts for best effect. Blocks of color are more effective than individual flowers dotted here and there in the garden.

Although most spring-flowering bulbs prefer a sunny location, avoid planting them in extremely warm areas, such as near the foundations on the south side of a building. Chinooks or unseasonably mild late-winter days can cause bulbs planted in such spots to sprout prematurely, only to have the leaves frozen when temperatures plummet.

Add a bit of bone meal to the soil in the planting hole or a fertilizer high in potassium and phosphorus. Plant bulbs nose end up at a depth of at least three times the bulb height. Water at planting time, throughout the fall and spring, and until the leaves die back completely. Mark the spot where your bulbs are planted (so you don't dig them up by mistake), then mulch them generously for the winter to conserve moisture and keep the ground from thawing too early.

Fertilize bulbs when foliage emerges in the spring. Once blooming has finished, cut off old flower heads and allow the foliage to die down before removing it. Browning foliage may be disguised with strategic plantings of perennials and shrubs that leaf out as the bulbs are finishing their spring show, or with annuals.

year-round winners, offering fiery fall foliage, beautiful bark color and texture, and spring blossoms.

Plant at a Glance

Each entry contains a summary that enables readers to quickly review plant characteristics and cultural requirements. Plants are classified by type: bulb, annual, perennial, groundcover, vine, shrub, or tree. Where applicable, plants are noted as either deciduous or evergreen.

Plant height and width measurements represent the expected rate of growth provided the plant's cultural requirements are met. These dimensions will vary from garden to garden, depending on light, soil, and microclimate.

Soil preferences are classified as poor, average, or fertile. Few prairie soils are naturally fertile or rich in organic matter; many locations have high clay content and may be on the alkaline side. We recommend incorporating compost, peat moss, or well-rotted manure to improve soil fertility and tilth. This will also aid in moderating soil alkalinity. In addition, gypsum (calcium sulphate) may also be added to help lighten clay soils.

We have also noted moisture and drainage requirements where they are important to a plant's well-being. Some plants require consistently moist soil; in these cases, evaporation can be minimized by using a 5- to 10-cm (2- to 4-in.) layer of organic mulch. Shredded leaves, compost, or wood chips all work well. Most plants prefer well drained soils; the addition of organic matter to clay soils will also help improve drainage. In some cases it may be necessary to dig in a quantity of coarse sand.

Light requirements are indicated as full sun (over eight hours of direct sun per day), part sun (four to eight hours of direct sun per day), light shade (less than four hours of direct sun per day or bright filtered light), and full shade (no direct or filtered sunlight).

Flowering times are classified as spring (April to May), early summer (June to mid-July), mid-summer (mid-July to mid-August), late summer (mid-August to mid-September), and fall (mid-September to hard frost).

Acer tataricum var. *ginnala*

(*ay*-ser tah-*tahr*-ih-cum var. jin-*a*-lah)

Amur maple, Ginnala maple

The large, three-lobed leaves of the graceful sugar maple (*Acer saccharum*) have long been a beloved Canadian symbol, and few sights are more spectacular than the blazing red autumn foliage of these lovely trees. However, although some prairie gardeners have grown sugar maples successfully in sheltered locations, they are not reliably hardy in our harsh climate. Fortunately, there are other maples that are both ornamental and hardy, such as *Acer tataricum* var. *ginnala*, a native of China, Siberia, and Japan.

Tapping maples for their sweet sap is not a North American innovation—the practice originated in China, home to over 100 maple species. The generic name *Acer* comes from the Latin term for "sharp" or "pointed." This may be descriptive of the leaf shape, or a reference to the Roman use of hard maple wood for spear hafts.

Portrait

Acer tataricum var. *ginnala*, the Amur maple (also sold as *A. ginnala*), is among the best prairie-hardy trees for brilliant orange or red fall foliage color. It may be grown as a large, multi-stemmed, upright shrub or as a single-trunked small tree. The attractive gray bark is a notable feature year-round. Amur maples have glossy, three-lobed leaves with red leaf veins and petioles (leaf stalks). Scented, greenish white flowers appear in spring that by fall have transformed into bright red, winged, paired seed pods, called samaras or keys.

Several cultivars of *Acer tataricum* var. *ginnala* are available; 'Flame', 'Redwing', and 'Embers' have outstanding autumn color. Shorter varieties, ideal for hedges, include 'Durand Dwarf', 'Bailey's Compact', and 'Compactum'.

Where to Grow

Amur maple is a little tree with a big impact, which makes it a perfect specimen tree for small gardens. Use it as a centerpiece in a shrub bed, or plant several in a row as a hedge or screen.

How to Grow

Amur maple is tough, vigorous, and easy to grow, although it may suffer some winter kill in severe winters. Plant it in well-drained soil of average fertility, in full or part sun; the best fall color is achieved in a sunny location. Once established, this tree is drought tolerant.

Although the Amur maple may be

Plant at a Glance

TYPE: deciduous tree
HEIGHT: 6 m (20 ft.)
WIDTH: 4.5 m (15 ft.)
SOIL: average, well drained
LIGHT: full to part sun
FLOWERING TIME: spring

PHOTO – PAGE 73

heavily pruned to shape it into a tree form, like all members of its genus, it will "bleed" sap if pruned too early in the year. Wait until the new leaves have fully emerged before undertaking any pruning.

Amur maples are susceptible to lime-induced chlorosis, which occurs when iron is unavailable to plants because of high soil pH. The symptoms of this condition are pale leaves with darker green veining. Treat affected plants with chelated iron, either in a foliar spray or added to the soil. The addition of sulphur or epsom salts ($MgSO_4$) will help lower the soil pH, as will peat moss and other organic material.

Perfect Partners
Create an attractive grouping by planting Amur maple with 'Dart's Gold' ninebark, red osier dogwood (*Cornus sericea*), 'Blizzard' mock orange (*Philadelphus lewisii*), and American highbush cranberry (*Viburnum trilobum*). Evergreens provide a wonderful contrast to the Amur maple's fiery fall colors. Choose dwarf cultivars that will not overwhelm the maple: Scotch pine, *Pinus sylvestris* 'Nana'; Colorado blue spruce, *Picea pungens* f. *glauca* 'Globosa' and 'Pendula'; juniper, *Juniperus scopulorum* 'Cologreen' and 'Tolleson's Weeping'.

Collectors' Choice
Try these other prairie-hardy maples, keeping in mind their mature size when choosing a location.

- *Acer negundo* (12 m, 40 ft.), commonly called Manitoba maple or box elder, is a fast-growing prairie native. This hardy tree thrives in full sun, and tolerates a wide range of soil conditions. It is an ideal tree for large lots or rural settings, and can even be tapped for sap. However, these versatile trees have a few nasty habits: the pollen can cause allergic reactions, the winged seed pods

are messy, the seedlings are annoying, and the trees are susceptible to aphids and leafhoppers. Manitoba maple cultivars include 'Baron', a seedless male clone developed in Morden, Manitoba; 'Sensation', with bright red fall color; and 'Kelly's Gold', which produces golden new foliage while older leaves are green.

- *Acer saccharinum* 'Silver Cloud' (18 m, 60 ft.), developed in Manitoba, is the hardiest silver maple for prairie growing conditions. The leaves are light green above, with silvery undersides. An excellent shade tree for large spaces, it has an upright and symmetrical crown form. Plant it in well-drained soil and provide adequate moisture.

- *Acer tataricum* (5 m, 16 ft.), tatarian maple, may be grown as a single- or multi-trunked tree. It has a pleasingly shaped low, open canopy. Bright red leaf petioles, red winged fruit, and orange or yellow fall color characterize this eye-catching maple. Plant it in fertile soil, in a sunny location.

> "*Amur maple is definitely the hardiest maple for the northern prairie region. It's one of our few trees with scarlet red fall color—a mark of distinction on the prairies.*"
>
> DALE HERMAN
> FARGO, NORTH DAKOTA

Achillea Galaxy Series
(ah-*kill*-ee-ah)

Yarrow, Milfoil

Renowned in ancient myth and medieval lore, yarrow has served mankind as a medicinal herb for untold centuries. According to legend, the Greek hero Achilles used yarrow to heal the wounds of his soldiers during the Trojan War, hence, the generic name *Achillea*. Many folk names testify to the herb's efficacy as a styptic—a substance to stop bleeding—nosebleed, staunchweed, soldier's woundwort, knight's milfoil, and carpenter's herb. Yarrow was also credited with curing many other ills, including toothache, digestive disorders, and colds.

In Britain, yarrow was sacred to the Druids, who used it to predict weather; the Chinese used it to foretell the future. Yarrow also reputedly had powers as a love oracle, and protected against evil spirits. Obviously a plant that belonged in every herb garden, yarrow was even said to strengthen the aromatic oils of other herbs.

It is now possible for prairie gardeners to grow a veritable rainbow of yarrows. Beneficial as well as beautiful, the flat flower heads (called corymbs) attract butterflies, predatory wasps, and other helpful garden insects. Fortunately, one creature yarrow does not attract is deer, who do not find the aromatic foliage to their taste.

Portrait
The Galaxy Series was bred in Germany and introduced by Blooms of Bressingham in England. The result of crosses between *Achillea millefolium* and *A.* x 'Taygetea', this series offers many more colors, stronger stems, and larger flower heads than older varieties of common yarrow. Although colors will fade as the flowers mature, plants continue to bloom all summer, providing superb cut flowers for both fresh and dried arrangements.

Galaxy Series cultivars range from 60 to 90 cm (24 to 36 in.) in height. They include 'Appleblossom' (light pink), 'Heidi' (clear pink), 'The Beacon' (red), 'Great Expectations' or 'Hope' (buff yellow), 'Orange Queen' (salmon), 'Salmon Beauty' (salmon pink), 'Paprika' (bright red), 'Snow Taler' (white), and 'Weser River Sandstone' (rose pink). Some of these cultivars may also be sold under their German names.

Where to Grow
Galaxy Series yarrows are outstanding ornamental perennials for hot, sunny borders, large rock gardens, and cutting gardens.

Plant at a Glance

TYPE: perennial
HEIGHT: 60 to 90 cm (24 to 36 in.)
WIDTH: 60 cm (24 in.)
SOIL: average, well drained
LIGHT: full sun
FLOWERING TIME: early summer to fall

PHOTO – PAGE 73

How to Grow

Galaxy Series cultivars prefer full sun and average, well-drained soil. Plants may be susceptible to root rot if drainage is poor. Although adequate water is essential until plants are established, mature specimens are tolerant of hot, dry weather. Like all yarrows, these require little fertilizing; in fact, too much nitrogen will cause the plants to become floppy.

Make sure to deadhead faded flowers so the plants will continue to bloom all summer. Yarrows do have a tendency to spread—some worse than others—but most cultivars, including those in the Galaxy Series, can be kept in check by dividing plants every three or four years, or more often if necessary. These cultivars may also be propagated by basal or stem cuttings.

Perfect Partners

The long blooming period of the Galaxy Series yarrows allows them to be combined with a host of hardy perennials. As summer approaches its climax, daylilies (*Hemerocallis* spp.), irises, campanula, and spiky blue veronica and nepeta bring out the best in these enduring plants. Ornamental grasses, garden phlox, Shasta daisies (*Leucanthemum* x *superbum*), coreopsis, and helenium are compatible late-summer companions.

Collectors' Choice

Pick a posy of yarrows from the many trouble-free varieties that love the warm, dry prairie summers.

- *Achillea* 'Anthea' (90 cm, 36 in.) is an upright, long-blooming hybrid with gray-green foliage and primrose yellow flowers that fade to creamy yellow.
- *Achillea* 'Coronation Gold' (90 cm, 36 in.) produces mustard yellow flowers all summer, and is one of the best yarrows for dried flower production.

- *Achillea filipendulina* (1.2 m, 4 ft.), also called fernleaf yarrow, has deeply divided leaves and golden yellow blooms; 'Gold Plate' is the best-known cultivar.
- *Achillea millefolium* (60 cm, 24 in.), common yarrow, offers the widest color range. Best cultivars include 'Summer Pastels', a mixture of shades of pink, rose, red, apricot, cream, beige, purple, and white; 'Lavender Lady' (pastel lavender); 'Red Beauty' (crimson red); and 'Terra Cotta' (deep orange).
- *Achillea* 'Moonshine' (60 cm, 24 in.) is a compact, non-invasive hybrid with silvery gray foliage and sulphur yellow flowers. It is an excellent choice for small gardens and will bloom all summer.
- *Achillea tomentosa* (20 cm, 8 in.), woolly yarrow, forms mats of soft, finely cut gray-green foliage; yellow flowers appear in June and July. Plant this heat-loving and drought tolerant yarrow as a groundcover or tuck it into a rock garden. 'Aurea' (golden yellow) and 'King Edward VIII' (pale yellow) are recommended cultivars.

Aconitum 'Bressingham Spire'
(ahk-oh-*neye*-tum)

Monkshood, Wolf's bane

Just when you think you've seen the last of summer's vibrant blue flowers fade, along comes monkshood, with its slender spires of unique hooded blossoms that span a range of hues from azure to indigo. Monkshood, a staple of monastery and cottage gardens since the thirteenth century, presents a vivid contrast in late-summer borders where perennials with yellow or purple, daisylike blossoms usually preside.

All parts of monkshood are poisonous so it is not surprising that its history is dotted with sinister tales. Legend has it that the very first monkshoods sprouted from saliva dripping from the maw of Cerberus, a hideous three-headed guard dog that stood sentinel at the gates of Hades.

In medieval times, the plant's poisons were used in evil ways. They were often mixed with bait to destroy wolves and badgers, hence, the common name wolf's bane. Armies were decimated by drinking water from wells tainted with monkshood; even wives and husbands occasionally came to a sorry end, thanks to the powers of this plant.

Regardless of its shady reputation, monkshood has great ornamental value and is well suited for perennial and mixed borders on the prairies.

Portrait

'Bressingham Spire' is an indispensable cross between a bicolored *Aconitum* x *cammarum* and 'Newry Blue'. It produces mounds of durable, shiny, deeply cut foliage and showy spikes of vivid violet-blue flowers. Individual blossoms are striking; they consist of three rounded, lower petals and an upper hoodlike structure very reminiscent of a monk's hood, hence, its common name of monkshood.

Other reliable hybrid cultivars include 'Bicolor' (two-toned, blue and white), 'Blue Sceptre' (blue touched with cream), and 'Newry Blue' (inky navy blue).

Where to Grow

Plant 'Bressingham Spire' at the back of lightly shaded perennial and mixed borders, in a woodland or wildflower garden, or as a tall foundation planting between windows. Because it is poisonous, make sure it is not planted within easy reach of children or inquisitive pets.

How to Grow

'Bressingham Spire' appreciates fertile, moist, well-drained soil, in a lightly shaded

❦
Plant at a Glance

TYPE: perennial
HEIGHT: 90 cm (36 in.)
WIDTH: 30 cm (12 in.)
SOIL: fertile, moist, well drained
LIGHT: light shade to full sun
FLOWERING TIME: mid-summer
to fall

PHOTO – PAGE 73

12

location, sheltered from the wind. It also performs in full sun if adequate moisture levels are maintained. When stricken with drought, the plant looks diseased; its leaves turn black, wither, and die. An organic mulch around the plant helps conserve valuable soil moisture.

Deadheading 'Bressingham Spire' prevents self-seeding and tidies the plant after blooming, but rarely results in additional flowers. This cultivar should not require staking unless it has been planted in a very windy spot.

All monkshoods, including 'Bressingham Spire', dislike being transplanted. Only divide them if they start to languish, if the number of flowers diminishes significantly, or for propagation purposes (in spring or fall). Wear rubber gloves and avoid rubbing your face and eyes when handling monkshood roots as they are very poisonous. Afterward, wash both your hands and gloves to prevent accidental poisoning.

Perfect Partners

In light shade, 'Bressingham Spire' is a friendly comrade for bugbane (*Cimicifuga* spp.), meadow rue (*Thalictrum* spp.), ferns, and hostas. In full sun, deep blue 'Bressingham Spire' pairs beautifully with yellow-blooming sneezeweed (*Helenium autumnale*), sunflowers (*Helianthus* spp.), coreopsis, goldenrod (*Solidago* spp.), and false sunflower (*Heliopsis helianthoides*).

Collectors' Choice

Monkshood species, although similar in appearance, bloom at different times. Their colors also vary; the blue-flowering types are the hardiest of the bunch.

§ *Aconitum carmichaelii* (90 cm, 36 in.), azure monkshood, is the latest-blooming monkshood; a sturdy plant, it produces spikes of deep blue hooded flowers from late summer to fall, above

"Monkshood is an excellent hardy perennial for the back of the border. The blue, blue and white, or ivory blossoms also look great in cut flower arrangements."

MITCHELL WLOCK
YORKTON, SASKATCHEWAN

lustrous, deep green, divided foliage. 'Arendsii' has dark blue blossoms; 'Barker's Variety' and *A. c.* var. *wilsonii* both have amethyst blossoms.

§ *Aconitum henryi* (1.2 m, 4 ft.) produces spires of vivid dark blue flowers in late summer. 'Spark's Variety' blossoms are a rich violet blue.

§ *Aconitum napellus* (1 m, 3.3 ft.), garden monkshood, is an old-fashioned favorite that produces deep blue, helmet-shaped flowers from mid to late summer. Good cultivars include 'Album' (gray white), 'Carneum' (light pink), and 'Rubellum' (pink). Pink-blooming cultivars require consistently cool nights to develop their best color.

§ *Aconitum* 'Stainless Steel' (1.5 m, 5 ft.) is a new cultivar with glossy green foliage and unique bicolor flowers of silvery gray-blue and white. It blooms mid-summer. Ivory and cream-colored monkshoods are shorter, on average, than the blue ones.

§ *Aconitum lycoctonum* subsp. *neopolitanum* (syn. *A. lamarkii*, *A. pyrenaicum*) (76 cm, 30 in.), has unusual creamy yellow, hooded flowers and blooms in mid-summer.

§ *Aconitum septentrionale* 'Ivorine' (90 cm, 36 in.) is an early blooming, compact monkshood that produces short spikes of ivory white flowers.

Aesculus glabra
(eye-skew-luss *glah*-brah)

Ohio buckeye,
American horse chestnut

Prairie gardeners are pioneers in "pushing the limits" and testing previously untried plants for reliability in a challenging climate. Thanks to their perseverance, exotic-looking trees such as the Ohio buckeye have been proven hardy and are gradually being introduced into the prairie landscape.

The Ohio buckeye, also called American horse chestnut, is a native of the American midwest. It is a close relative of the common horse chestnut (*Aesculus hippocastanum*), whose smooth nuts were a favorite among British school children for playing the infamous game of conkers.

The nuts of both the buckeye and horse chestnut are poisonous and not to be confused with the edible fruit of chestnut trees (*Castanea* spp.). Even so, when food was scarce, resourceful American Natives used to roast buckeye nuts, grind them into flour, leach the poisons with water, and use the end product to bake nutritious breads.

Early residents of Ohio, the Buckeye State, gave these nuts their name because of a perceived resemblance to the eyes of a buck deer. Today, Ohio residents themselves are often affectionately called buckeyes. It is good luck to carry a buckeye in your pocket; its charms are reputed to ward off rheumatism, piles, and chills.

Portrait

The Ohio buckeye is a medium-sized tree that in its native habitat is accustomed to growing in the shade of taller neighbors. It is one of the first trees to leaf out in spring, producing large, palm-shaped, compound leaves that give it a decidedly tropical aspect. Each leaf consists of five to seven smooth, shiny leaflets, 10 to 15 cm (4 to 6 in.) long, with pointy tips and wedge-shaped bases. New leaves are frost resistant, and although a hard freeze may cause them to droop, they always recover as the temperature rises. Buckeye leaves are poisonous and release an unpleasant odor when bruised; this explains one of its common names, the stinking buckeye.

Large, vertical, yellowish green flower clusters, 15 cm (6 in.) tall, reminiscent of plump, tapering candles, appear at the ends of branches in late spring, and provide a feast for the local hummingbirds. They soon turn into small clusters of smooth, brown nuts, 5 cm (2 in.) long, encased in prickly, green husks.

Just as it is one of the first trees to leaf

Plant at a Glance

TYPE: deciduous tree
HEIGHT: 12 m (40 ft.)
WIDTH: 12 m (40 ft.)
SOIL: fertile, moist, well drained
LIGHT: full to part sun
FLOWERING TIME: late spring
to early summer

PHOTO – PAGE 73

14

out in the spring, the buckeye is also one of the first to lose its foliage; its leaves are brilliant orange by the time they start to fall in late summer. By early September, only ornamental buckeyes remain dangling from the branches, a perfect meal for hungry squirrels.

Where to Grow
Use Ohio buckeye as a feature shade tree on average to large properties, or include it as a visual anchor in a shrub border. Situate these trees away from seating areas or walkways as much as possible, so that prickly buckeyes do not rain down from above onto unsuspecting individuals.

How to Grow
Plant Ohio buckeye in fertile, moist, well-drained soil in a sunny or lightly shaded, sheltered site. Keep it well watered at all times, to prevent scorching and premature leaf drop during hot, dry summers. Mulching around the tree base helps retain valuable soil moisture and protects the roots from hot sun.

The Ohio buckeye produces a long taproot, so does not transplant well when mature; however, young buckeyes may be moved in early spring or after they have shed their leaves and entered dormancy in late summer.

Perfect Partners
Because Ohio buckeye produces heavy shade and a strong rain shadow, it's best left to its own devices or underplanted with woodland perennials that thrive in deep shade such as lily-of-the-valley (*Convallaria majalis*), bleeding heart (*Dicentra* spp.), or Solomon's seal (*Polygonatum* spp.).

Collectors' Choice
Two other exotic-looking trees that are proving hardy on the prairies are the white

"I love Ohio buckeye's racemes of creamy blossoms that sit at the ends of branches like big, wide candles. This is the perfect choice for people who would like a long-lived, beautiful, large shade tree in their garden."

KATRINA DIEBEL
BLACK DIAMOND, ALBERTA

and black walnuts. They both require fertile, moist, well-drained soil, and a sheltered site in full sun. Male catkins and inconspicuous female flowers are produced separately but on the same tree in spring. Walnut trees are allelopathic; that is, they produce chemicals that may inhibit the growth of other plants in the vicinity or affect aquatic life in ponds infiltrated by groundwater.

- *Juglans cinerea* (12 m, 40 ft.), white walnut or butternut, makes a beautiful feature tree with its pinnate leaves consisting of bright green, aromatic leaflets. Its edible, buttery nuts are the earliest of all nuts to ripen in North America.
- *Juglans nigra* (15 m, 50 ft.), black walnut, is a globe-shaped, long-lived specimen tree with coarse, fernlike foliage that produces tasty, edible nuts in as few as 10 years. Black walnut hardwood and dark stains derived from walnut husks are both valued commercially.

Ajuga reptans 'Burgundy Glow'

(ah-*jew*-gah *rep*-tans)

Ajuga, Creeping bugleweed

Groundcovers offer many benefits to the prairie gardener. They conserve moisture, suppress weeds, and are much less work than a lawn. Many of these practical plants are also beautiful, providing flowers as well as a carpet of foliage.

Shade-tolerant groundcovers are a particularly useful group, flourishing in tough spots where many other plants, including grass, are unsuccessful. One of the best for the prairie climate is *Ajuga reptans*, creeping bugleweed. *A. reptans* 'Burgundy Glow' is one of many decorative members of this species, chiefly grown for variegated or richly colored foliage, but also bearing dainty flower spikes, usually violet-blue.

Portrait

'Burgundy Glow' is notable for its outstanding foliage, marbled in pink, white, and green. The rounded, somewhat spoon-shaped leaves grow in densely clustered rosettes that spread by means of stolons. In late spring to early summer, spikes of tiny, violet-blue flowers rise above the lovely mat of foliage.

Other *Ajuga reptans* cultivars also offer intriguing foliage. 'Tricolor' has variegated cream, pink, and yellow leaves; those of 'Variegata' are white, green, and yellow. 'Atropurpurea' (purple), 'Bronze Beauty' (bronze), and 'Braunherz' (mahogany brown) have richly shaded leaves. 'Jungle Beauty' and 'Catlin's Giant' are larger, growing up to 30 cm (12 in.).

Where to Grow

'Burgundy Glow' lights up shaded areas under deciduous trees, around shrubs, and along pathways. The unique foliage lends season-long color to the front of perennial or mixed borders, and hard-to-maintain slopes.

How to Grow

Although 'Burgundy Glow' grows in full sun or full shade, part sun is preferable. Plant it in average to fertile, moist but well-drained soil, allowing 30 cm (12 in.) between plants. A layer of organic mulch around the plants will help prevent the soil from becoming overly dry. Trim off old flower spikes to tidy the plant and showcase the splendid foliage.

'Burgundy Glow' and similar variegated forms spread more slowly than other creeping ajugas, which can become invasive if left unchecked. It may suffer some winterkill if planted in an exposed location that receives little snow cover.

Plant at a Glance

TYPE: perennial groundcover
HEIGHT: 15 cm (6 in.)
WIDTH: 90 cm (36 in.)
SOIL: average to fertile, moist, well drained
LIGHT: full shade to full sun
FLOWERING TIME: spring to early summer

PHOTO – PAGE 74

Like many ajugas, 'Burgundy Glow' is easily propagated by stolon cuttings or division; simply separate the leaf rosettes and replant.

Perfect Partners

Combine 'Burgundy Glow' with other shade-loving groundcovers; however, avoid planting it in close proximity to other variegated plants or the effect will be too busy. Blue-green hostas, such as 'Elegans', 'Blue Angel', or the smaller 'Love Pat', are excellent choices, as is *Geranium phaeum* 'Mourning Widow'. Other possibilities include astilbes, ferns, bleeding hearts, and foamflower (*Tiarella cordifolia*).

Collectors' Choice

Although less vigorous than *Ajuga reptans*, other ajugas are useful groundcovers with equally striking foliage.

- *Ajuga genevensis* (30 cm, 12 in.) tolerates drier conditions than other species. It has rounded leaves and blue flowers, and it spreads by underground stolons; 'Pink Beauty' is a pink-flowered cultivar.
- *Ajuga pyramidalis* 'Metallica Crispa' (10 cm, 4 in.) has fascinating crinkled, shiny leaves of darkest green shaded with bronze and purple. The blue flower spikes are incidental to the eye-catching foliage. This slow-growing ajuga likes sun and is suitable for rock gardens.

Try these other perennial groundcovers for full to light shade.

- *Convallaria majalis* (20 cm, 8 in.), the fragrant lily-of-the-valley, has pointed leaves and produces delicate, white bells in the spring, followed by red berries. Lily-of-the-valley spreads by an underground rootstock and may need to be confined to avoid overwhelming other perennials. All parts of this plant are poisonous.

> *"Ajuga is almost an all-season plant: it has pretty blue flowers in spring and colorful foliage throughout summer and fall. I grow ajuga in the shade of a large tree and find it is a very hardy groundcover."*
>
> SUE LAFONTAINE
> HALFMOON LAKE, ALBERTA

- *Lamium galeobdolon* (25 cm, 10 in.), also known as yellow archangel, has toothed, silver-splashed leaves and whorls of yellow flowers in the spring. 'Hermann's Pride' is a vigorous, clump-forming cultivar with silver leaves veined with green.
- *Lamium maculatum* (20 cm, 8 in.), spotted dead nettle, is undeserving of its ugly common name. This pretty groundcover has pointed, toothed leaves marked with silver, and clusters of tiny, pink or white flowers. There are several excellent cultivars, particularly 'White Nancy', with predominantly silver foliage and pure white flowers, and 'Beacon Silver', which has silvery white leaves rimmed with green, and pink flowers.
- *Omphalodes verna* (15 cm, 6 in.), also known as blue-eyed Mary, has pointed, medium green leaves on creeping stems. The small, blue flowers of this dainty woodland gem appear in the spring.
- *Vinca minor* (15 cm, 6 in.), common periwinkle, is a trailing plant with shiny, oval, dark leaves and small, blue, purple, or white flowers. Periwinkle stems develop roots where they touch the ground. A good snow cover or mulch layer is essential to protect the evergreen leaves from desiccation in winter.

Alchemilla mollis
(al-ke-*mil*-ah *maw*-lis)

Alchemilla, Lady's mantle

Lady's mantle, a lovely and good-natured plant, is much admired in prairie gardens. Always in accord with the landscape, it is as dependable as the day is long. Its unique soft green foliage and airy veil of delicate, chartreuse flowers make it a fascinating plant in its own right, but its appearance also brings out the best in flashier neighbors. Indeed, blossom colors seem to intensify with a drift of lady's mantle close by.

Medieval alchemists believed lady's mantle to be a magical plant. They used extracted juices and dewdrops collected from its leaves in their quest for a universal cure for disease, the means for prolonging life indefinitely, and the transformation of base metals into gold. This explains the botanical name *Alchemilla*, which derives from the Arabic *al kimiya* or *alkemelych*, meaning alchemy.

Although the magic of lady's mantle never translated into success for the alchemists of old, modern gardeners succumb to its spell of beauty and charm every day.

Portrait
Lady's mantle produces mounds of pleated, soft, gray-green foliage with gently scalloped edges. Individual leaves are covered with downy, silvery hairs that collect the early morning dew in sparkling droplets—pure magic for gardeners and garden photographers alike. Frothy sprays of tiny, petal-less, star-shaped blossoms form a lacy, chartreuse mantilla over the entire plant. Florists value lady's mantle for its excellent long-lasting cut flowers.

'Thriller' is a named selection that forms spreading clusters of soft, gray-green foliage and myriad sprays of small, star-shaped, greenish yellow flowers.

Where to Grow
Use lady's mantle as a specimen plant at the front of perennial and mixed borders, as a groundcover, as edging along pathways, or in summer containers.

How to Grow
Lady's mantle adapts to most garden conditions, but it thrives in fertile, moist, well-drained soil, in a cool spot that experiences morning sun and afternoon shade. Too much hot afternoon sun results in thin flowering, wilted and scorched leaves, or dead plant centers. Even though lady's

Plant at a Glance

TYPE: perennial
HEIGHT: 45 cm (18 in.)
WIDTH: 60 cm (24 in.)
SOIL: fertile, moist, well drained
LIGHT: full to part sun
FLOWERING TIME: late spring
to mid-summer

PHOTO – PAGE 74

mantle is drought tolerant, it should still be watered regularly during dry spells to look its best. An organic mulch around the plant helps preserve valuable soil moisture.

Lady's mantle sets seed with great abandon, spreading its offspring far and wide. If this habit is not to your liking, deadhead fading flowers before they set seed. Self-seeding is, however, an excellent means of propagation for lady's mantle since it grows true from seed. It may also be propagated by stem cuttings in spring, or root division in spring or fall.

If lady's mantle languishes or needs tidying mid-season, cut it back and before long, fresh foliage will grow to form a neat, vigorous mound.

Perfect Partners
The colors of all flowers are subtly enhanced and intensified in the presence of lady's mantle. An ideal foil for white, yellow, purple, and blue flowers, pair lady's mantle with white hardy roses, bellflowers (*Campanula* spp.), lilies (*Lilium* spp.), irises, coral bells (*Heuchera* spp.), columbine (*Aquilegia* spp.), and hostas. It also makes an excellent transition between plants of clashing colors.

Collectors' Choice
In addition to the familiar lady's mantle of gardens, there are several low-growing species that are perfect for the rock garden or for planting among paving stones. They all prefer sun and fertile, moist, well-drained soil.

- *Alchemilla alpina* (20 cm, 8 in.), alpine lady's mantle, is a mat-forming perennial with deep-green, shiny, five-lobed leaves (hairy underneath), smothered with tiny, lime green flowers in summer.
- *Alchemilla erythropoda* (30 cm, 12 in.) produces clumps of lobed, toothed, hairy, bluish green leaves and sprays of

> 🐦
>
> *"It's worth getting up early to see the dewdrops in the leaf fringes of alchemilla. I love combining it with red-flowering coral bells. Alchemilla flowers are also great fillers for bouquets."*
>
> JUNE MINISH
> SELKIRK, MANITOBA

yellowish green flowers from late spring to late summer.
- *Alchemilla glaucescens* (25 cm, 10 in.), dwarf lady's mantle, forms mounds of kidney-shaped leaves with silvery undersides that are topped with a froth of tiny, chartreuse flowers.

Two other perennials that produce masses of tiny, delicate flowers are German statice and sea lavender. Both are reliable, long-lived summer bloomers that thrive in full sun or light shade.
- *Goniolimon tataricum* (40 cm, 16 in.), German statice, produces spikelike clusters of tubular-trumpet-shaped, everlasting white, pink, purple, or red flowers on short, winged stems in mid to late summer. Large, smooth, fleshy leaves form a basal rosette. This plant prefers a sunny site. German statice flowers are excellent for cutting or drying, but the plant is also useful for edging perennial or mixed borders.
- *Limonium latifolium* (60 cm, 24 in.), sea lavender, forms large basal rosettes of leathery, spoon-shaped leaves; hazy dome-shaped sprays of tiny, lavender-blue flowers top tall, wiry, branched stems. 'Violetta' produces darker, violet-colored flowers; 'Blue Cloud' bears mauve flowers.

Allium aflatunense 'Purple Sensation'
(*al*-ee-um a-flah-toon-*en*-see)

Allium, Persian onion

Although definitely a member of the onion genus, 'Purple Sensation' is no lonely little onion in the petunia patch. Quite the contrary, it is a showstopper, with its large globes of stunning violet-purple, star-shaped flowers that create a stir wherever it is planted. It's easy to see why this plant has earned itself the common name Persian onion—its regal bearing and majestic appearance instantly conjure up images of an exotic Middle East ancestry.

Onions, leeks, scallions, and chives have been grown for highly practical culinary and medicinal purposes since the earliest days of civilization; for centuries, however, no thought was given to growing these or other alliums for their highly ornamental value. Today's gardeners have a different attitude, as more and more of them cultivate ornamental onions for their exceptional beauty in perennial and mixed borders.

Plant at a Glance

TYPE: hardy bulb
HEIGHT: 60 cm (24 in.)
WIDTH: 45 cm (18 in.)
SOIL: fertile, moist, well drained
LIGHT: full sun
FLOWERING TIME: spring to
early summer

PHOTO – PAGE 74

Portrait

The shiny, broad, strappy foliage of 'Purple Sensation' is unremarkable; it emerges from the ground a blue-green with light undersides, and like all bulb foliage, soon fades away. It has all but disappeared by the time sturdy, 90-cm (36-in.), ribbed flower stalks are maturing and the burgeoning flower buds, encased in thin, papery sheaths, are bursting at the seams. 'Purple Sensation' produces one of the largest flowers among the ornamental onions; it forms an incredible 10-cm (4-in.) starburst globe of dozens of tiny, violet-purple flowers, radiating from a central point.

Where to Grow

'Purple Sensation' grows best in full sun, closely interplanted with other medium-sized inhabitants of informal cottage gardens and mixed or perennial borders.

How to Grow

'Purple Sensation', like all alliums, grows from a hardy bulb and must be planted in early fall, at the same time as tulips, narcissus, and other hardy bulbs. Plant bulbs, pointed end up, about 10 cm (4 in.) deep, in fertile soil amended with a handful of bone meal. Keep them moist until the ground freezes, and then cover them with organic mulch before winter sets in, to prevent them from emerging too early in spring.

Apply a fertilizer high in phosphorus and potassium (4–8–10) when tender shoots emerge in the spring, and again when the plant has finished blooming, to help replenish the nutrients in the bulb. Do not remove foliage until it has died back completely.

You may deadhead 'Purple Sensation' as flowers fade, but its decorative seed heads are dazzling in the winter garden. They also look lovely in dried flower arrangements.

Propagate this plant by digging up mature bulbs, separating the small bulblets that have formed, and planting them as you would all bulbs.

Perfect Partners

'Purple Sensation' looks best when paired with bushy plants that hide its fading foliage and soften the lines of bare flower stalks. Geraniums, lady's mantle (*Alchemilla mollis*), lavender (*Lavandula* spp.), and catmint (*Nepeta* spp.) are good choices, as are blue flax (*Linum perenne*), lilies (*Lilium* spp.), and false sunflowers (*Heliopsis helianthoides*).

Collectors' Choice

There are ornamental onions to suit every garden situation. Most bloom in late spring or early summer, and require full sun and fertile, moist, well-drained soil. These miniatures are suitable for the rock garden.

- ❧ *Allium karataviense* (15 cm, 6 in.) has a grapefruit-sized globe of tiny, lilac-blue flowers nestled in broad, gray-green foliage.
- ❧ *Allium oreophilum* (20 cm, 8 in.), also sold as *A. ostrowskianum*, produces loose clusters of bell-shaped, rose-purple flowers above linear, medium green leaves.

These short alliums can be naturalized or massed in borders.

- ❧ *Allium flavum* (30 to 45 cm, 12 to 18 in.) produces loose clusters of bright yellow, sweetly scented, bell-shaped

flowers with prominent stamens; the cylindrical foliage is gray-green.

- ❧ *Allium moly* (45 cm, 18 in.), also known as golden garlic or lily leek, was once regarded as a sign of prosperity. It produces loose clusters of lemon yellow, star-shaped flowers above paired, lance-shaped, green leaves.

These tall alliums are welcome additions to mixed or perennial borders.

- ❧ *Allium atropurpureum* (90 cm, 36 in.) produces a flat, 8-cm (3-in.) cluster of deep wine-purple, star-shaped flowers on stiff stems.
- ❧ *Allium bulgaricum* (90 cm, 36 in.) produces graceful green spires, topped with clusters of arching, blue-green and purple, bell-shaped flowers.
- ❧ *Allium christophii* (60 cm, 24 in.), star of Persia, produces the largest blossoms of all the alliums—striking 30-cm (12-in.) globes of over 100 perfectly star-shaped flowers radiating from a central point like some botanical sparkler or fireworks. The blossoms are pale mauve and have an exquisite metallic iridescence that is hard to describe. This is a spectacular accent plant, and even though it may languish or disappear altogether after several years, it is always worth replacing.

Amelanchier alnifolia 'Northline'

(am-el-*lang*-kee-ur all-ni-*foe*-lee-ah)

Saskatoon, Western serviceberry

It would be difficult to find a plant more suited to prairie gardens than the saskatoon, *Amelanchier alnifolia*. For many prairie folk, the mid-summer trek to harvest the sweet fruit for pies and jams is a pleasurable summer ritual. Saskatoon fruit is often compared to blueberries in appearance and texture, but it has a distinctive almondlike flavor all its own.

The saskatoon is a large shrub native to western North America. Extremely hardy and adaptable, it grows from near the Arctic Circle to New Mexico, in open woods and prairie coulees, on hillsides, and along streambanks. In spring the saskatoon produces clusters of white blossoms followed by the dark blue-purple fruit in late July. The species name *alnifolia* means "with leaves like an alder," referring to the dark green foliage that changes to warm shades of yellow, orange, or red in autumn.

The common name of the shrub is adapted from the Cree word for the fruit, *mi-sakwato-min*, meaning "fruit from the tree of many branches." The city of Saskatoon, Saskatchewan, was named for the plant, which is plentiful in the area. The saskatoon was an important food source to indigenous plains peoples, who used it in pemmican and dried it in cakes for later use. The summer harvest was a significant annual event marked with ceremonies and feasts.

Native saskatoons are extremely variable in size and form, their growth habits largely dependent on local habitat, but new selections have resulted in varieties that are more reliable and productive for home or commercial use. As a result, saskatoons are increasingly being appreciated as attractive additions to the home landscape.

Portrait

'Northline' is a superb saskatoon variety that combines ornamental value and heavy fruit production. The upright shape and neat form are more compact and less sprawling than many other varieties, making it an excellent shrub for prairie gardens. The dark green leaves are oval and serrated and offer impressive yellow to red fall color.

In the spring, 'Northline' bears masses of fragrant, white flowers; the dark purple fruit is approximately 1.5 cm (0.5 in.) in diameter. The plants flower and fruit on the current year's growth and are self-pol-

Plant at a Glance

TYPE: deciduous shrub
HEIGHT: 2.5 m (8 ft.)
WIDTH: 1.8 m (5.5 ft.)
SOIL: average, well drained
LIGHT: full sun
FLOWERING TIME: spring

PHOTO – PAGE 74

linating. Botanically speaking, the sweet fruits are not berries but pomes, like apples. This variety will produce fruit in three years and reach maturity in six years.

Other saskatoons suitable for ornamental and culinary use include 'Honeywood' (2.5 m, 8 ft.), another compact variety with large fruit; 'Smoky' (3 m, 10 ft.), a widely grown older selection with sweet, flavorful fruit; and 'Altaglow' (3 m, 10 ft.), which is columnar in form, produces white fruit, and has exceptional fall color ranging from orange to red to purple.

Where to Grow

'Northline' may be used as a feature shrub or as part of a shrub border. Where space allows, it makes an excellent hedge, and is also a good choice for shelterbelts.

How to Grow

'Northline' thrives in full sun. It performs well in many soil types, provided they are well drained, and is drought tolerant once established. To maintain soil moisture, mulch around plants with an organic material such as compost, which will also provide nutrition, shredded bark, or wood chips. Like most native plants, saskatoons do not require any additional fertilizer. This variety is noted for its good disease and pest resistance.

Mature shrubs should be pruned every few years to remove stems greater than 2.5 cm (1 in.) in diameter. Cut these off at the base while shrubs are dormant to encourage vigorous new fruit-bearing growth, and to keep the plants healthy.

Perfect Partners

'Jumping Pound' pin cherry (*Prunus pensylvanica*), European red elder (*Sambucus racemosa*), and cherry prinsepia (*Prinsepia sinensis*) are fine companions for 'Northline' in an informal shrub border that will also provide shelter and food for

"Saskatoon bushes produce clusters of flavorful, sweet fruit in great profusion. As well, they are valuable ornamental shrubs with masses of showy flowers in spring and brilliant fall foliage."

PAUL HAMER
DeWINTON, ALBERTA

many species of birds. For striking foliage contrast, plant it with 'Dart's Gold' golden ninebark (*Physocarpus opulifolius*).

Collectors' Choice

Saskatoons are not the only hardy and decorative fruit-bearing shrub native to the prairies—currants and gooseberries also offer an abundant berry harvest.

- *Ribes aureum* (2 m, 6 ft.), golden flowering currant, is named for its fragrant, yellow flowers. It bears black currants in mid to late summer and has bright orange-red autumn foliage. Plant it in a sunny location; it spreads by suckering so is best suited to a large garden.
- *Ribes oxycanthoides* (1 m, 3.3 ft.), wild gooseberry, is a low shrub with thin, prickly stems clothed with light green leaves that turn orange-red in fall. The smooth fruit is reddish purple. 'Pixwell' bears green fruit that turns pink when ripe; 'John's Prairie Gooseberry' has reddish pink fruit.

Antennaria rosea

(an-ten-*nair*-ee-ah rose-*ay*-ah)

Pussytoes, Early everlasting

The variety of groundcovers available in prairie nurseries increases every year, but one that is often conspicuous by its absence is the delightful antennaria. A North American wildflower, it is ideally suited for the dry, sunny conditions that prevail across the prairies. About 12 species of this genus live on the prairies, but they are all so similar they are difficult to identify. The pink-flowered *Antennaria rosea* is the species of choice for most converts.

Portrait

Early summer hikes in the prairies or foothills may have led you across endless low-lying mats of gray-green, woolly foliage smothered with small, white or pink flower clusters perched on top of erect, downy stems. These flower clusters bear a strong resemblance to cat's paws or pussytoes, the most common "common name" for *Antennaria*. It has also been called songbird, dog toes, four toes, love's nest, Indian tobacco, and poverty weed. This last assignation is often used to refer to plants that survive or even thrive in poor-quality soil.

Antennaria usually grow in long colonies interconnected by underground runners called stolons. The small, silvery leaves grow to about 2 cm (0.75 in.) and are often arranged in rosettes, from which emerge fuzzy 6-cm (2.5-in.) stems. The rosy flower heads consist of tight clusters of tubular, cream or pinkish colored, everlasting flowers that produce flyaway seeds just like those of dandelions.

Antennaria have both male and female flowers growing in separate but adjacent colonies. The male flowers (which have swollen tips resembling the antennae of butterflies, hence, the botanical name) produce pollen, which is transported by bees and flies to the female flowers. Unfertilized female flowers can still produce seeds, but these are generally of poor quality. The likelihood of having adjacent female and male colonies in the artificial environment of a home garden is low, so chances are that the flying seeds won't germinate.

Where to Grow

Antennaria are an excellent solution for carpeting dry, sunny areas where nothing else will grow. Plant them between paving stones or as a groundcover to edge pathways, at the front of perennial borders, or in rock gardens.

Plant at a Glance

TYPE: perennial groundcover
HEIGHT: 15 cm (6 in.)
WIDTH: 45 cm (18 in.)
SOIL: poor to average, well drained
LIGHT: full sun
FLOWERING TIME: early summer

PHOTO – PAGE 75

How to Grow

Full sun and a fairly lean, well-drained soil are essential for growing antennaria; a sunny, gravelly location would be perfect. Without enough sun you become the proud keeper of vast expanses of beautiful foliage, barren of flowers. In overly rich soil, the flower stems grow excessively long and tend to flop.

Growing antennaria from seed is easy; propagating them from self-rooted pieces of creeping stems also works well. Plants spread slowly but steadily, and can be divided and replanted every few years.

Perfect Partners

The blue-green, fuzzy mat of antennaria foliage is a perfect carpet for spring bulbs and makes a pretty background for small rock garden plants such as thrift (*Armeria juniperifolia*, or *A. maritima* 'Alba', 'Dusseldorf Pride'). Large thrift (*A. pseudoarmeria* 'Formosa Hybrids') is a taller companion in shades of carmine, pink, and white. Plant antennaria with creeping thymes and golden oregano for a tapestry of foliage, or beside clump-forming grasses such as *Festuca glauca*. It also contrasts vividly with the smooth, rounded leaves and blossoms of *Geranium cinereum* 'Ballerina', and complements blue *Salvia superba*.

Collectors' Choice

Other antennaria species may be available through nurseries specializing in native plants.

- *Antennaria aprica*, commonly known as low everlasting, is a white-flowered species that grows wild on the prairies; *A. parvifolia*, small-leaved pussytoes, and *A. pulcherrima*, showy everlasting, are two other native species.

The following groundcovers are ideal for sunny and rock gardens.

- *Achillea tomentosa* (30 cm, 12 in.), woolly yarrow, has fernlike, soft, gray-green foliage crowned with flat clusters of golden or pale yellow flowers in June and July.
- *Androsace sarmentosa* (15 cm, 6 in.), commonly called rock jasmine, forms rosettes of leaves and spreads by stolons. It produces pink or white flowers in May.
- *Veronica* spp., creeping veronicas or speedwells, have dainty blooms and tiny leaves. *V. repens* (10 cm, 4 in.) produces pale blue flowers in spring; *V. pectinata* (10 cm, 4 in.), comb speedwell, has gray leaves and produces blue or rose flowers with a white eye in June or July. *V. prostrata* (15 cm, 6 in.), harebell speedwell, has white ('Alba'), sapphire blue ('Heavenly Blue'), and pink ('Mrs Holt', 'Rosea') cultivars that bloom in late spring and early summer. *V.* x 'Waterperry Blue' (15 cm, 6 in.) has striking bronze-tinted foliage and sky blue flowers in June and July.

Antirrhinum majus Floral Showers Series

(an-tee-*ree*-num *may*-uss)

Snapdragon, Lion's mouth

Snapdragons, which rank among the top 10 favorite annuals in North America, are an enduring favorite among children, who love to squeeze the jawlike blossoms of the friendliest little dragon in town. Its gently snapping, lobed petals and snoutlike seed pods inspired both its common name and its botanical name, *Antirrhinum*, which derives from the Greek *anti* (like) and *rhin* (snout).

Perennial, purple, and unscented in their native Mediterranean habitat, snapdragons were at one time harvested for their oily seeds, which were pressed to provide a cheap alternative to olive oil. It was believed that people anointed with snapdragon oil would not only become famous some day, but would also be protected for all time against witchcraft and sorcery.

The snapdragons of old probably arrived in Great Britain via the Romans. They were originally perceived as vulgar plants, but became fashionable in Victorian gardens where they were grown as showy giants, 2 m (6.5 ft.) tall and 1.5 m (5 ft.) across! Modern hybrids are a much more manageable size; many introductions made since 1963 are even deliciously scented.

Portrait

Floral Showers Series snapdragons are early blooming and form short, bushy mounds of glossy, deep green, lance-shaped leaves. Upright flower spikes bloom from the bottom up and are smothered all summer long in fragrant, tubular, two-lipped blossoms. Named cultivars come in a range of cheerful colors and include: 'Crimson', 'Lilac', 'Deep Bronze', 'Purple', 'Rose Pink', 'Scarlet', 'White', 'Yellow', and 'Mix'. Bicolors in lavender/white, apricot/white, and wine/white combinations are also available.

Where to Grow

Charming Floral Showers Series snapdragons are ideally suited for mass-planting at the front of perennial and mixed borders or as an edging along informal pathways. You can also tuck them into summer containers or a sunny rock garden.

How to Grow

Floral Showers Series snapdragons require little more than fertile, moist, well-drained soil, in a sunny or lightly shaded location. They are frost tolerant and can be planted outdoors in early spring just like pansies, when the weather is still too cool for most other annuals. However, be prepared to

Plant at a Glance

TYPE: annual
HEIGHT: 20 cm (8 in.)
WIDTH: 30 cm (12 in.)
SOIL: fertile, moist, well drained
LIGHT: full sun to light shade
FLOWERING TIME: early summer to fall

PHOTO – PAGE 75

provide protection if hard frost threatens.

Remove the first bloom spike at the time of planting to encourage branching and multiple flower spikes. Then water, fertilize with a balanced fertilizer (20–20–20), and cut blossoms on a regular basis to encourage flowering all summer long.

Perfect Partners

In flowerbeds, Floral Showers Series snaps combine well with most annuals and a variety of perennials including geraniums, chrysanthemums, poppies (*Papaver* spp.), *Scabiosa columbaria*, and the short bell-flower, *Campanula carpatica*. In summer containers, try these snaps with *Bacopa*, licorice plant (*Helichrysum petiolare*), *Osteospermum*, and 'Blue Splash' lobelia.

Collectors' Choice

Hybridizers have had a field day with ever-popular snapdragons, which now come in a wide range of heights, flower shapes, bloom times, and colors. Tall snaps (60 to 90 cm, 24 to 36 in.) are perfect for a strong vertical accent in perennial borders, but may require staking. Intermediate types (30 to 60 cm, 12 to 24 in.) produce long stems for cutting and require no support. Dwarf varieties (15 to 30 cm, 6 to 12 in.) are perfect for rock gardens, edging, or carpet bedding. The following series feature traditional tubular snapdragon flowers.

- 'Floral Carpet Mixed' (20 cm, 8 in.) forms bushy plants with numerous flower spikes; 'Tahiti Mix' (25 cm, 10 in.) is similar, but taller and blooms two weeks earlier; 'Magic Carpet Mixed' (15 cm, 6 in.) is slightly shorter, but equally lovely.
- Lampion Series snapdragons (30 cm, 12 in.), with their trailing habit, are an exciting innovation for connoisseurs; they make delightful additions to sum-

mer containers and hanging baskets. Remove faded flowers to prolong blooming. Cultivars developed to date come in a range of pastel shades.

- Liberty Series snapdragons (60 cm, 24 in.) are early blooming and produce tall flower spikes perfect for cutting.
- Rocket Series snapdragons (90 cm, 36 in.) produce long, strong flower spikes of beautifully colored blossoms on sturdy stems.

These snapdragons highlight non-traditional, open-faced flowers.

- 'Bright Butterflies Mixed' (76 cm, 30 in.) forms stocky, branching plants that produce from 10 to 12 long-stemmed flower spikes smothered with open-faced, azalealike flowers. 'Little Darling' (30 cm, 12 in.) is the short equivalent of 'Bright Butterflies' and shows good wind tolerance. Bells Series snapdragons (20 cm, 8 in.) are shorter still; they bloom earlier than 'Little Darling' and produce long-lasting, open-faced flowers.
- 'Madame Butterfly Mixed' (70 cm, 28 in.) produces double, open-faced flowers on vigorous base-branching plants. It blooms five days earlier than 'Bright Butterflies Mixed' and is perfect for cutting. 'Sweetheart Mix' (30 cm, 12 in.) is the dwarf equivalent of 'Madame Butterfly Mixed'.

> *"I've always liked snapdragons because they are colorful, reliable, and bloom for a long season. Some years I've picked snapdragon bouquets at Thanksgiving."*
>
> EDITH WADDELL
> NEWDALE, MANITOBA

Aquilegia canadensis

(ack-will-*ee*-gee-ah ca-na-*den*-sis)

Columbine, Granny's bonnet

For centuries, the charming flowers and dainty foliage of *Aquilegia*, the columbine, have graced English gardens. Always a pretty sight dancing in the breeze, the uniquely shaped blooms have inspired many fanciful common names, including granny's bonnet, doves-round-a-dish, and meetinghouses. The nodding flowers are composed of five cupped petals, which narrow into spurs that protrude behind the bloom, and five petal-like sepals that are a different color in bicolored columbines.

Portrait

Aquilegia canadensis, the Canadian columbine, is native from Nova Scotia to the Northwest Territories and down to Texas and Florida. Among the first columbines of the season to bloom, it produces 5-cm (2-in.) flowers with yellow petals extending into short red spurs and scarlet sepals. This fine plant has deeply lobed leaflets resembling the delicate foliage of a maidenhair fern. Beloved by bees and hummingbirds, it is also a rich source of nectar.

The cultivar 'Corbett' (60 cm, 24 in.) is smaller than the species and has pale yellow flowers. *Aquilegia formosa*, the western or crimson columbine, is similar to *A. canadensis*.

Where to Grow

Plant *Aquilegia canadensis* in the dappled or light shade of a woodland garden. It also easily adapts to life in a perennial border, looking particularly at home in a cottage-style garden.

How to Grow

Aquilegia canadensis prefers part sun or light shade; however, it will grow in full sun provided the soil is kept evenly moist. Best results will be achieved in fertile, well-drained soil amended with liberal amounts of compost or well-rotted manure. Mulch around the plants to retain soil moisture, unless you wish them to self-seed.

Pesky leaf miners are the bane of all columbines, although native species are less likely to be attacked than hybrids. The larvae of these insects burrow in the leaves, making telltale white tracks. Remove affected leaves immediately, and dispose of them in the garbage, not the compost bin. Tidy the plant by cutting back spent flowering stems and any foliage that turns yellow. New green leaves usually appear when temperatures become cooler in the fall.

Plant at a Glance

TYPE: perennial
HEIGHT: 90 cm (36 in.)
WIDTH: 30 cm (12 in.)
SOIL: average to fertile, moist, well drained
LIGHT: light shade to full sun
FLOWERING TIME: spring to early summer

PHOTO – PAGE 75

Columbines cross-pollinate promiscuously, so hybrid seedlings may pop up unless *Aquilegia canadensis* is isolated from other columbines in the garden. Seedlings transplant easily, unlike mature plants that develop a tough, deep taproot. The species is generally more durable than its hybrid cousins, which may only survive three or four years.

Perfect Partners

Plant *Aquilegia canadensis* in dappled shade with bleeding hearts, hostas, ferns, coral bells (*Heuchera* spp.), creeping phlox (*Phlox stolonifera*), and masterwort (*Astrantia major*). They also make splendid cottage garden compositions with campanula, shrub roses, hardy geraniums, peonies, irises, and short delphiniums such as the 'Magic Fountain Hybrids'.

Collectors' Choice

Other *Aquilegia* species are equally appealing.

- *Aquilegia alpina* (45 cm, 18 in.), alpine columbine, has violet-blue flowers and deep green foliage.
- *Aquilegia caerulea* (60 cm, 24 in.), Rocky Mountain or Colorado columbine, has blue and white flowers, and is more tolerant of heat and drought than many others of its genus.
- *Aquilegia chrysantha* (76 cm, 30 in.), or golden columbine, is a North American native with upward-facing, yellow flowers. Cultivars include 'Yellow Queen' and the heat-tolerant 'Texas Gold'.
- *Aquilegia flabellata* (45 cm, 18 in.), fan columbine, produces long-spurred, blue and white flowers. Look for 'Mini Star' (15 cm, 6 in.) and 'Alba' (25 cm, 10 in.), an exceptional white form.
- *Aquilegia flavescens* (50 cm, 20 in.), a native of western North America, has nodding, lemon yellow flowers.
- *Aquilegia jonesii* (10 cm, 4 in.), Jones or

limestone columbine, is an exquisite little Rocky Mountain alpine plant. It produces 5-cm (2-in.) wide violet-blue flowers, held just above the silver-blue foliage.

There are also a host of lovely *Aquilegia* hybrids. Extravagant double-pleated forms are also available, but these petticoats on stems lack the dainty charm of simpler varieties.

- Biedermeier Hybrids (30 cm, 12 in.) are compact plants with short stems and upward-facing flowers.
- Cameo Series (15 cm, 6 in.) are dwarf rock garden columbines in blue, purple, rose, and bicolors with white.
- McKana Hybrids (76 cm, 30 in.), or 'McKana's Giants', have large, long-spurred, and flared flowers in mixed pastel shades.
- 'Nora Barlow' (76 cm, 30 in.) is an unusual double columbine with narrow petals tinged with pink, green, and white. Formerly called the rose columbine, it has been cultivated for roughly 300 years.
- Songbird Hybrids (40 cm, 16 in.) are available as a mix or as individually named cultivars bearing cheerful and evocative names such as 'Blue Jay', 'Robin', 'Goldfinch', and 'Cardinal'.

"Of the many columbines I grow, my favorite is the scarlet-and-yellow-flowered Aquilegia canadensis, *whose delicate blue-green foliage makes a graceful addition to my sunset-colored garden."*

SHARON LANIGAN
SASKATOON, SASKATCHEWAN

Artemisia ludoviciana 'Valerie Finnis'

(ar-tuh-*meej*-ah loo-doh-vich-ee-*a*-nah)

Artemisia, Wormwood

Not all plants are grown for their floral splendor. Gardeners value many perennials for their appealing foliage color and texture, more enduring characteristics than bloom alone. Artemisia and other silver-foliaged plants are among the most useful of these garden stalwarts; they light up the evening garden with an ethereal glow and blend effortlessly with more floriferous companions. Silver-gray perennials are invaluable additions to any garden, enhancing blues, pinks, magentas, and yellows, and mediating between incompatible colors.

The name artemisia comes from Artemis, chaste Greek goddess of hunting and the moon. The genus *Artemisia*, used for medicinal purposes for 2,500 years, may be named for a historical woman, sister and wife of the Greek/Persian King Mausolus. Although Artemisia was renowned as a botanist and medical researcher, she is most famous for supervising the construction of one of the seven wonders of the ancient world, her husband's splendid tomb at Halicarnassus, known as the Mausoleum.

Artemisia ludoviciana is native to western North America, the species name meaning "of Louisiana." The silvery foliage of this artemisia and many other plants native to hot and dry environments is due to tiny hairs on leaf surfaces, which often give them a downy or fuzzy texture. These hairs trap moisture, reduce transpiration, and shade the leaf surface. Silver also tends to reflect, rather than absorb, heat.

Portrait

Artemisia ludoviciana 'Valerie Finnis' is an upright, clump-forming perennial clothed with jagged, silver-gray leaves. Insignificant gray flowers appear in late summer. The aromatic, dried foliage is most attractive in flower arrangements and can also be used in potpourri.

'Silver Queen' (60 cm, 24 in.) and 'Silver King' (76 cm, 30 in.), both commonly available cultivars, tend to be more aggressive than 'Valerie Finnis', and should therefore be used with caution in a perennial border.

Where to Grow

Place 'Valerie Finnis' in perennial borders or use it in combination with small shrubs. Both heat and drought tolerant, it is an ideal plant for naturalized prairie gardens.

Plant at a Glance

TYPE: perennial
HEIGHT: 60 cm (24 in.)
WIDTH: 60 cm (24 in.)
SOIL: poor to average, well drained
LIGHT: full sun

PHOTO – PAGE 75

How to Grow

'Valerie Finnis' thrives in full sun and requires little water once established. Like all silver-leaved artemisias, this cultivar prefers poor to average, well-drained soil, and should not be fertilized. Rich soil, too much nitrogen, or overwatering cause it to become floppy or lanky. It may be cut back during the growing season to maintain bushier growth.

Divide 'Valerie Finnis' regularly, both to limit spreading and to keep plants vigorous. After dividing, replant the new shoots from the outside of the plant, discarding the old woody growth from the center. New plants may also be started from basal or stem cuttings.

Perfect Partners

'Valerie Finnis' is particularly striking with the blue spikes of 'Six Hills Giant' nepeta, veronicas such as 'Sunny Border Blue' or 'Crater Lake Blue', the rich pink of 'Heidi' yarrow, and sunny golden yellow 'Zagreb' coreopsis.

Collectors' Choice

Other species of silver-leaved artemisia have different foliage types and growth habits.

- *Artemisia absinthium* 'Lambrook Silver' (76 cm, 30 in.), also called common wormwood, has finely cut, silver-gray leaves and small, gray flowers.
- *Artemisia schmidtiana* 'Silver Mound' (also called 'Nana') (30 cm, 12 in.) grows into a fragrant silver-gray mound of soft, feathery foliage that spreads about 45 cm (18 in.). Cut it back during the summer to maintain its compact shape.
- *Artemisia stelleriana* 'Silver Brocade' (30 cm, 12 in.), also called perennial dusty miller or beach wormwood, is a low-growing, spreading artemisia with many-lobed, silver-gray leaves and

> *"One of my favorite plant combinations is silvery artemisia and bright red geraniums. The foliage color of artemisia is so beautiful that it doesn't even need its own blooms. It also grows rapidly."*
>
> Lorraine Boyle
> Swift Current, Saskatchewan

small, yellow flower spikes.

- *Artemisia versicolor* 'Sea Foam' (30 cm, 12 in.), misty sage, forms a mound of frosty, blue-green, lacy foliage; yellow flowers appear in late summer.

Artemisias are not the only plants that will add the cool lustre of gray or silver to a perennial garden.

- *Lavandula angustifolia* (45 cm, 18 in.), English lavender, is renowned for the soothing fragrance of both its narrow, gray-green leaves and its spikes of tiny, lavender-blue flowers. Other species of lavender are not generally hardy on the prairies; 'Munstead' is the best blue selection, and 'Jean Davis' has pale pink flowers. Lavender requires a sunny, sheltered location and will tolerate poor to fertile soils provided drainage is excellent. Mulch around plants in winter, and prune them back to new shoots in the spring.
- *Perovskia atriplicifolia* (90 cm, 36 in.), commonly known as Russian sage, is a sun-loving, shrubby plant with silver-green leaves and hazy spikes of lavender-blue flowers. It prefers poor to average, well-drained soil, and requires winter mulching. On the prairies, plants may die back to the ground in winter, but new shoots often grow from the base in the spring.

Aster novi-belgii 'Audrey'

(*ass*-ter no-vee-*bell*-jee-ee)

Michaelmas daisy, New York aster

When the starry blossoms of asters start to sparkle on the prairies, gardeners know that the chilly days of autumn are drawing near. They also know that the splendid purples, pinks, reds, and whites of asters present a spectacular finale to summer. Even as the days shorten noticeably, asters continue to enchant and inspire through the first light frosts and beyond. Gardeners revel in their longevity, adaptability, and carefree nature; butterflies and birds appreciate asters as a valuable food source. With so much to commend it, who wouldn't love an aster?

It is said that the goddess of the stars, Asterea (named for the Greek *aster*, meaning star), looked down from Mount Olympus in ancient times and saw there were no stars on earth to light the way. With that realization, tears welled up in her eyes, and everywhere Asterea's tears fell, a radiant aster sprouted. This is a charming legend, but Mount Olympus must have towered majestically over North America instead of Greece when Asterea shed her tears, because most of the world's aster species are North American natives. As with many other North American native plants, they were not appreciated on the home front until Europeans discovered their virtues and raved about them.

Portrait

'Audrey' is an aster that forms dense, compact mounds of medium green, lance-shaped foliage. Slender, self-supporting, branched stems display a profusion of showy clusters of lavender-blue flower heads. Individual flower heads grow to 2.5 cm (1 in.) and are composed of a radiating ruffle of very narrow ray florets that encircle a tight central button of bright yellow, tubular disk florets.

Other Michaelmas daisies to try include 'Alert' (deep crimson red), 'Little Pink Beauty' (semi-double, bright pink), and 'Professor Kippenberg' (semi-double, bright blue). *A. novi-belgii* is a parent of the compact *A.* x *dumosus* hybrids. 'Coombe Rosemary' (double, violet-purple) and 'Winston Churchill' (red) are good choices. These asters may not bloom in years of exceptionally early hard frost.

Where to Grow

'Audrey' provides vivid fall color at the front of perennial and mixed borders; it is also at home in wildflower gardens and sunny meadows. Like some chrysanthe-

Plant at a Glance

TYPE: perennial
HEIGHT: 35 cm (14 in.)
WIDTH: 45 cm (18 in.)
SOIL: fertile, moist, well drained
LIGHT: full to part sun
FLOWERING TIME: late summer to fall

PHOTO – PAGE 76

mums, asters form flower buds as daylight diminishes, so do not plant this hybrid where it is exposed to bright light at night, or flowering may be delayed.

How to Grow

Plant 'Audrey' in full sun, in fertile, moist, well-drained soil. Provide plenty of moisture and good air circulation as it will succumb to powdery mildew when stressed. Thinning early in the season aids air circulation. Apply an organic mulch around the plant to help conserve valuable soil moisture.

All Michaelmas daisies, including 'Audrey', are heavy feeders. Top dress with compost in spring as plants emerge from the ground, and fertilize again with a balanced fertilizer in mid-summer.

This aster does not require staking as do many of its taller cousins. However, it does require deadheading during a long, warm fall to prevent self-seeding; 'Audrey' does not grow true from seed and less-desirable offspring will grow vigorously and eventually compete with the parent plant. If you are prepared to rogue out seedlings in the spring, then leave seed heads in place for the birds to enjoy during the winter.

Divide this plant every three or four years to maintain vigor and prevent centers from dying out. 'Audrey' may be propagated both by division and stem cuttings.

Perfect Partners

Lavender-blue 'Audrey' puts on a dazzling display when paired with yellow bloomers such as goldenrod (*Solidago* spp.), false sunflower (*Heliopsis helianthoides*), sneezeweed (*Helenium autumnale*), coneflower (*Rudbeckia* spp.), and chrysanthemums.

"Our fall asters are absolutely gorgeous balls of purple color at the end of September and beginning of October. I think everyone should grow asters!"

IRENE CONNAUGHTY
SEDLEY, SASKATCHEWAN

Collectors' Choice

The following aster species make beautiful ornamental plants; all require fertile, moist, well-drained soil, and full sun.

- *Aster alpinus* (25 cm, 10 in.), alpine aster, produces large, yellow-centered, pink or purple daisylike flowers in early summer. It is excellent for the rock garden.

- *Aster ericoides* (90 cm, 36 in.), heath aster, forms small-leaved, bushy mounds smothered in masses of tiny, starry flowers in early fall. Many are disease resistant. 'Blue Star' (sky blue) and 'Esther' (pink) are recommended cultivars.

- *Aster lateriflorus* (90 cm, 36 in.) produces attractive mahogany foliage and clouds of tiny, red-eyed, starry, white flowers in early fall. 'Prince' is a choice cultivar.

- *Aster novae-angliae* (1.5 m, 5 ft.), New England aster, is a tall, fall-blooming plant that produces showy clusters of purple, pink, or white flowers that close at night. Lovely cultivars include 'Alma Potschke' (rose), 'Hella Lacy' (pink), 'September Ruby' (red), and 'Purple Dome' (deep purple). This aster may not bloom in years of exceptionally early hard frost.

Astilbe x *arendsii* 'Fanal'

(ah-*still*-bee x ah-*rend*-see-ee)

Astilbe, False spirea

Astilbe is a misnomer, if ever there was one. The plant name originates from two Greek words: *a* (without) and *stilbos* (brilliance)—without brilliance. This probably describes the dull flowers and leaves of some native species, but when it comes to lighting up shady corners, most astilbe hybrids absolutely glow. Their showy plumes of red, magenta, pink, lavender, salmon, and white flowers float airily above clumps of divided foliage, adding welcome splashes of color to the serene green of shade gardens. Uniformly hardy and long-lived, cultivars vary so widely in height, plume shape, bloom period, and color that a perfect one can be found for every garden circumstance.

Portrait

'Fanal' is a particularly fine cultivar of the hybrid *Astilbe* x *arendsii*, with its delicate, pyramidal plumes of tiny, dark crimson red flowers that appear on tall stems by mid-summer. The flower plumes eventually develop small, dry fruits containing abundant seeds that disperse when the fruit splits open.

The foliage of 'Fanal' and most other red-flowering astilbes emerges from the ground a dark bronze-green in early spring, transforming to pure green during the growing season. Deeply divided leaves with sharply toothed edges form a tidy clump that spreads slowly.

Where to Grow

'Fanal' can be planted singly as an accent plant or grouped in the middle of lightly shaded borders. It is also at home in woodland gardens or naturalized by a pond or damp creekside. Dwarf varieties go well in rock gardens or massed at the front of flowerbeds.

Avoid planting 'Fanal' and other astilbes against exposed south- or west-facing fences, walls, and foundations, since sunlight reflected from these surfaces will scorch the foliage.

How to Grow

Plant 'Fanal' with its woody crown at ground level in very fertile, moist, well-drained soil. Because this plant is shallow rooted, its crown becomes exposed above ground level over time. When this happens, top dress lightly with a mixture of soil and compost to cover it, or divide clumps and replant them with their crowns back at soil level.

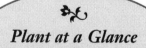

Plant at a Glance

TYPE: perennial
HEIGHT: 60 cm (24 in.)
WIDTH: 45 cm (18 in.)
SOIL: fertile, moist, well drained
LIGHT: part sun to light shade
FLOWERING TIME: early to
mid-summer

PHOTO – PAGE 76

The key to health for astilbes is providing sufficient moisture; keep 'Fanal' well watered and mulched at all times to prevent drying, or the leaves will quickly become crisp, curl, and turn brown. If you maintain adequate moisture levels, it will tolerate full sun, but it is happier with just a few hours of morning sun or light shade.

'Fanal' stands up well to wind and rain, as all astilbes do, and requires no staking. Deadheading does not encourage a second flush of bloom, so instead of removing dried flower stalks, leave them be until spring to provide year-round interest in the garden.

Divide this plant every three to four years in the spring or fall to maintain its vigor and encourage profuse blooming. Also divide to propagate, since named astilbe cultivars such as 'Fanal' will not grow true from seed.

Perfect Partners

'Fanal' looks lovely in the company of bold-leaved, shade-loving pulmonaria, hostas, bergenia, ferns, and bleeding heart (*Dicentra* spp.). It is also an excellent companion for hardy bulbs, effectively disguising their dying foliage.

Collectors' Choice

Astilbe hybrids and cultivars abound, making choices difficult for gardeners. Here are a few suggestions.

- *Astilbe* x *arendsii* hybrids (to 1.2 m, 4 ft.) are the best-known astilbes. Try 'Bressingham Beauty' (rose pink), 'White Gloria' (creamy white), 'Glow' (intense red), or 'Hyacinth' (lilac).
- *Astilbe chinensis* hybrids (to 90 cm, 36 in.) are late-season bloomers. They can be short (less than 50 cm, 20 in.) like 'Pumila' (lavender purple), 'Veronica Klose' (red-purple), and 'Visions' (raspberry red), or tall (90 cm, 36 in.) like 'Purpurkerze' (red-purple).

- *Astilbe japonica* hybrids (to 60 cm, 24 in.) are early bloomers of average height. 'Queen of Holland' (white) and 'Washington' (white) have lovely bronzy foliage.
- *Astilbe simplicifolia* hybrids (to 45 cm, 18 in.) are dwarf, late-season bloomers. 'Sprite', with its soft pink flowers and dark green, glossy foliage, was the Perennial Plant Association's 1994 plant of the year.
- *Astilbe thunbergii* hybrids (to 90 cm, 36 in.) are tall, late bloomers with large flower plumes. 'Professor van der Wielen' is a favorite cultivar.

Goatsbeard is very similar in appearance and habit to astilbe.

- *Aruncus aethusifolius* (40 cm, 16 in.) is a compact, dwarf goatsbeard with glossy, fernlike foliage and short plumes of creamy white flowers.
- *Aruncus dioicus* (2 m, 6 ft.) produces large mounds of divided, toothed, fern-like medium green leaves and long, airy plumes of tiny, creamy white flowers in mid-summer. 'Kneifii' is a shorter cultivar that produces cream flowers on arching stems.

Bergenia 'Sunningdale'

(ber-*geen*-ee-ah)

Bergenia, Elephant ears

Long-lived and easy to please, this attractive but tough perennial adapts readily to most prairie growing conditions and insists on looking its best from spring to fall, regardless of where it is planted. Bergenia is not fussy about where it grows; its large rosettes of shiny, green foliage and clusters of pink, bell-shaped flowers make a handsome groundcover in sun or shade, and in soil that is alkaline, acidic, fertile, lean, moist, or dry. The foliage of some cultivars turns a beautiful coppery bronze or deep mahogany in autumn. Where snow cover is reliable, bergenia is evergreen and greets gardeners with "instant green" after long prairie winters.

Bergenias, named for the German botanist Karl August von Bergen, are giant members of the saxifrage family and were introduced into western horticulture from their native Siberia and Mongolia in the eighteenth century. They were given the unlovely nickname pigsqueak when it was discovered that a swinelike grunt could be elicited from their large leaves by stroking them firmly between thumb and forefinger (try it!). In the past, a dye extracted from the roots of some bergenias was used to tan leather, earning bergenia another descriptive name—leatherleaf.

Portrait

'Sunningdale', an exceptionally cold-tolerant bergenia cultivar, forms rosettes of 15-cm (6-in.), elliptical, shiny, medium to dark green leaves that spread into lovely clumps through underground rhizomes. The leaf undersides are reddish, and the whole plant turns a coppery red in winter, especially when grown in a sunny spot. In early spring, clusters of small, lilac-magenta, bell-shaped flowers appear above the foliage on sturdy, red stalks.

Where to Grow

Use 'Sunningdale' bergenia massed as a groundcover under shrubs and trees, or as edging at the front of perennial or mixed borders. Like all bergenias, this one grows well in dry, shady spots next to fences, walls, and buildings, and it is lovely planted in long ribbons to soften the hard edges of paving. It also looks attractive planted next to ponds or streams.

How to Grow

Although 'Sunningdale' is not fussy and will grow almost anywhere, it produces luxuriant foliage when planted in light

Plant at a Glance

TYPE: perennial
HEIGHT: 45 cm (18 in.)
WIDTH: 60 cm (24 in.)
SOIL: fertile, moist, well drained
LIGHT: light shade to full sun
FLOWERING TIME: spring

PHOTO – PAGE 76

shade, in fertile, moist soil. Planted in full sun and lean soil, it produces fewer and smaller leaves than shade-grown specimens; however, as if to compensate, it also undergoes a more dramatic change in autumn leaf color than it would otherwise.

Plant 'Sunningdale' with its crown at soil level, in a location sheltered from the wind to protect the foliage. Deadhead to prolong the period of bloom and water well, especially during dry, hot weather. Once established, this plant will tolerate some drought.

'Sunningdale' is evergreen and its foliage requires excellent snow cover to survive the winter unscathed. In areas of poor snow cover, such as Alberta's Chinook zone, apply winter mulch around the plant for protection. Pull back the mulch in spring and remove any scruffy-looking leaves.

Propagate 'Sunningdale' bergenia by division after flowering in spring or in autumn; alternatively, take rhizome cuttings. Plants started from seed will take several years to bloom.

Apparently slugs love bergenia, but according to one prairie gardener, given the choice between bergenia and hostas, the slugs go for hostas every time.

Perfect Partners

The shiny, round leaves of 'Sunningdale' contrast beautifully with the feathery foliage of bleeding heart (*Dicentra* spp.), corydalis, astilbe, and ferns. Blue-flowered blue-eyed Mary (*Omphalodes verna*) and Siberian bugloss (*Brunnera macrophylla*) also make good companions, as do all spring-flowering bulbs and ornamental grasses.

Collectors' Choice

The following species of bergenia are widely available and bloom in the spring.

- *Bergenia cordifolia* (60 cm, 24 in.), also

> *"Thankfully, bergenia was one of my first garden plants. It remains a favorite for its evergreen leaves that greet me in the spring, contrast beautifully with the foliage of my other shade-lovers, and redden up with the cool fall nights."*
>
> LINDA GOH
> CALGARY, ALBERTA

called heart-leaved bergenia, produces rosettes of heart-shaped, glossy, 30-cm (12-in.) leaves that turn bronzy purple in the fall. Pink, bell-shaped flowers form clusters at the end of sturdy, red stalks. 'Perfecta' has deep rosy red flowers; 'Purpurea' has magenta flowers.

- *Bergenia crassifolia* (45 cm, 18 in.), also called Siberian tea, produces 15-cm (6-in.), elliptical leaves that stay green all year. Branched, reddish green flower stems bear pinkish purple, nodding flowers. 'Aureo-marginata' has medium green leaves edged in cream.

- *Bergenia purpurascens* (45 cm, 18 in.) produces clumps of deep green, 25-cm (10-in.), oval leaves with purple-red undersides; the foliage turns deep purple or beet red in the fall. Upright, brownish red stems bear clusters of nodding, purple-red flowers.

- Most bergenia cultivars available today are hybrids of the species *B. cordifolia*, *B. crassifolia*, and *B. purpurascens*. Look for 'Baby Doll' (soft pink), 'Bell Tower' (deep reddish pink), 'Bressingham Ruby' (intense red), 'Morning Red' (reddish pink), and 'Silver Light' (white, aging to pink), to name a few.

Betula papyrifera
(*bet*-ewe-lah pa-py-*riff*-er-ah)

Paper birch, Canoe birch

Although birch trees are denizens of cool, moist northern forests, they have long been popular in drought-prone prairie gardens. For sheer beauty and a sense of drama in the landscape, birches have no equal among other prairie-hardy trees.

Birch trees boast a practical and venerable history in society. They were revered by ancient Celts and Germans as holy trees with powers of purification, and to this day many churches are still decorated with birch branches on Whit Sunday. In the Middle East, some of the oldest manuscripts still in existence are made of birchbark, which has maintained its resistance to water damage and decomposition for centuries. Its water-repellant qualities also made birchbark indispensable to North American Natives for constructing shelter, watertight canoes, bowls called "rogans," and cone-shaped horns to summon local moose. Even pioneers relied on birch trees; they tapped them for sap, which was used to make medicinal tonics, wine, and a sweet syrup similar to maple syrup.

Portrait
Paper birch, the "lady of the forest" in northern climates, is a medium-sized tree with single or multiple trunks and a delicate limb structure. Trunks and large branches are covered with papery, self-peeling bark that starts out pale orange-yellow, but turns the familiar bright white after several years' growth. Bright green, oval leaves average 10 cm (4 in.) in length and turn a lovely golden yellow in autumn.

Both male and female flowers, in the form of catkins, are produced on the same tree. Showy male catkins set bud in August and expand the following spring, reaching a maximum length of about 10 cm (4 in.). Wind-pollinated female catkins are less conspicuous, but stay on the tree well into fall, long after the seeds have set.

'Chickadee' is an attractive narrow, upright cultivar, perfect for small gardens; it is not yet readily available, but will be in the future.

Where to Grow
Because of its relatively large size and moderately fast growth habit, use paper birch as a specimen tree on average-sized to large properties.

How to Grow
Plant paper birch in fertile, moist, well-

Plant at a Glance

TYPE: deciduous tree
HEIGHT: 12 m (40 ft.)
WIDTH: 6 m (20 ft.)
SOIL: fertile, moist, well drained
LIGHT: full sun

PHOTO – PAGE 73

drained soil, in full sun. Be prepared to water this birch on a regular basis; it is not drought tolerant and will suffer severe stress if left to dry out. Drought stress weakens these trees and often results in die-back at the top. Stressed trees are also more susceptible to pests—the bronze birch borer and birch leaf miner in particular.

Bronze birch borers only attack trees that are already failing for other reasons. They tunnel under the bark, girdling and eventually killing entire branches. Remove affected parts and burn them or dispose of them in the garbage. Leaf miners disfigure foliage but rarely cause a birch to die.

Paper birch seldom requires pruning. However, if you must, prune it after foliage is completely developed. Earlier pruning results in sap "bleeding" from the tree.

Perfect Partners

The snowy white bark of birch trees shows to advantage in front of dark green ever-greens. Aspens (*Populus tremuloides*) and pin cherries (*Prunus pensylvanica*), with which it is associated in the wild, also make natural-looking partners.

Collectors' Choice

All birch trees, regardless of the species, require generous supplemental watering when grown on the prairies to maintain their health and vigor.

- ❧ *Betula nana* (60 cm, 24 in.), dwarf or arctic birch, is a tough, spreading shrub that produces small, finely toothed, medium green, glossy leaves that turn brilliant yellow or red in autumn. This birch is covered with yellow-brown catkins in spring and is perfect for growing in a shrub border or rock garden.
- ❧ *Betula pendula* (15 m, 50 ft.), European white birch, has a broad, upright,

"Graceful birches remind me of the play of light and shadow in a woodland forest. To me, clumps of birch giving the effect of a grove always look better than a single tree."

EDZARD TEUBERT
MILLARVILLE, ALBERTA

pyramidal form and slightly weeping branches that droop increasingly with age. Diamond-shaped, sharply toothed leaves are glossy green and turn yellow in fall. The bark on twigs, branches, and developing trunks starts out a golden brown, maturing to pure white broken by black ridges. It is more sus-ceptible to bronze birch borer and birch leaf miner than paper birch. 'Fastigiata' is columnar when young and develops a more pyramidal or oval profile with age. The cutleaf weeping birch is sold interchangeably as 'Crispa', 'Gracilis', or 'Laciniata'; it has pendulous branches and deeply incised, toothed leaves. 'Purple Rain' foliage emerges a dark purple and gradually changes to a dark bronze-green, then turns a coppery bronze in fall. 'Trost's Dwarf' forms a small bush covered with threadlike, green leaves. 'Youngii', which has a pronounced weeping habit, is often grafted onto a straight trunk; stake the trunk until it reaches the desired height and then let the branches cascade freely.

Campanula persicifolia 'Chettle Charm'
(cam-*pan*-you-lah pur-sick-i-*foh*-lee-ah)

Peach-leaved bellflower

For many gardeners a perennial border would be incomplete without the graceful blue bells of at least one species of long-blooming campanula. The genus *Campanula* comprises nearly 300 species, some of which are admirably suited to prairie gardens. The generic name, Latin for "little bell," was inspired by the bell-shaped flowers that characterize most species.

Campanulas come in many forms; they may be upright, clump-forming, spreading, or even trailing. The flowers may be tiny fairy thimbles or huge cups and saucers. Tall types make excellent cut flowers for fresh arrangements.

It must be noted here than not all campanulas are well-mannered garden citizens. Some aggressive species, such as the clustered bellflower (*Campanula glomerata*), simply need to be disciplined with the sharp edge of a shovel each year. Others, such as the spreading bellflower *C. rapuncu-loides*, are almost impossible to completely eradicate once they have colonized a garden. *C. cochlearifolia*, the spiral bellflower or fairy bells, displays similar tendencies, although its miniature bells are a delightful sight growing in cracks and crevices. *C. punctata* is another thuggish species that will overrun less-rambunctious perennials.

Portrait
From late June to early September, *Campanula persicifolia* 'Chettle Charm' bears pale porcelain blue, bell-shaped flowers, with a darker blue edge. The tall stems bearing the outward-facing flowers rise above basal rosettes of toothed leaves. Smaller, narrow leaves on the flower stems resemble those of a peach tree, hence, the species name *persicifolia*, or "peach-leaved."

Other charming cultivars of this old-fashioned favorite are 'Alba' (white), 'Blue Gardenia' (double, silver-blue), 'Telham Beauty' (violet-blue), and 'White Pearl' (double, white).

Where to Grow
Plant 'Chettle Charm' in the middle of a perennial or mixed border, especially with other cottage garden favorites. For a more striking display, plant it in groups of three or more.

How to Grow
'Chettle Charm' thrives in fertile, moist, well-drained soil in part to full sun. Like many campanulas, it dislikes extreme heat and is not particularly drought tolerant. Mulch around their base to keep the soil

Plant at a Glance

TYPE: perennial
HEIGHT: 1 m (3.3 ft.)
WIDTH: 30 cm (12 in.)
SOIL: fertile, moist, well drained
LIGHT: part to full sun
FLOWERING TIME: late spring to mid-summer

PHOTO – PAGE 76

cool and to conserve moisture. If dead-headed regularly, these plants will reward the gardener with summer-long bloom. Divide them every three or four years to keep them healthy and to obtain new plants.

Although 'Chettle Charm' and other peach-leaved bellflowers are reliably hardy, the basal foliage often stays green during the winter and should be protected by snow or a layer of organic mulch in areas of unreliable snow cover.

All campanulas are relatively pest and disease free, but slugs may be a problem in moist areas.

Perfect Partners

The pale, porcelain blue flowers of 'Chettle Charm' complement the showy, bold colors of many mid-summer bloomers. Painted daisies (*Tanacetum coccineum*), oriental poppies (*Papaver orientale*), daylilies (*Hemerocallis* spp.), monarda, and cranesbill (*Geranium* spp.) are all pleasing companions. Subtler combinations can be achieved with pink garden phlox, yellow or pale pink foxgloves (*Digitalis grandiflora*), or lady's mantle (*Alchemilla mollis*).

Collectors' Choice

Hardy campanula species offer versatility and reliability, not only in the perennial border, but also in the rock garden. Most prefer part to full sun.

- Campanula x 'Birch Hybrid' (15 cm, 6 in.) is a long-blooming, deep blue-flowered hybrid of *C. portenschlagiana* and *C. poscharskyana*.
- Campanula carpatica (30 cm, 12 in.), Carpathian harebell, rewards gardeners with a profusion of upward-facing, bell-shaped flowers above mounds of foliage, and is suitable for rock gardens or the front of borders. 'Blue Clips' and 'White Clips' are the most popular cultivars.

> *"Peach-leaved bellflowers are hardy and pest-free, with beautiful spikes of flowers that are perfect for cutting. After the flowers are finished, the foliage remains attractive all summer."*
>
> MARCUS OLSEN
> BRANDON, MINNESOTA

- Campanula medium (90 cm, 36 in.) is the familiar Canterbury bells of cottage gardens. These biennial plants produce huge, pink, blue, lilac, or white bells; there is also a double form. 'Calycanthema' has cup-and-saucer-style flowers.
- Campanula portenschlagiana (15 cm, 6 in.), Dalmation bellflower, is a low-growing, spreading species with violet-blue flowers. *C. poscharskyana* (30 cm, 12 in.) is similar with starry, lavender-blue flowers. 'E. H. Frost' has white flowers with a blue eye. Both are attractive, vigorous groundcovers and are suitable for rockeries. *Campanula trachelium* 'Bernice' (30 in., 76 cm) bears double, violet-blue flowers on sturdy stems and is tolerant of dry soil.
- Campanula rotundifolia (30 cm, 12 in.), bluebells of Scotland, is a pretty prairie native with nodding, blue flowers. 'Olympica' is a bright blue cultivar; 'Alba' is white.

Similar to campanula, the blooms of this perennial are sure to delight young gardeners.

- Platycodon grandiflorus (45 cm, 18 in.), commonly known as balloon flower, is named for the flower buds resembling inflated balloons that pop open into flared, bell-shaped flowers; blooms are usually blue, but there are also white and pink shades.

Caragana arborescens 'Lorbergii'

(ka-ra-*gah*-nah ar-bo-*res*-kens)

Fern-leaved caragana, Siberian pea tree

During the Dirty Thirties, when all else was withered and brown across the prairies, caragana windbreaks still strutted their stuff, clothed in refreshing green, dotted with cheerful yellow flowers, and covered with brown, pealike pods that shattered with a snap! crackle! pop! when dispersing seeds. Obviously, caragana is a survivor. It hails from the steppes of Mongolia and Siberia and, not surprisingly, is tolerant of very harsh conditions, especially the cold, dry surroundings typical of prairie habitats.

Portrait

Caragana arborescens 'Lorbergii', a mutant of the species, begins as a tidy, columnar shrub but soon acquires an ungainly sprawl. This makes it an excellent candidate for grafting onto a standard either of the species or of 'Sutherland' caragana, which results in a treelike shrub with an unusual, but very attractive shape.

The slender 'Lorbergii' branches that emerge from the vertical standard curve every which way and look very much like the tentacles of an octopus. They are clothed in lime green, linear, threadlike leaves reminiscent of asparagus fern foliage, which gives them a soft glow, especially when backlit by the sun. After blooming in late spring with the yellow, pealike blossoms common to caraganas, its blossoms develop into flat pods that are medium brown at maturity.

Several other cultivars of *Caragana arborescens* are agreeable additions to mixed and shrub borders; all produce yellow, pealike flowers in spring. 'Tidy' is an upright, seed-free version of the fern-leaved 'Lorbergii'. 'Nana' is a dwarf shrub with twisted branches suitable for rock gardens. 'Sutherland' is a tall (3 m, 10 ft.), non-suckering, upright shrub with non-branching stems; it makes a perfect accent "tree" in small gardens. 'Pendula' and 'Walker' both have graceful, weeping branches, usually grafted onto 90-cm (36-in.) standards of the species or of 'Sutherland', to create small, weeping trees. Like 'Lorbergii', they both make a dense, woody groundcover that is perfect for stabilizing steep, dry, exposed slopes when left on their own rootstock. 'Pendula' also sports distorted stems, which give it a fascinating profile in the winter garden.

Where to Grow

Plant 'Lorbergii' as a feature tree in small spaces or as part of a larger mixed or shrub border.

Plant at a Glance

TYPE: deciduous shrub
HEIGHT: 4 m (13 ft.)
WIDTH: 3 m (10 ft.)
SOIL: average to poor
LIGHT: full sun
FLOWERING TIME: late spring

PHOTO – PAGE 77

How to Grow

'Lorbergii' survives in almost all soil types, although it prefers average, well-drained soil, in a sunny spot. It should always be planted with the graft union above the ground. Once established, it is a tough, drought-tolerant shrub that requires no supplemental water.

This shrub rarely needs pruning although its branches may be trimmed; early spring is the best time for this. Keep an eye out for suckers appearing at the base of standards; trim them back to the ground when they appear.

Propagate 'Lorbergii' by softwood cuttings in summer; winter is a good time for grafting if you want to create your own standard.

Perfect Partners

Low-growing, full-leaved shrubs such as saskatoon (*Amelanchier alnifolia*), cotoneaster, dogwood (*Cornus* spp.), and potentilla look splendid at the feet of airy 'Lorbergii', as do dark green, contrasting junipers and mugo pines (*Pinus mugo*).

Collectors' Choice

The following caragana species make excellent, low-growing, maintenance-free hedges.

- *Caragana frutex* 'Globosa' (90 cm, 36 in.), globe caragana, is a slow-growing, globe-shaped shrub with spineless branches covered in dark green leaves, each consisting of four leaflets, but is devoid of flowers and fruit. It maintains its globular shape without pruning and makes an attractive low hedge. It is also a perfect substitute for boxwood (*Buxus* spp.), which is not hardy on the northern prairies.

- *Caragana pygmaea* (90 cm, 36 in.), pygmy caragana, is a thorny shrub that makes an impenetrable low hedge. It produces arching branches covered in

"Don't be fooled by the name caragana. This hardy but delicate-looking, graceful, small tree should be in every garden. Its light green, needlelike foliage, arching branches, and yellow pea flowers will brighten and soften any landscape."

SHELLEY BARKLEY
BROOKS, ALBERTA

yellowish green leaves, each consisting of four lance-shaped, spine-tipped leaflets. The flowers, borne singly, are pealike, two-tone yellow, with occasional red markings on the outside. This caragana does not sucker.

Two other shrubs that are commonly used for hedges on the prairies are cotoneaster and alpine currant. Both are lovely left in their natural shape, but are also amenable to shearing for a more formal look. They prefer full sun, and fertile, moist, well-drained soil.

- *Cotoneaster lucidus* (2 m, 6.5 ft.), hedge cotoneaster, produces rounded, shiny green foliage, slightly hairy underneath, which puts on a spectacular display of orange-red fall color. Small, cup-shaped, pinkish white flowers turn into black, berrylike fruit in late summer.

- *Ribes alpinum* 'Schmidt' (2 m, 6.5 ft.), alpine currant, is a mildew-resistant shrub with deeply lobed, maplelike, shiny green foliage and unobtrusive greenish yellow flowers that turn into small, round, shiny red fruit in midsummer. Since currants may host a pathogen fatal to pines, do not plant it in their vicinity.

Chrysanthemum x *rubellum* 'Clara Curtis'

(kriss-*an*-the-mum x roo-*bell*-um)

Hardy mum

Chrysanthemums provide the gift of bright color to fall gardens when most other prairie-hardy plants are hanging up their faded hats for the season. Cultivated in Asia for more than 2,500 years and named for the yellow-flowering varieties of long ago (from the Greek *chrysos anthemon*—gold flowers), chrysanthemums are one of the most familiar and best-loved plants among gardeners and non-gardeners alike. For this reason it is unlikely that the word chrysanthemum will ever disappear from common usage, even though the genus *Chrysanthemum* has recently been dismantled and its members reclassified among several others, including *Leucanthemum* and *Tanacetum*. Garden chrysanthemums had also found a temporary home elsewhere—in the genus *Dendranthema*—but are now again officially classified as *Chrysanthemum*. During this time of transition, labelling may be inconsistent in nurseries and greenhouses, so both names are given here to avoid confusion.

Portrait

'Clara Curtis' is a fine example of *Chrysanthemum* x *rubellum* (also listed as *Dendranthema* x *rubellum*), the earliest and hardiest, fall-blooming chrysanthemum to grow on the prairies. This plant has lovely rich green, bushy, aromatic foliage that is often edged in red. The five-lobed leaves are toothed and slightly hairy. Single, rose-pink, daisylike flowers (8 cm, 3 in.) with bright yellow centers are produced in profusion on stiff stems from mid-summer until after the first frost. They make excellent cut flowers.

Other lovely cultivars to try are 'Mary Stoker' (pale apricot, fades to yellow), 'Duchess of Edinburgh' (muted red), 'Pink Procession' (soft pink), and 'Paul Boissier' (white).

Where to Grow

Plant 'Clara Curtis' as a specimen plant in the front or middle of perennial borders or mass-plant as edging in front of hedges and shrub borders.

How to Grow

'Clara Curtis' thrives in full sun and average to fertile, moist, well-drained soil. Excellent drainage is essential; locate it in a raised bed if regular flowerbeds have a tendency to become waterlogged. This plant also has a shallow, fibrous root sys-

Plant at a Glance

TYPE: perennial
HEIGHT: 60 cm (24 in.)
WIDTH: 60 cm (24 in.)
SOIL: average to fertile, moist, well drained
LIGHT: full sun
FLOWERING TIME: mid-summer to fall

PHOTO – PAGE 77

tem that dries out quickly, so maintain soil moisture with the help of organic mulch.

'Clara Curtis' produces a dense cluster of stems; the stems should be thinned when they are about 15 cm (6 in.) high. Pinch back stem tips to encourage bushy growth and abundant flowers, but refrain from doing so after the beginning of July, or the plant may not bloom before the arrival of killing frosts. Deadhead to keep it looking tidy.

Propagate 'Clara Curtis' by separating and replanting soil-level offshoots in spring or by cuttings later in the season. All chrysanthemums require frequent division to maintain plant vigor and bloom capability. They are also heavy feeders and should be nourished with a balanced fertilizer on a regular basis.

Perfect Partners
Agreeable companions for 'Clara Curtis' include daylilies (*Hemerocallis* spp.), delphinium, globe thistle (*Echinops* spp.), sneezeweed (*Helenium autumnale*), sage (*Artemisia* spp.), 'Autumn Joy' sedum, and ornamental grasses.

Collectors' Choice
Several other members of the former genus *Chrysanthemum* make excellent key players in perennial and mixed borders.

- *Chrysanthemum* x *morifolium* (45 cm, 18 in.), also labelled *Dendranthema* x *grandiflora*, are the well-known garden mums, which put on a fabulous display of fall color above compact, bushy mounds of aromatic, lobed foliage. Thanks to the wizardry of Canadian plant breeders at the horticultural research station in Morden, Manitoba, a series of early-flowering mums was developed; when properly labelled, cultivar names include 'Morden'. Try 'Morden Canary' (double, yellow), 'Morden Eldorado' (double, yellow),

'Morden Everest' (double, white), 'Morden Fiesta' (double, purple), and 'Morden Gaiety' (double, orange bronze).

- *Chrysanthemum weyrichii* (25 cm, 10 in.) is a mound-forming plant with five-lobed leaves and daisylike flower heads with pink or white ray florets and yellow disk florets. 'Pink Bomb' and 'White Bomb' are attractive cultivars.

- *Leucanthemum* x *superbum* (60 cm, 24 in.), formerly *Chrysanthemum* x *superbum*, is the popular white Shasta daisy that blooms all summer long. It produces lovely dark green, toothed basal foliage that becomes sparse toward the tips of stiff stems. These are topped by pure white, yellow-centered, many-petalled, daisylike flowers of "he loves me, he loves me not" fame. 'Alaska' (single), 'Mount Shasta' (double), and 'Polaris' (single) are cultivars of standard size; 'Little Miss Muffet' (single, semi-double) and 'Silver Princess' (single) are dwarf cultivars growing to 30 cm (12 in.).

- *Tanacetum coccineum* (60 cm, 24 in.), formerly *Chrysanthemum coccineum*, is the brilliant magenta-pink painted daisy that blooms in late spring and early summer. It produces large, pink, red, or white daisies on lax stems above a low mound of deep green, ferny foliage.

Clematis viticella 'Purpurea Plena Elegans'

(*klem*-ah-tiss or klem-*ah*-tiss vi-ti-*chell*-ah)

Italian clematis, Virgin's bower

Lovely clematis is often called the "Queen of Vines." Few garden sights are more spectacular than trellises curtained with masses of clematis flowers, whether they are large-flowered hybrids, or species with dainty, bell-shaped blossoms.

Clematis are divided into three groups based on pruning requirements and blooming time. Group A blooms in the spring on old wood only. Remove dead wood in the spring, then prune lightly after flowering to tidy wayward shoots.

Group B includes large-flowered hybrids that bloom in early summer on old wood, and sometimes later in the season on new growth. However, since cold prairie winters frequently kill old wood to the ground and any flowers produced on new growth are inevitably sparse and late, this group is not recommended for the prairies. Some Group B cultivars are labelled as Group B/C or B2. These are a better choice; while they bloom on both old and new wood, numerous flowers appear on the new growth in July and August. Prune these back to 90 cm (36 in.) in fall or spring.

Group C—the best choice for prairie gardens—includes summer-blooming, large- and small-flowered clematis that produce masses of bloom on new growth. Prune these close to the ground in fall or early spring.

Portrait

'Purpurea Plena Elegans' is a splendid *Clematis viticella* hybrid belonging to Group C. From mid to late summer it is covered with nodding, 6-cm (2.5-in.), double, rose-purple blossoms.

Most clematis listed as *Clematis viticella* cultivars are likely of hybrid origin. The group includes many gorgeous single-flowered hybrids, including 'Kermisina' (deep crimson), 'Little Nell' (white and mauve), 'Mme Julia Correvon' (rose-red), 'Polish Spirit' (deep purple), and 'Venosa Violacea' (purple and white).

Where to Grow

'Purpurea Plena Elegans' looks spectacular climbing on a trellis against a wall, or on an arbor or fence. Plant it beneath a deciduous tree or large shrub, training the new growth up into the branches.

Plant at a Glance

TYPE: perennial vine
HEIGHT: 3 m (10 ft.)
WIDTH: 1.2 m (4 ft.)
SOIL: fertile, moist, well drained
LIGHT: full to part sun
FLOWERING TIME: mid to late summer

PHOTO – PAGE 77

How to Grow

'Purpurea Plena Elegans' does best in full sun, requiring at least four hours of sun daily. Before planting, erect a strong trellis or other supporting structure for the vine. Dig a hole 45 cm (18 in.) deep that is 30 cm (12 in.) from the wall or other support. Add a layer of bone meal and well-rotted manure or compost to the bottom of the hole, then cover with a thin layer of good topsoil. Place the plant in the hole, with about 15 cm (6 in.) of stem below the soil line, and spread out the roots. Fill the hole with topsoil, firm the soil, and water. Add a layer of organic mulch around the plant to keep roots cool and moist.

Pinch back growing tips periodically to promote root development and bushy growth, especially in the first year. Once established, 'Purpurea Plena Elegans' benefits from an application of compost to the soil surface every spring, or it may be fed with a balanced water soluble fertilizer. Keep it well watered, especially during dry spells.

'Purpurea Plena Elegans' may be divided in early spring, shortly after new growth has appeared.

Perfect Partners

Like all clematis, 'Purpurea Plena Elegans' prefers a cool root run, so it pairs well with plants that shade its base. Cranesbill (*Geranium* spp.), lady's mantle (*Alchemilla mollis*), and *Heuchera micrantha* 'Palace Purple' are all fine choices. Small hardy shrub roses such as 'Winnipeg Parks', 'Morden Blush', and 'Henry Hudson' also make elegant companions.

Collectors' Choice

The following clematis are proven prairie performers and are listed by pruning group. New hybrids are available every year; check to see which pruning group they belong to before you buy. To enjoy

"Of all the clematis in my garden, this is my favorite. The double flowers are a gorgeous pink and very long lasting. It's not easy to find, but the search is worth it."

RUTH STAAL
CALGARY, ALBERTA

these lovely vines from spring until late summer, choose from groups with different blooming times.

Group A (Stick to hybrids of these two species; others in this group usually die back to the ground in winter.)

- *Clematis alpina* (2.5 m, 8 ft.) is shade tolerant, bearing nodding, bell-shaped flowers with four large sepals. Good cultivars include 'Frances Rivis' (blue), 'Ruby' (mauve-red), and 'Willy' (pale pink).
- *Clematis macropetala* (3.6 m, 12 ft.) produces double, open, bell-shaped flowers. Try 'Blue Bird' (lavender-blue), 'Markham's Pink' (light pink), and 'White Swan' (white).

Group B/C

- 'General Sikorski' (mid-blue), 'Henryi' (white), 'Lincoln Star' (pink with pale edges), 'Niobe' (dark wine red), 'Ville de Lyon' (deep red).

Group C

- 'Ascotiensis' (sky blue), 'Comtesse de Bouchaud' (mauve-pink), 'Hagley Hybrid' (shell pink), 'Jackmanii' (rich purple), 'Star of India' (purple with red bars).
- Other prairie-hardy Group C clematis species include *Clematis* x *durandii*, *C. orientalis*, *C. tangutica*, and *C. texensis*.

Consolida ajacis 'Dwarf Hyacinth Flowered'
(con-*sahl*-i-dah ah-*jack*-iss)

Larkspur

The stately spires of tall annual larkspur are often mistaken for small delphiniums. Indeed, this romantic cottage garden annual used to be classified as *Delphinium ajacis*, but now has its own genus, *Consolida*. It has recently undergone a name change from *C. ambigua* to *C. ajacis*.

Larkspur has much to offer prairie gardeners. It has good frost tolerance and is useful for filling in gaps in a newly planted perennial border. A long-lasting fresh cut flower, it also retains its color well when dried. Many cultivars are available, some with double blooms, ranging in height from 30 to 120 cm (12 to 48 in.). Dwarf larkspurs are the most versatile as they adapt well to container culture and do not require staking. Tall larkspurs produce more flowering branches per plant.

Portrait

'Dwarf Hyacinth Flowered' features finely cut, bright green foliage and showy, compact flower spikes; each flower bears a curved spur, hence, the common name. The complementary mixed pastel shades of the flowers include white, blue, lilac, lavender, and pink. Like delphiniums, the blooms on larkspur open from the bottom to the top. Cut flowers for drying when half the buds are open.

Look for the elegant tall 'Giant Imperial Mixed' (1.2 m, 4 ft.), which includes white, pink, blue, and violet blooms; the equally tall 'Exquisite Series' is available in individual colors, such as 'Blue Bell' (light blue), 'Blue Spire' (dark blue), and 'Scarlet Spire' (scarlet red). 'Giant Double Hyacinth Flowered Mixed' (90 cm, 36 in.) is an early-blooming larkspur mixture with large, double flowers in a pleasing array of colors.

Where to Grow

Plant 'Dwarf Hyacinth Flowered' in mixed borders with perennials and other cottage-garden annuals. It will also add height and a spiky element to container plantings.

How to Grow

'Dwarf Hyacinth Flowered' dislikes being transplanted so is best seeded directly outside in early spring, as soon as the soil can be worked. If you do start plants indoors, plant the seeds in peat pots about eight weeks before the planting-out date for your area. Cover the

Plant at a Glance

TYPE: annual
HEIGHT: 30 cm (12 in.)
WIDTH: 20 cm (8 in.)
SOIL: fertile, well drained
LIGHT: full to part sun
FLOWERING TIME: early summer

PHOTO - PAGE 77

seeds as they need darkness to germinate.

Although 'Dwarf Hyacinth Flowered' likes a sunny to partly sunny location, it thrives in cool weather and evenly moist soil. Keep it well watered during hot spells and deadhead spent blooms to prolong flowering.

Unlike taller larkspurs, which can become top-heavy and snap, 'Dwarf Hyacinth Flowered' does not require staking.

All parts of larkspur are poisonous and should be handled with care!

Perfect Partners

Create a romantic, old-fashioned bed of mixed annuals in shades of blue, pink, rose, purple, and white by combining 'Dwarf Hyacinth Flowered' larkspur with *Cosmos bipinnatus* 'Sea Shells'; pure white *Nicotiana alata*; clarkia; 'Ten Week Mixed' stocks (*Matthiola incana annua*); 'Giant White Hyacinth' candytuft (*Iberis umbellata*); and single or double Shirley poppies (*Papaver rhoeas*).

Collectors' Choice

Many other annuals may be gathered and dried to make exquisite flower arrangements. Except for nigella, which grows best when seeded directly outdoors, the following annuals are easy to grow indoors from seeds started six to eight weeks before planting-out time. All are quite frost tolerant and prefer a sunny location.

- *Helichrysum bracteatum*, strawflower, has an orange-yellow button center surrounded by stiff, petal-like bracts that may be white, yellow, pink, rose, red, or orange. Pick the flowers before the bracts are fully open. Try 'Bikini Mixed' (38 cm, 15 in.), individual colors in the Bikini Series, and 'Monstrosum' (90 cm, 36 in.). Choose 'Pastel Mixed' (90 cm, 36 in.) or 'Silvery Rose' (76 cm, 30 in.) for a change from the

> *"Larkspur, with its spires of pink, blue, and white blossoms, is one of the prettiest annuals for flower arrangements. It dries very well, too."*
>
> MARY YAKEM
> LAC DU BONNET, MANITOBA

more commonly available strong, bright shades of yellow or orange.

- *Limonium sinuatum*, commonly called statice, has tiny, papery flowers borne in clusters on stiff, triangular, winged stems. 'Petite Bouquet' (20 cm, 8 in.) is available in mixed or single colors. Also recommended are Fortress Series (60 cm, 24 in.), 'Pastel Shades' (76 cm, 30 in.), and 'Sunset Shades' (60 cm, 24 in.). 'Iceberg' (60 cm, 24 in.) is a pure white cultivar.

- *Nigella damascena* (40 cm, 16 in.), also called love-in-a-mist, has cornflower-like blooms framed with tangled, ferny foliage. Use blooms in fresh floral arrangements, or allow seed pods to mature for drying. 'Persian Jewels' has mixed white, blue, violet, pink, and rose flowers; 'Miss Jekyll' produces sky-blue, semi-double flowers.

- *Salvia viridis* syn. *Salvia horminum*, clary sage, has tiny flowers hidden in the leaf axils, but is distinguished by long-lasting blue, violet, pink, or white, petal-like bracts. 'Claryssa' (45 cm, 18 in.) is a compact strain available in blue, pink, white, and mixed colors. Other cultivars include 'Oxford Blue', 'Pink Sundae', and 'Tricolor Mix'.

Coreopsis verticillata 'Zagreb'

(cor-ee-*op*-siss ver-ti-sil-*lah*-tah)

Coreopsis, Thread-leaved tickseed

The family *Asteraceae* includes an abundance of annual and perennial, yellow, daisylike flowers. Many are native to North America, including one of the best of the bunch, *Coreopsis verticillata*, thread-leaved tickseed. This species boasts many fine attributes: it is tolerant of dry conditions, produces masses of flowers over several weeks during the summer, and attracts butterflies.

The generic name *Coreopsis* is from the Greek words *koris*, meaning "bug," and *opsis*, "vision" or "looking at." Like the common name "tickseed," this refers to the black seeds that resemble little bugs. The species name *verticillata* refers to the whorled arrangement of the leaves about the stem.

Portrait
Coreopsis verticillata 'Zagreb' is robust and compact, ranking among the hardiest of all coreopsis cultivars. Forming mounds of fine-textured, needlelike foliage, 'Zagreb' shines with a multitude of eight-petalled, golden yellow flowers, each measuring roughly 5 cm (2 in.) across.

'Golden Shower' (60 cm, 24 in.), which may also be referred to as 'Grandiflora', is a taller thread-leaved cultivar. The most popular of the species is 'Moonbeam', named the Perennial Plant of the Year in 1992 by the Perennial Plant Association. 'Moonbeam' (60 cm, 24 in.) displays lovely pale lemon yellow blossoms, and is heat and drought tolerant. Not quite as hardy as 'Zagreb', 'Moonbeam' requires gritty soil for excellent drainage and should be mulched for winter protection.

Where to Grow
Plant 'Zagreb' in large groups at the front of perennial borders for a showy display. This compact, long-blooming coreopsis is also an ideal rock garden or summer container plant.

How to Grow
'Zagreb' blooms beautifully in full sun. The soil should be well drained and of average fertility. Too much fertilizer, water, or shade will cause it to become lanky. Although not completely drought resistant, this plant is tolerant of hot, dry weather.

Diligent deadheading will keep 'Zagreb' blooming all summer, and plants may be cut back to a few inches once blooming has ceased. Divide plants every three years to maintain vigor and obtain new plants. It

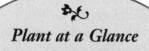

Plant at a Glance

TYPE: perennial
HEIGHT: 40 cm (16 in.)
WIDTH: 40 cm (16 in.)
SOIL: average, well drained
LIGHT: full sun
FLOWERING TIME: early to
late summer

PHOTO – PAGE 78

cannot be grown from seed and must be propagated by division or cuttings.

Perfect Partners

Like most yellow daisies, 'Zagreb' is easy to place in a perennial border. Team it with other members of the *Asteraceae* family that bloom in contrasting shades of purple or blue. Fleabane (*Erigeron* hybrids), purple coneflower (*Echinacea purpurea*), and smooth asters (*Aster laevis*) are all fine choices. Spiky blue salvia or *Veronica spicata*, the bottle-brush flowers of *Liatris spicata*, and the bell-shaped blooms of campanula or balloon flower (*Platycodon grandiflorus*) offer pleasing and complementary variations in flower form.

Collectors' Choice

Always deserving of trial, other coreopsis may, however, be more short-lived, or slightly less hardy than 'Zagreb'. Dead-head them regularly, and divide every two or three years. If they are planted in an exposed location or if snowfall is scarce, apply a layer of organic mulch over the plants for winter protection.

- *Coreopsis auriculata* 'Nana' (20 cm, 8 in.), the delightfully named mouse ear tickseed, is a petite, creeping plant with orange-yellow blooms, suitable for rock gardens.
- *Coreopsis grandiflora*, large-flowered tickseed, is a superb species for cut flowers; 'Early Sunrise' (45 cm, 18 in.), an All America award winner, has double, golden yellow blooms.
- *Coreopsis lanceolata* (60 cm, 24 in.), lance-leaved tickseed, is similar to *C. grandiflora*, but longer-lived. 'Goldfink' (single, gold) and 'Rotkehlchen' (double yellow, with red centers) are compact cultivars (25 cm, 10 in.).
- *Coreopsis rosea* (45 cm, 18 in.), pink tickseed, produces rose pink flowers with yellow centers.

> *"Coreopsis will survive and thrive in places where it's hot and dry—places where many other plants don't do well. It has starry flowers and interesting feathery foliage."*
>
> MONA HUGHSON
> PILOT MOUND, MANITOBA

Other perennial members of the *Asteraceae* family are stellar late-summer and fall performers. All do best in evenly moist soil, in a sunny location.

- *Helenium autumnale* hybrids, commonly known as sneezeweeds, have richly colored, daisylike flowers consisting of notched ray florets around a rounded central disk. Recommended shorter sneezeweeds (1 m, 3.3 ft.) include 'Moerheim Beauty' (dark orange-red), 'Butterpat' (deep yellow), and 'Wyndley' (yellow striped with dark orange). If you have the space for more substantial sneezeweeds (1.5 m, 5 ft.), try 'Flammenrad' (yellow overlaid with copper) or 'Sonnenwunder' (deep yellow).
- *Helianthus salicifolius* (1.5 m, 5 ft.), willow-leaved sunflower, has lance-shaped leaves and golden yellow flowers. With a width of 1.5 m (5 ft.), this plant is an impressive addition to the back of a large perennial border.
- *Heliopsis helianthoides*, false sunflower, has bright golden yellow flowers that actually do resemble small sunflowers. Choice cultivars are 'Summer Sun' (90 cm, 36 in.), with semi-double blooms, 'Karat' (1.2 m, 4 ft.), and 'Loraine Sunshine' (76 cm, 30 in.), which has variegated creamy white and green foliage.

Cornus alba 'Sibirica'

(*core*-nuss *all*-bah)

Siberian coral dogwood

The genus *Cornus* includes 50 species of trees, shrubs, and groundcovers. The most common species grown on the prairies are the native red osier, *C. sericea*, and *C. alba*, the Tatarian or red-twig dogwood, indigenous to eastern Asia from Siberia to North Korea.

These hardy, clump-forming species are highly valued for year-round appeal: they bear white flowers in the spring, produce clusters of fruit in summer, have excellent fall color, and, best of all, enliven the winter garden with their brightly colored stems.

Portrait

Cornus alba 'Sibirica', the Siberian coral dogwood, is noted for its erect thicket of coral-red stems that stand in striking contrast to the muted grays and browns of the winter landscape. Deeply veined, pointed, oval leaves are enhanced by corymbs of creamy white flowers that appear in late spring to early summer. The clusters of white to blue-white fruit produced in summer resemble berries, but are actually drupes, which contain a hard stone in a fleshy coating, like peaches or plums. Purple-red fall foliage provides a preview to the winter show.

Other fine red-stemmed cultivars of *Cornus alba* include 'Aurea', the yellow-leaf dogwood; 'Elegantissima' (also sold as 'Argenteo-marginata'), the silver-leaf dogwood, with variegated silver and gray-green leaves; 'Ivory Halo', a compact variegated form; 'Gouchaultii', the golden variegated or golden-edged dogwood, with green, yellow, and pink variegated leaves; and 'Siberian Pearls', which produces white berries with blue-black tips.

'Kesselringi', the purple-twig dogwood, has outstanding deep purple winter stem color, dark bronzy green leaves, and blue-white berries.

Where to Grow

'Sibirica' is a fine addition to a mixed shrub border, and may be mass-planted where space allows. Planted as a hedge, it makes a bold band of winter color and a pleasing spring and summer screen. Use it as a specimen plant in small gardens.

How to Grow

Plant 'Sibirica' in average to fertile, well-drained soil, in full sun to light shade; the red stems will be most colorful in sunny locations. Water regularly during the first

Plant at a Glance

TYPE: deciduous shrub
HEIGHT: 2 m (6 ft.)
WIDTH: 2 m (6 ft.)
SOIL: average to fertile, well drained
LIGHT: full sun to light shade
FLOWERING TIME: spring to early summer

PHOTO – PAGE 78

season, and mulch around the plant to keep the soil moist and cool. Once established, it will tolerate drier conditions. Well-rotted manure or compost may be added around this shrub each spring, but should not touch the stems.

In late winter or early spring, cut half of the old stems to within a few inches of the ground to encourage new growth, which has the most brilliant red color. To rejuvenate overgrown shrubs, cut all stems back to within 15 cm (6 in.) of the ground.

'Sibirica' is easy to transplant and may be propagated from stem cuttings.

Perfect Partners

The eye-catching red stems of 'Sibirica' show up beautifully against a backdrop of evergreens. Plant it with dwarf Colorado spruce, *Picea pungens* f. *glauca* 'Montgomery'; black spruce, *Picea mariana* 'Nana'; or 'Arcadia' juniper. Add a yellow-twig dogwood for a festive winter scene.

Collectors' Choice

Hardy native dogwoods make fine additions to moist garden locations.

§ *Cornus canadensis* (20 cm, 8 in.), bunchberry, is a useful non-aggressive groundcover for woodland gardens. The attractive oval leaves are arranged in whorls, with small flowers framed with showy white bracts appearing at the centers. The small fruit turns red in fall.

§ *Cornus sericea* (syn. *C. stolonifera*) (3 m, 10 ft.), red osier dogwood, spreads by stolons and requires plenty of space. Cultivars include 'Cardinal', noted for its cherry-red winter stems; 'White Gold', with variegated white and green leaves and bright gold stems; and 'Flaviramea', yellow-twig dogwood. If space is limited, try 'Isanti' (1 m, 3.3 ft.), a compact form with red shoots.

> *"The Siberian coral dogwood is a very hardy shrub. I plant it for its colorful red twigs and their outstanding winter effect. This shrub is especially lovely when planted in groups of three or five, in parks, large gardens, and acreages."*
>
> ALBERTHA VAN WAGENINGEN
> VERMILION, ALBERTA

For vivid color from spring to fall, try these other lovely shrubs.

§ *Euonymus nanus* 'Turkestanicus' (1 m, 3.3 ft.) is commonly called Turkestan burning bush for its red-pink fall foliage. It bears unusual bright pink fruit with orange seeds. *E. alatus* (2 m, 6.5 ft.), winged burning bush, is a larger shrub with corky ridges on the branches, colorful fruit, and vivid crimson-pink fall foliage. 'Compacta' (1 m, 3.3 ft.) is a dwarf cultivar.

§ *Forsythia* x 'Northern Gold' (2.5 m, 8 ft.), forsythia, produces golden yellow blooms in spring before its dark green leaves emerge. Plant forsythia in a sunny, sheltered location, since in very severe winters the flower buds may succumb to the cold.

§ *Physocarpus opulifolius* 'Dart's Gold' (1.2 m, 4 ft.), golden ninebark, has three-lobed, golden yellow leaves and cinnamon-colored shredding bark. It produces pinkish white flowers in early summer, followed by attractive red seed pods. Golden ninebark prefers moist soil, and sun to part sun. 'Diablo' is a striking, new purple-leaved ninebark worthy of further trial on the prairies.

Corydalis lutea

(ko-*ry*-dah-lis or *ko*-ry-dah-lis *lew*-tee-ah)

Yellow corydalis, Golden bleeding heart

Attractive yet undemanding, yellow corydalis is fast becoming a staple of the prairie shade garden. There is much to commend it: this plant is hardy, blooms over a long period, and has extremely attractive feathery foliage that makes it an asset to the garden whether it is blooming or not. In recent years its cousin, *Corydalis flexuosa*, a blue-flowered native of China, has also become a widely sought-after treasure for woodland gardens. Luckily, as increasing numbers of prairie gardeners grow to appreciate the cool green elegance of shade gardens, plants that thrive in these conditions, including corydalis, are becoming more widely available.

All corydalis flowers are spurred, or at least come to a spurlike point, so they take their botanical name from the Greek word for lark, a family of birds distinguished by sharp, elongated hind toenails that look like spurs. Until recently a member of the fumitory family (*Fumariaceae*), corydalis is also sometimes referred to by the rather unlovely names of fumitory or fume-root, so designated because of the slightly smoky smell that results from crushing its roots. Today corydalis belongs to the poppy family (*Papaveraceae*).

Portrait

Yellow corydalis has the same delicate, lacy blue-green foliage that distinguishes fern-leaf bleeding heart, and to which it is closely related. It is even called yellow bleeding heart by some. The finely divided, ferny leaves form a 40-cm (16-in.) mound sprinkled with clusters of buttery yellow, snapdragonlike flowers that bloom from June through August. The flowers are tubular, distinctively spurred, and terminate in broad upper and lower lips; they grow to 3 cm (1.2 in.) and appear on stems held just above the feathery foliage.

Where to Grow

Plant corydalis under trees or shrubs, along pathways, on the lightly shaded banks of a pond, or at the front of a partly shaded border. Because of its self-seeding habit, *Corydalis lutea* is ideal for naturalizing in a woodland garden. It also thrives in cracks between paving stones or cascading from crevices in old stone walls.

How to Grow

Plant yellow corydalis in fertile, moist, well-drained soil. Although it will flourish in part or dappled shade, it is not at all

Plant at a Glance

TYPE: perennial
HEIGHT: 40 cm (16 in.)
WIDTH: 45 cm (18 in.)
SOIL: average to fertile, moist, well drained
LIGHT: light shade
FLOWERING TIME: early summer to fall

PHOTO – PAGE 78

fussy, and will also perform well in sunny locations and average soil. However, the hotter the location, the shorter the season of bloom. Also, corydalis foliage appears to stay a fresher, deeper green when not exposed to bright sunlight all day.

Yellow corydalis is a reliable self-seeder and has a habit of popping up in unexpected places. Luckily, seedlings are both easy to transplant or to pull up if you want to get rid of them altogether. Plants may also be divided in early spring or in the fall, after they have finished blooming.

Perfect Partners
Blue and yellow always make a striking combination, so try planting both colors of corydalis together. Other suitable companion plants include Jacob's ladder (*Polemonium* spp.), 'Johnson's Blue' geranium, dwarf or intermediate-sized bearded irises, leopard's bane (*Doronicum columnae*), primulas, and lady's mantle (*Alchemilla mollis*). For an equally lovely effect, partner corydalis with an assortment of late spring-blooming bulbs such as grape hyacinth, dwarf daffodils, and Darwin or lily-flowered tulips.

Collectors' Choice
The following corydalis are also worth trying. Note that even though most corydalis are fibrous-rooted, *Corydalis solida* and *C. cava* are tuberous-rooted and somewhat more difficult to obtain and grow than *C. lutea*.

§ *Corydalis aurea* (15 cm, 6 in.) produces yellow flowers, and *C. sempervirens* (15 cm, 6 in.) produces lovely yellow and pink flowers. Both are low, spreading biennials native to the prairies, and when left to their own devices, will romp through your garden putting on a great show of color in late spring and early summer.

§ *Corydalis cava* (20 cm, 8 in.), also sold as

C. bulbosa, has purple or white flowers. It prefers light shade, thrives in moderately fertile, humus-rich, moist, well-drained soil, and goes dormant in the summer.

§ *Corydalis flexuosa* (30 cm, 12 in.) prefers cooler, moister conditions than *C. lutea*, and a soil richer in organic matter. The deep blue flowers of *C. flexuosa* 'Blue Panda', and 'China Blue' appear in early June; 'Blue Panda' foliage forms a mound, whereas 'China Blue' foliage has more of a spreading habit. In a hot, dry location they will go dormant until cooler weather returns. Propagate by division.

§ *Corydalis nobilis* (60 cm, 24 in.) is a robust plant that produces bluish green foliage and upright stems of up to 30 yellow flowers, each with a brown spot and a short, downward-pointing spur.

Crocus chrysanthus 'Cream Beauty'
(*kro*-kus kri-*san*-thus)

Snow crocus

To many prairie gardeners the most precious flowers of the year are those that herald the end of a long, dreary winter. Fresh, delicate, and ephemeral, few blooms are more welcome than the small crocuses that remind us of the miracle of spring.

Members of the *Crocus* genus are among the first to bloom, usually emerging in early April. The botanical name is derived from *krokos*, the Greek word for saffron. Indeed, the source of this prized spice, *Crocus sativus*, is the oldest cultivated species, mentioned in the Song of Solomon, written over 3,000 years ago, and portrayed in Minoan paintings dating from 1600 BC. Although *C. sativus* is not suitable for prairie gardens, *C. chrysanthus* and many of its other relatives are perfectly hardy in the region, including some fall-blooming species.

Plant at a Glance

TYPE: hardy bulb
HEIGHT: 8 cm (3 in.)
WIDTH: 5 cm (2 in.)
SOIL: poor to average, well drained
LIGHT: full to part sun
FLOWERING TIME: spring

PHOTO – PAGE 78

Portrait

Crocus chrysanthus 'Cream Beauty' has fragrant, cupped, cream and gold flowers with green bases; the foliage is grasslike. This and other crocuses grow from corms, which are swollen underground stems that resemble bulbs.

There are other lovely *Crocus chrysanthus* cultivars, among them: 'Snow Bunting' (white); 'Eye-catcher' (pale gray with purple on outside); 'Blue Bird' (pale blue with purple marks on outside); 'Blue Pearl' (white with lilac on outside); 'Ladykiller' (white with deep violet marks on outside); and 'E. A. Bowles' (yellow with purple marks on outside).

Where to Grow

Plant 'Cream Beauty' in rock gardens, beside paths, or even in large gaps between stones in pathways. Always enchanting in perennial beds or under deciduous trees, they may also be naturalized in turf or tucked in amidst low-growing groundcovers.

How to Grow

'Cream Beauty' prefers full sun, but will tolerate a partly sunny location. The soil should be of poor to average fertility and well drained. Grit may be added if necessary. Plant corms 10 cm (4 in.) deep in early fall. As with all small bulbs, the best effect is achieved by mass-planting; the sunlit shimmer of drifts of 'Cream Beauty' is truly spectacular.

If your garden is prone to raids by

hungry rodents, it may be necessary to take steps to protect all crocuses, considered a great delicacy by squirrels.

Perfect Partners

Pale gold 'Cream Beauty' and rich royal purple *Iris reticulata* are indeed a combination fit for a queen. Combine 'Cream Beauty' with groups of purple or golden orange crocuses, and add plantings of delightful early spring bulbs, such as deep blue Siberian squill (*Scilla sibirica*), striped squill (*Puschkinia scilloides* var *libanotica*), snowdrops (*Galanthus* spp.), and glory-of-the-snow (*Chionodoxa luciliae*).

Collectors' Choice

Other species and varieties of crocus are suitable for prairie gardens.

- *Crocus ancyrensis* 'Golden Bunch' (5 cm, 2 in.) produces scented, richly colored orange-yellow flowers in clusters of five.
- *Crocus speciosus* (15 cm, 6 in.) blooms in the fall, producing violet-blue flowers veined with dark blue. Two attractive cultivars are 'Oxonian' (deep mauve) and 'Conqueror' (sky blue). Plant these bulbs in August.
- *Crocus tommasinianus* (10 cm, 4 in.) has slender, long flowers and dark green leaves with a white stripe. Two favorite cultivars are 'Ruby Giant', with red-purple flowers, and 'Whitewell Purple', with flowers that are red-purple on the outside and pale silvery purple inside. *C. tommasinianus* f. *albus* is a pure white form.
- *Crocus vernus* (13 cm, 5 in.), commonly known as Dutch crocus, has white or lilac-purple, cup-shaped flowers and white-striped leaves. Named varieties include 'Remembrance' and 'Purpureus Grandiflorus' (both violet), 'Queen of the Blues' (lilac-blue), and 'Pickwick' (white striped with lilac).

The following are among the earliest dainty blooms to welcome spring, often appearing well before the snow has melted.

- *Chionodoxa luciliae* (10 cm, 4 in.), also known as glory-of-the-snow, produces small racemes of blue, star-shaped flowers with white centers. *C. forbesii* 'Pink Giant' (20 cm, 8 in.) is a delicate pale pink cultivar.
- *Galanthus nivalis* (15 cm, 6 in.), common snowdrop, has sweetly scented, pendant, white blooms dangling from a green base. There are some lovely common snowdrop cultivars, among them 'Sandersii', which has yellow markings and base, and 'Pusey Green Tip', which has white petals tipped with green. 'Flore Pleno', the double common snowdrop, is white with green marks inside. Somewhat less petite is *G. elwesii* (23 cm, 9 in.), the giant snowdrop, also white marked with green. Snowdrops prefer light or dappled shade and moist, well-drained soil.
- *Iris reticulata* (15 cm, 6 in.) is a diminutive fragrant iris with violet-purple blooms. Named varieties include 'Cantab' (pale blue with orange markings), 'Harmony' (sky blue with yellow markings), and 'J. S. Dijt' (red-purple).

Delphinium x *elatum* 'Magic Fountain Hybrids'

(dell-*fin*-ee-um x ay-*lah*-tum)

Delphinium, Bee delphinium

It's easy for gardeners to see eye to eye with magnificent delphiniums—many are at least as tall as their keepers! Classic delphiniums, which are *elatum* hybrids, paint a familiar picture. Their stately scepters of brilliant blue, spurred flowers reach for prairie skies in late spring and early summer, towering above nearby plants without hesitation. The best-known *elatum* hybrids are the 'Pacific Giant Group'; true to their name, they are gigantic, showy inhabitants of perennial and mixed borders, often growing to 2 m (6.5 ft.) or more.

Portrait

Charming 'Magic Fountain Hybrids' delphiniums are short, compact members of the 'Pacific Giant Group' that produce mounds of deeply divided, maplelike leaves in spring. Self-supporting, sturdy flower spikes are densely packed with 2.5-cm (1-in.), single or double flowers, properly called florets, in a range of colors including true blue, lavender, rosy pink, and white. Each floret consists of at least five colored, petal-like sepals; the top one sports a large, recurved spur. At the center of each floret is a little cluster of true petals, often of a contrasting color; these are the famous delphinium "bees."

Where to Grow

Plant 'Magic Fountain Hybrids' in the middle of sunny perennial and mixed borders. They make excellent specimen plants, but also look stunning when grouped in clusters.

How to Grow

'Magic Fountain Hybrids' require fertile, moist, well-drained soil, and a spot in full sun, preferably sheltered from prevailing winds. They do not require staking as their larger cousins do; however, delphinium stems are hollow and brittle, and even short ones occasionally suffer the effects of strong prairie breezes.

All delphiniums, including these hybrids, are heavy feeders. Give them a balanced fertilizer, such as 10–10–10, as they emerge from the ground in spring and follow up with regular biweekly feedings until they start to bloom.

'Magic Fountain Hybrids' are susceptible to powdery mildew; to prevent it, provide good air circulation, water regularly, especially during dry spells, and put all plant debris in the garbage instead of the composter.

The delphinium moth caterpillar, left

Plant at a Glance

TYPE: perennial
HEIGHT: 75 cm (30 in.)
WIDTH: 45 cm (18 in.)
SOIL: fertile, moist, well drained
LIGHT: full sun
FLOWERING TIME: late spring to early summer

PHOTO – PAGE 79

unchecked, can also wreak havoc on these plants. Look for these pests on flower buds and under leaves; signs of infestation include caterpillar droppings and leaves that seem to be tied together. To eradicate them, handpick caterpillars or cut new growth, caterpillars and all, back to the ground after it has reached 30 cm (12 in.). The plant will quickly regenerate, although bloom may be delayed by a few weeks.

Deadhead the main flower spike after blooming to prevent self-seeding and to encourage the formation of smaller, secondary flower spikes that bloom well into summer.

'Magic Fountain Hybrids' grow true from seed; they can also be propagated by division and stem cuttings.

All parts of delphinium are poisonous and should be handled with care!

Perfect Partners
'Magic Fountain Hybrids' look lovely in the company of clematis vines and large shrub roses. Silvery artemisia, peonies (*Paeonia* spp.), yarrow (*Achillea* spp.), oriental poppies (*Papaver orientale*), and coral bells (*Heuchera* spp.) also make interesting combinations.

Collectors' Choice
Many other delphiniums are worthy of prairie gardens.

- *Delphinium* x *belladonna* (1.5 m, 5 ft.) are hybrids that produce deep blue, nodding flowers on wide-open, multi-branched stems in mid-summer. Popular cultivars include 'Belladonna' (light blue), 'Bellamosum' (dark blue), 'Casa Blanca' (white), and 'Cliveden Beauty' (azure blue); 'Connecticut Yankee Hybrids' come in a mix of colors.
- *Delphinium elatum* (1.8 m, 6 ft.), bee delphinium, is the main parent of many delphinium hybrids. It is smothered in blue florets, each adorned with a bee, in

early summer; it requires staking.

- *Delphinium elatum* hybrids are divided into several groups. Some cultivars in the 'Pacific Giant Group' are named after characters in the Arthurian legends and are loosely grouped into a Round Table Series. They include 'Black Knight' (midnight purple, black bee), 'Galahad' (white), 'Guinevere' (lavender pink, white bee), 'King Arthur' (dark violet, white bee), and 'Lancelot' (lavender, white bee). Other outstanding 'Pacific Giant Group' cultivars are 'Blue Bird' (clear blue), 'Blue Jay' (medium blue, dark bee), and 'Summer Skies' (sky blue, white bee). In addition to the 'Pacific Giant Group', look for 'Blackmore and Langdon Hybrids' (1.8 m, 6 ft.), 'Fantasia Hybrids' (76 cm, 30 in.), and 'New Century Hybrids' (90 cm, 36 in.).
- *Delphinium grandiflorum* (syn. *D. chinense*) (60 cm, 24 in.), Chinese delphinium, is a short-lived perennial that produces very loose, branched spikes of single, deep blue, spurred florets above finely divided and dissected foliage; it does not require staking. Popular cultivars include 'Album' (white), 'Blue Butterflies' (blue), 'Blue Mirror' (brilliant blue), 'Blue Elf' (medium blue), 'Dwarf Blue' (dwarf, gentian blue), and 'Butterfly' (rich blue).

Dianthus gratianopolitanus 'Tiny Rubies'

(die-*an*-thuss gra-tee-an-oh-paul-i-*tah*-nuss)

Cheddar pink, Mountain pink

Pinks have long occupied a place of pride in prairie gardens, treasured for their exquisite blooms and spicy clove perfume. Members of the *Dianthus* genus, which also includes carnations, they are true aristocrats of the plant world. Prized in ancient Greece, the generic name means "flower of Zeus," while the Romans called them "Jove's flowers."

Although carnations are not hardy on the prairies, there are plenty of suitable pinks. The common name "pink" comes from an old word meaning "to pierce" and probably refers to the jagged edges of the flowers; the term "pinking" as a decorative finish on cloth has the same derivation. The color pink was likely named from the flower, popular since before Elizabethan times, as the adjective is not seen in print in England until 1678.

Most pinks cultivars are hybrids between species, usually *Dianthus plumarius*, *D. chinensis*, and *D. gratianopolitanus*. Some date back to the seventeenth century, although many pinks sold under the old names are more recent look-alikes. Nonetheless, who could resist welcoming 'Sops-in-Wine', 'Old Crimson Clove', or 'Mrs. Sinkins' into their garden? Single or double, fringed or laced, these sweet-scented little flowers are treasures that connect us to gardeners of old.

Dianthus gratianopolitanus (formerly *D. caesius*) is also called mountain pink or Cheddar pink, from the place in England where it grows on limestone rocks. The tongue-twisting species name means "from Grenoble."

Portrait

Dianthus gratianopolitanus 'Tiny Rubies' forms tidy, little mounds of grassy, blue-gray foliage. The leaves not only remain fresh looking all summer, but are evergreen year-round. Delightfully fragrant, the small, rose-pink, double flowers look like miniature carnations.

Other cultivars of note include 'Blue Hills' (blue-gray foliage, single, rose pink flowers), 'Bath's Pink' (steel blue foliage, fringed single, pink flowers with a darker eye), and 'Badenia' (fringed red flowers).

Where to Grow

'Tiny Rubies' is perfect for rock gardens, and as an edging for borders or pathways. These petite beauties are also charming additions to alpine trough gardens. Like

Plant at a Glance

TYPE: perennial
HEIGHT: 10 cm (4 in.)
WIDTH: 30 cm (12 in.)
SOIL: average to fertile, well drained
LIGHT: full to part sun
FLOWERING TIME: early to mid-summer

PHOTO – PAGE 79

all pinks, plant them where you can savor their captivating fragrance.

How to Grow
'Tiny Rubies' thrives in full sun, although light shade during hot afternoons will help blooms last longer. Provide average to fertile, well-drained soil. Once established, this plant will tolerate dry conditions, despite preferring evenly moist soil. Overly soggy soil may cause crown rot.

Cut off individual flower stems as blooms fade, leaving new buds and foliage intact. In the spring, trim dead leaves away from around and underneath the crown of the plant and feed with a balanced fertilizer.

The evergreen foliage requires a good winter snow cover; alternatively, cover the plants with branches from evergreen shrubs or trees.

'Tiny Rubies' should be divided every two or three years, or when the center begins to die out. This task is best accomplished in the spring as new growth starts. Like all pinks, this one is easy to propagate from cuttings.

Perfect Partners
Plant 'Tiny Rubies' with suitable rockery companions such as alpine aster, alpine columbines, creeping 'Birch Hybrid' campanula, sedums, thymes, and woolly yarrow (*Achillea tomentosa*).

Collectors' Choice
Other hardy species of pinks are also superb choices for prairie gardens.
- *Dianthus alpinus* (15 cm, 6 in.), alpine pink, has flat, pink flowers above mounds of narrow bright green leaves.
- *Dianthus barbatus* (45 cm, 18 in.), sweet William, bears clusters of perfumed, fringed blooms in a wide range of colors, including striped varieties. Sweet William is biennial but will frequently

"'Tiny Rubies' is just spectacular. It produces masses of showy pink flowers in spring and continues to bloom all summer."

HUGH SKINNER
ROBLIN, MANITOBA

self-seed. Cultivars include 'Indian Carpet Mixed', 'Snowy' (pure white), and 'Sooty' (deep maroon chocolate).
- *Dianthus deltoides* (20 cm, 8 in.), maiden pink, has low-growing, dark green foliage and abundant pink, red, or white flowers. Look for 'Albus' (white), 'Zing Rose' (deep rose red), 'Flashing Light' (bright pink), and 'Brilliant' (bright red).
- *Dianthus plumarius* (45 cm, 18 in.), also called cottage, grass, or border pink, has sweetly scented, fringed, pink flowers. This centuries-old species is the ancestor of many hardy garden pinks.

Not all pinks cultivars are hardy on the prairies; however, many have proved deserving of a prominent place in the garden.
- 'Pike's Pink' (15 cm, 6 in.), semi-double, pale pink flowers with a darker pink center.
- 'Pink Princess' (38 cm, 15 in.), double, salmon pink flowers.
- 'Rainbow Loveliness' (30 cm, 12 in.), deeply fringed, white, lilac, pink, and carmine flowers.
- 'Spring Beauty' (30 cm, 12 in.), fringed, double, pink, rose, salmon, and white flowers.
- 'Swarthmore' (20 cm, 8 in.), single, white flowers with a raspberry eye.

Dicentra x 'Luxuriant'
(di-*ken*-trah)

Fernleaf bleeding heart

Every June gardens across the prairies are awash with the eye-catching magenta and white of bleeding hearts (*Dicentra* spp.). Of all the old-fashioned flowers, bleeding heart is one of the loveliest and easiest to grow, requiring minimal care when properly planted. Most familiar is the common bleeding heart (*D. spectabilis*), which at maturity can be several feet tall and wide, giving it the appearance of a good-sized shrub.

Dicentra formosa, the western bleeding heart, is native to western North America. It is often called fernleaf bleeding heart because of the finely cut, delicate foliage. *D. eximia*, or fringed bleeding heart, is an eastern North American native that shares many characteristics with *D. formosa*, although it seems to be slightly less tolerant of the dry prairie climate. There is some confusion between *D. eximia* and *D. formosa*; some authorities claim certain cultivars belong to one species, while others classify them under the other. It is likely that many are in fact hybrids.

Bleeding heart blossoms grow on arching stems above clumps of blue-green, deeply divided foliage. As the name suggests, the inflated, paired lobes of each flower look like a small heart with a drop of blood dangling from the tip. The intriguing flower shape has inspired a host of evocative common names, among them lyre plant, lady's locket, and lady-in-a-bath.

Belying their charming appearance, all bleeding hearts are poisonous. However, this is a great advantage to prairie gardeners as the plants are left untouched by grazing deer and nibbling rodents.

Portrait

'Luxuriant' is a fernleaf bleeding heart that is likely a hybrid of *Dicentra formosa* and *Dicentra eximia*. Starting in late spring and throughout most of the summer, it is covered in cherry red, heart-shaped flowers set above compact mounds of ferny, blue-green foliage. Although even moisture is advisable for extended bloom, this and other fernleaf bleeding hearts tolerate sun and drought better and bloom longer than common bleeding hearts, which have a tendency to die back unattractively in our dry prairie summers.

Other notable fernleaf bleeding hearts are 'Adrian Bloom' (crimson red), 'Alba' (white), 'Bacchanal' (burgundy), 'Bountiful' (bright pink), 'Langtrees'

Plant at a Glance

TYPE: perennial
HEIGHT: 30 to 40 cm (12 to 16 in.)
WIDTH: 45 to 60 cm (18 to 24 in.)
SOIL: fertile, moist
LIGHT: part sun to light shade
FLOWERING TIME: spring to
late summer

PHOTO – PAGE 79

(white), 'Stuart Boothman' (pink), and 'Zestful' (rose red).

Where to Grow

'Luxuriant' is most at home in the dappled shade beneath deciduous trees, in lightly shaded perennial borders, or along the north and east sides of buildings. It will also perform well in rock gardens and perennial borders in partly sunny locations, preferring morning sun.

Although the larger *Dicentra spectabilis* is best used as an accent plant, use 'Luxuriant' or other fernleaf bleeding hearts in groups for a lush effect.

How to Grow

'Luxuriant' and all other bleeding hearts grow from brittle rhizomes similar to peony rootstocks; handle them with care as they snap very easily. Soak the bare-root rhizomes in room-temperature water overnight before planting them in fertile, moist soil, in part sun to light shade. Place the crown of the plant 2.5 cm (1 in.) below soil level. Bare-root bleeding hearts may be planted in the spring or in the fall while rhizomes are dormant.

'Luxuriant' and other bleeding hearts are also available as potted plants that can be set in the garden immediately after purchase. After planting, use an organic mulch around the plants to help maintain soil moisture.

All bleeding hearts may be divided every few years if you desire more plants, but, left undisturbed, they will bloom happily for many years. Divide them in the spring as soon as new growth emerges, or in early fall to allow the new plants time to become established before winter and to bloom the following spring.

Regular deadheading will prolong the blooming period of 'Luxuriant' and other fernleaf bleeding hearts.

"Bleeding hearts can't be beaten. They are simply gorgeous and start to bloom well before many other perennials."

MONA HUGHSON
PILOT MOUND, MANITOBA

Perfect Partners

The dainty foliage of 'Luxuriant' is stunning with spring flowers such as daffodils, tulips, peonies, irises, and primroses (*Primula* spp.). This plant also suits woodland companions such as columbine (*Aquilegia* spp.), creeping phlox, cranesbill (*Geranium* spp.), meadowsweet (*Filipendula* spp.), and hostas.

Collectors' Choice

Try these other hardy bleeding hearts.

- *Dicentra cucullaria* (30 cm, 12 in.) is called Dutchman's breeches after the shape of its white and yellow flowers. It has ferny foliage and prefers a shady, woodland location.
- *Dicentra spectabilis* (90 cm, 36 in.), common bleeding heart, produces 2.5-cm (1-in.), pink or white blooms in June and July. The white form 'Alba' is slightly less hardy than the pink form. The white cultivar 'Pantaloons' is more robust than 'Alba'. Since *D. spectabilis* may die back in hot weather or if it becomes too dry, plant it close to perennials such as lungwort (*Pulmonaria* spp.) and ferns, which will happily occupy the spaces vacated by dormant neighbors.

Doronicum columnae 'Miss Mason'

(do-*ron*-i-kum co-*lum*-neye)

Leopard's bane

Delightful yellow daisies are common in prairie gardens in mid-summer, when golden Marguerites, heliopsis, and rudbeckia brighten perennial borders with their sunny blooms. If you are a daisy devotee and would like the cheerful effect of these wonderful flowers in a spring garden, find a spot in your flowerbeds for leopard's bane. This striking perennial, native to the mountain forests of southeast Europe, Turkey, and Lebanon, will bring summer sunshine to your spring perennial borders.

Leopard's bane has no reputation of being poisonous, although a tale persists that its common name derives from the long-ago practice of hunting leopards with spears dipped in leopard's bane juice.

Portrait

Doronicum columnae (syn. *D. cordatum*) 'Miss Mason', also called 'Mme Mason', features attractive mounds of vivid green, heart-shaped, toothed leaves that appear early in spring. A few more-rounded leaves also clasp otherwise bare flower stems above the basal leaf cluster. For a leopard's bane, the foliage is long lasting; in other cultivars, the leaves sometimes falter during hot, dry summers.

Showy, yellow, daisylike blossoms, up to 8 cm (3 in.) across, are produced singly, high above the foliage, on numerous 60-cm (24-in.) stems and make excellent cut flowers. On the prairies, leopard's bane blooms a spirited yellow in May and June.

This plant's notable height, unusual among spring bloomers, is accentuated by its ground-hugging, leafy mounds and gives it a remarkable presence in the spring garden.

Where to Grow

Plant 'Miss Mason' in drifts at the edge of a woodland garden, under deciduous trees, or in the middle of a partly shaded border. It is also an ideal perennial to plant in an east-facing location that receives morning sun only. Avoid planting 'Miss Mason' in hot, dry areas, such as south- or west-facing beds in full sun.

How to Grow

'Miss Mason' prefers a partly shaded location, with cool, moist, rich soil. Before planting, amend the soil with plenty of organic matter, such as compost, rotted manure, leaf mould, or peat moss. After planting, top dress with organic mulch

Plant at a Glance

TYPE: perennial
HEIGHT: 60 cm (24 in.)
WIDTH: 60 cm (24 in.)
SOIL: fertile, moist, well drained
LIGHT: light shade to full sun
FLOWERING TIME: spring

PHOTO – PAGE 79

around the base of the plant to keep the shallow root mass cool, and the soil moist. Keep plants well watered and remove faded flowers and stems after they have finished blooming. Provide them with a protective winter mulch or cover them with snow whenever possible.

To propagate leopard's bane, divide the plants soon after flowering, or grow them from seed. They will spread slowly by means of underground rhizomes.

Perfect Partners
For striking color combinations, plant 'Miss Mason' with purple or lavender tulips, grape hyacinth (*Muscari* spp.), forget-me-nots (*Myosotis* spp.), squill (*Scilla* spp.), Siberian bugloss (*Brunnera macrophylla*), or 'Johnson's Blue' geranium. Leopard's bane also looks terrific paired with primulas, such as the delicate pink *Primula cortusoides*, lady's mantle (*Alchemilla mollis*), or the bronze-leaved astilbes.

Collectors' Choice
The many cultivars of *Doronicum orientale*, with their cheerful, large blossoms, also clearly announce the arrival of spring on the prairies.

❧ *Doronicum orientale* (syn. *D. caucasicum*) (60 cm, 24 in.) is very similar in appearance to *D. columnae*. Try 'Finesse' and 'Magnificum', which both grow to 50 cm (20 in.) and produce 5-cm (2-in.) flowers, or the shorter 'Spring Beauty', with its lovely double flowers. 'Little Leo' (40 cm, 16 in.) is a recent introduction that also is very popular.

If yellow blossoms give you pleasure in the spring garden, then you might also give these proven perennials a try.

❧ *Aurinia saxatilis* (25 cm, 10 in.), basket-of-gold, grows in full sun and produces alyssumlike, yellow flowers that

"This yellow daisy is a ray of sunshine in my shady garden. I have no fear of it spreading rampantly like the dandelion, and even after the blooms have faded, it has a nice mound of heart-shaped leaves all summer long."

ANGELA DU TOIT
BRAGG CREEK, ALBERTA

smother cascading, silvery foliage. It is ideal for rock gardens or edging. 'Compactum' has bright yellow flowers, 'Citrinium' bears pale sulphur yellow flowers, and 'Sunny Border Apricot' produces pale apricot yellow flowers.

❧ *Thermopsis lupinoides* (30 cm, 12 in.), false lupine, similar in appearance to lupines, produces spikes of lemon yellow, pealike flowers in late spring. Plants are long-lived and very drought tolerant.

❧ *Trollius cultorum* hybrids (90 cm, 36 in.), globeflower, grows in light shade and produces large, golden, incurved, buttercuplike flowers above leafy clumps of deeply lobed foliage. 'Canary Bird' has pale yellow flowers; 'Lemon Queen' is vigorous and produces large, clear yellow flowers; and 'Orange Crest' and 'Orange Princess' produce showy orange flowers.

❧ *Uvularia grandiflora* (45 cm, 18 in.), merrybells, is a woodland plant that prefers light shade and produces nodding, bell-shaped, yellow flowers that hang delicately from the stems. The leafy mound spreads to form an excellent foliage plant after blooming has finished.

Echinacea purpurea 'Magnus'

(eck-in-*ay*-see-ah purr-*purr*-ee-ah)

Purple coneflower

*E*chinacea purpurea, the purple cone-flower, is a North American plant native to prairies and open woods. This long-lived and low-maintenance perennial bears large, daisylike blooms composed of a prickly, orange-brown center and purple-pink ray florets, usually called petals, that curve downward from the center. The generic name comes from the Greek *echinos*, meaning "hedgehog," which refers to the spiny seed heads.

Purple coneflowers are a rich source of nectar and pollen, and rank among the top hardy perennials for attracting butterflies and bees to the garden. The long-lasting blooms make splendid cut flowers: the conical seed heads, which darken as they mature, may also be harvested for use in dried flower arrangements.

Purple coneflower is noteworthy for more than its colorful flowers, though. It has been used for hundred of years as an herbal remedy—by Native peoples to treat snakebite and fevers, and later by settlers who employed it against colds and influenza. Medical research has confirmed its antiviral, antifungal, and antibacterial properties. It is reported to strengthen the immune system and has been used in AIDS therapy.

Portrait

Echinacea purpurea 'Magnus', the Perennial Plant Association's 1998 Perennial Plant of the Year, was selected and improved in Sweden by Magnus Nilsson, who desired to breed a purple coneflower with more horizontal, less drooping ray petals. 'Magnus' forms clumps of deep green basal foliage; each lance-shaped leaf is hairy and toothed. Above the foliage rise sturdy stems bearing flowers measuring up to 10 cm (4 in.) across, usually of a rich red-purple hue, with deep maroon disk florets in the center. White and pink forms are also available.

Several other *Echinacea purpurea* cultivars are commonly available to prairie gardeners. Like 'Magnus', most have more horizontal ray petals than the species. 'Springbrook Crimson Star' (60 cm, 24 in.) is a compact cultivar with abundant bold crimson red blooms. 'Bravado' (60 cm, 24 in.) has purple-pink flowers, while 'Bright Star' (90 cm, 36 in.) has wide, rose-red ray petals. 'Robert Bloom' (1.2 m, 4 ft.) is a deep mauve-crimson.

Elegant white cultivars include the honey-scented 'White Swan' (60 cm,

Plant at a Glance

TYPE: perennial
HEIGHT: 90 cm (36 in.)
WIDTH: 45 cm (18 in.)
SOIL: average, well drained
LIGHT: full to part sun
FLOWERING TIME: mid-summer to fall

PHOTO – PAGE 80

24 in.), which features a black center high-lighted with gold; 'White Lustre' (76 cm, 30 in.); and 'Alba' (90 cm, 36 in.).

Where to Grow
Once established, purple coneflowers are heat and drought tolerant, making them ideal candidates for a natural prairie garden. They are also splendid grouped in perennial borders or used as specimen plants.

How to Grow
'Magnus' prefers a sunny location and average, well-drained soil amended every spring with compost or well-rotted manure. Like all purple coneflowers, it will tolerate a range of conditions, including wind, heat, and drought, although it will bloom most abundantly if watered during particularly dry spells.

Staking should not be necessary; however, plants may become floppy if they are overfertilized, overwatered, or grown in an excessively shady location. Pinch growing tips in late spring to encourage side shoots, bushier growth, and more flowers. Conscientious deadheading will extend the blooming time, but as the summer draws to a close, you may wish to leave the seed heads to provide winter interest and a food source for birds.

Divide 'Magnus' every four or five years, or when clumps become crowded or die out in the center. Basal cuttings may be taken in the spring.

Like most perennials, 'Magnus' and other purple coneflowers appreciate a substantial winter snow cover, or organic mulch around the root area, especially during the first winter when they are just becoming established.

Perfect Partners
'Magnus' makes a dynamic team with the hazy lavender-blue flowers of Russian sage

"Echinacea is a great all-round prairie plant. It's hardy, non-invasive, and has lovely flowers that bloom from late summer well into fall. I leave the brilliant rusty brown cones on the plant to poke up through the snow all winter."

CHERYLL RAFFA
HALFMOON LAKE, ALBERTA

(*Perovskia atriplicifolia*), or the spiky, thistlelike blooms of 'Veitch's Blue' globe thistle (*Echinops ritro*), or amethyst sea holly (*Eryngium amethystinum*). Also combine it with ornamental grasses, pink 'Marshall's Delight' monarda, liatris, blue or pink veronica, and 'Appleblossom' or 'Heidi' yarrow (*Achillea* Galaxy Series). For an all-daisy garden, add short varieties of sunflowers ('Sunspot', 'Valentine'), rudbeckia, coreopsis, sneezeweed (*Helenium autumnale*), and false sunflower (*Heliopsis helianthoides*).

Collectors' Choice
Look for these other hardy coneflowers.
- *Echinacea angustifolia* (60 cm, 24 in.), narrow-leaved coneflower, is a native prairie plant found from Saskatchewan down to Texas. This upright, bristly perennial has lance-shaped leaves, and in early summer produces 15-cm (6-in.) flower heads consisting of a conical, orange-brown disk and narrow, drooping, pink, purple, or white ray petals.
- *Echinacea paradoxa* (90 cm, 36 in.), also called yellow coneflower, bears eye-catching flowers with a domed, chocolate brown disk and reflexed, golden yellow ray petals.

Echinops ritro 'Veitch's Blue'

(*eck*-ih-nops *rih*-tro)

Globe thistle

One way to add a little zip and intrigue to flower borders is to plant something unexpected, like the fascinating shiny, spiny globe thistle (*Echinops* spp.). Whether you choose compact *Echinops ritro* or the mighty *E. giganteus*, globe thistles are all points and angles, with nary a smooth curve to be seen. From the coarse, jagged, incised leaves to the metallic blue, spherical clusters of short, spiky flower buds, everything about the globe thistle contributes to textural diversity in the garden.

Not surprisingly, the genus name *Echinops* is derived from two Greek words: *echinos* (hedgehog) and *opsis* (appearance). The description is an apt one—the globe thistle flower head really does look like a little blue hedgehog, hanging on for dear life at the top of its swaying perch.

Plant at a Glance

TYPE: perennial
HEIGHT: 1.2 m (4 ft.)
WIDTH: 60 cm (24 in.)
SOIL: average, well drained
LIGHT: full to part sun
FLOWERING TIME: mid-summer
to fall

PHOTO – PAGE 80

Portrait

Stately 'Veitch's Blue' globe thistle forms tidy, long-lived clumps of several stout, fuzzy stems that arise from a thick, branching taproot. The stiff, prickly, dark green leaves are deeply cut and reach a length of 20 cm (8 in.); their undersides are a downy white. The round, tightly packed, thistlelike flower heads are dark metallic blue and appear in summer. Each blue globe consists of dozens of tiny flowers that start out as cone-shaped buds; eventually, individual cones burst open into delicate, pointy, star-shaped blossoms, which make excellent fresh or dried cut flowers.

Where to Grow

'Veitch's Blue' and other globe thistles are perfect accent plants for the middle or back of perennial and mixed borders. They are also at home in sunny wildflower meadows.

How to Grow

Plant 'Veitch's Blue' in average, well-drained soil with the crown at or slightly below soil level. Although it will tolerate part sun, this plant grows best in full sun, and once established, it is quite drought resistant. There is no need to fertilize; indeed, too much nutrition causes it to bolt and set seed, thus shortening its bloom period. It also becomes leggy and requires staking in soil that is too rich. Deadheading prevents self-seeding, though the pointy blue bracts that remain behind after seed dispersal provide some interest in the winter garden.

'Veitch's Blue' is not invasive and seldom needs dividing. In fact, because it grows from a central taproot, true root division will not succeed. The long taproot also makes it difficult to move, although it can be done. Just remember that root pieces left behind after the move continue to produce baby globe thistles for a long time. However, if you really want to expand your patch of 'Veitch's Blue', relocate the small leaf rosettes that form at soil level, take root cuttings, or start new plants from seed.

Perfect Partners

'Veitch's Blue' paints a splendid picture with late-blooming yellow perennials such as goldenrod (*Solidago* spp.), false sunflower (*Heliopsis helianthoides*), sunflower (*Helianthus* spp.), and sneezeweed (*Helenium autumnale*). Fine-textured plants such as lady's mantle (*Alchemilla mollis*), sea lavender (*Limonium* spp.), and annual baby's breath (*Gypsophila* spp.) contrast well with its spiky foliage. Peonies, daylilies (*Hemerocallis* spp.), and garden phlox are also excellent partners.

Collectors' Choice

Several species of globe thistle are hardy in the prairies and are worth growing if you can find them. There is some confusion in nomenclature, but don't worry—they are all lovely late bloomers that prefer full sun.

- *Echinops bannaticus* (1.2 m, 4 ft.) has gray, woolly stems and spiny, hairy, 25-cm (10-in.), thistlelike leaves. Blue-gray, globe-shaped clusters of starry flowers are 5 cm (2 in.) across. Named cultivars include 'Blue Glow', 'Blue Globe', and 'Taplow Blue'.
- *Echinops giganteus* (5 m, 16 ft.) produces bristly, 45-cm (18-in.) leaves with hairy, white undersides and large, 20-cm

(8-in.), grayish blue, spherical flower heads.
- *Echinops sphaerocephalus* (2 m, 6.5 ft.) produces 35-cm (14-in.), spiny, gray-green leaves and 5-cm (2-in.) globes of tiny, silvery gray flowers. 'Arctic Glow' has white flowers, red stems, and silvery gray foliage.

Another plant similar to globe thistle in appearance, effect, growing conditions, and care requirements, is sea holly (*Eryngium* spp.), with its thistlelike, metallic purple blooms, showy bracts, erect stems, and spiny, heart-shaped, green leaves. Sea holly self-seeds abundantly.

- *Eryngium alpinum* (60 cm, 24 in.), also called alpine sea holly, is the showiest sea holly and produces steel-blue or white, 4-cm (1.5-in.) flowers with softly spiny bracts.
- *Eryngium amethystinum* (90 cm, 36 in.), also called amethyst sea holly, produces a profusion of 3-cm (1.25-in.) metallic blue flowers with silvery green bracts.
- *Eryngium planum* (90 cm, 36 in.), also called flat sea holly, is one of the hardiest species and produces 2-cm (0.75-in.) light blue flowers with blue-green bracts.

Eschscholzia californica 'Thai Silk Mixed'
(esh-*sholts*-ee-ah ca-li-*for*-ni-cah)

California poppy

The shimmering golden petals of California poppies have inspired many poetic legends. It is said that when sixteenth-century Spaniards saw the California hillsides clothed with poppies, they named the land "Tierra del Fuego." Also, prospectors seeking riches in the California gold rush are said to have run forward shouting, "Gold! Gold!" at their first sight of the same glowing slopes.

This splendid native poppy, a perennial or biennial in its native habitat, gained its unwieldy botanical name from Dr. Friedrich von Eschscholz, a naturalist and physician who accompanied a Russian expedition up the California coast in 1815. It was named the California state flower in 1890.

Today, prairie gardeners treasure California poppies for their rich colors and carefree growth habits. Grown as annuals in northern climes, they have been hybridized to produce semi-double and double flowers in shades of white, cream, yellow, orange, red, bronze, salmon, and rose.

Portrait

'Thai Silk Mixed' is a lovely cultivar for natural gardens. The semi-double flowers have fluted, wavy-edged petals in shades of orange, red, and pink.

The single-flowered species California poppies have satiny, golden orange, four-petalled flowers, 6 cm (2.5 in.) across, with a central cluster of golden stamens. The saucer-shaped flowers close at night and in overcast weather. Blue-green and finely cut, the dainty foliage forms a mound, above which the pointed buds arise atop 25-cm (10-in.) stems.

Other worthwhile cultivars of *Eschscholzia californica* include: 'Aurantiaca' (single, deep orange); 'Apricot Flambeau' (double, creamy yellow edged with coral); 'Dalli' (scarlet with yellow centers); 'Ivory Castle' (pure white); 'Mission Bells Mixed' (double, cream, pink, orange, and yellow); and 'Pink Chiffon' (rich rose-pink with creamy yellow centers).

Where to Grow

'Thai Silk Mixed' is striking in mass-plantings and as a filler in annual or mixed borders. It adds a splash of warm, cheerful color to rock gardens, window boxes, and other containers. These drought-tolerant annuals are perfect for natural meadows or wildflower gardens.

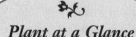

Plant at a Glance

TYPE: annual
HEIGHT: 25 cm (10 in.)
WIDTH: 25 cm (10 in.)
SOIL: poor to average, well drained
LIGHT: full sun
FLOWERING TIME: early summer to fall

PHOTO – PAGE 80

How to Grow

Since 'Thai Silk Mixed' resents being transplanted, sow the seeds directly outside in a sunny, warm location as soon as the soil may be worked in the spring. Poor to average, well-drained soil is ideal. Scatter the seed over the soil surface, rake in lightly, and water frequently to break the seeds' dormancy. Thin seedlings to 15 cm (6 in.) apart. Do not fertilize unless the plants are grown in extremely poor soil.

Deadhead plants regularly as blooms fade, and when flowering ceases, cut them back by half to encourage a new flush of flowers.

Plant new seeds each year. Although California poppies will self-seed, double forms are sterile, and hybrids will revert back to the single, orange originals.

Perfect Partners

The warm shades of 'Thai Silk Mixed' contrast beautifully with blue-flowered annuals such as bachelor's buttons (*Centaurea cyanus*), California bluebells (*Phacelia campanularia*), and Chinese forget-me-nots (*Cynoglossum amabile*). Also, combine them with dainty, white sweet alyssum (*Lobularia maritima*), Swan River daisies (*Brachycome iberidifolia*), or feverfew (*Tanacetum parthenium*).

Collectors' Choice

Other annual poppies may be graceful and delicate like California poppies, or big, bold, and blowsy. The following types all love a sunny location.

- *Eschscholzia caespitosa* 'Sundew' (15 cm, 6 in.), tufted California poppy, has fragrant, bright yellow, cup-shaped blooms.
- *Papaver commutatum* (60 cm, 24 in.), Flanders poppies, are closely related to Shirley poppies and sometimes considered members of the same species.

"California poppies are so cheerful—some are like neon lights in the garden. They also have lovely foliage that looks a bit like carrot tops."

HELEN DYCK
WINNIPEG, MANITOBA

They are glossy crimson poppies with a black blotch at the center of their cup-shaped flowers. 'Ladybird' (45 cm, 18 in.) is brilliant crimson red with bold, black basal spots resembling a ladybug's markings; the fringed, red blooms of 'Danebrog Laced' (60 cm, 24 in.) are marked with a large, white cross.

- *Papaver rhoeas* (60 cm, 24 in.), also known as Shirley poppies or corn poppies, may be single or double and appear in shades of pink, red, crimson, salmon, white, and bicolors. 'Mother of Pearl' (35 cm, 14 in.) blooms in unusual pastel shades of lilac, blue, gray, peach, pink, white, and speckled and picotee bicolors.
- *Papaver somniferum* (1.2 m, 4 ft.), opium poppies, have large flowers up to 18 cm (7 in.) across. Many are grown for their decorative seed pods, particularly 'Hen and Chickens', which has large, lilac flowers followed by an unusual central seed pod surrounded by smaller pods. *P. somniferum* var. *paeoniflorum*, or peony-flowered poppies, boast gorgeous double flowers. Some recommended cultivars are 'Pink Chiffon', 'White Cloud', and the fascinating 'Black Peony', which has purple blooms so dark they are almost black.

71

Fraxinus nigra 'Fallgold'

(fracks-in-us nee-grah)

Black ash

Hailing from the cool temperate zones of the Northern Hemisphere, the genus *Fraxinus* includes 65 species of deciduous trees. Commonly known as ash, many of these adaptable and fast-growing trees cast their dappled shade over parks and boulevards in North America and Europe. Ash trees were revered by peoples on both continents and appear in mythology as the tree of life. An Algonkian legend tells of the World Ash, the womb from which the first human beings emerged. At the heart of the Norse cosmos was the great ash Yggdrasil, whose leaves were eternally green and whose roots penetrated the worlds of gods and man. According to Norse myth, the first man was created from an ash tree.

Ash trees are tough, disease resistant, and long-lived. They generally leaf out later and lose their leaves sooner than many other deciduous trees. Most bear inconspicuous male and female flowers on separate trees in spring; if both sexes are planted close together, the female trees will produce clusters of winged seeds, called samaras. Because of the resultant weed problem caused by ash seedlings popping up in profusion, most gardeners now choose to grow seedless male clones.

Portrait

Fraxinus nigra 'Fallgold' is a seedless black ash that was introduced in 1969 by the Morden Research Station, selected from among native black ash seedlings near Portage la Prairie, Manitoba. 'Fallgold' has an upright, pyramidal form and is narrower than many other ash trees. Like all ash trees, it has compound, pinnate leaves, making it an ideal tree to plant where light or filtered shade is desired. 'Fallgold' is notable for golden yellow fall foliage, which persists for about two weeks longer than that of most black ash. The bark of young trees is smooth, becoming scaly as trees mature.

Where to Grow

Its uniform shape, seedless habit, and fine fall color make 'Fallgold' ash an excellent shade tree for medium to large gardens, boulevards, and parks.

How to Grow

'Fallgold' ash prefers a sunny location. It is not fussy about soil and will perform well in wet or dry sites.

The foliage of this ash is generally

Plant at a Glance

TYPE: deciduous tree
HEIGHT: 15 cm (50 ft.)
WIDTH: 10 cm (33 ft.)
SOIL: average to fertile
LIGHT: full sun

PHOTO – PAGE 80

Acer tataricum var. *ginnala*
(Amur maple, ginnala maple) page 8.

Achillea Galaxy Series,
'Apple Blossom' (yarrow, milfoil) page 10.

Left: *Betula papyrifera* (paper birch, canoe birch)
page 38. Center: *Larix sibirica* (Siberian larch)
page 114. Right: *Aesculus glabra* (Ohio buckeye,
American horse chestnut) page 14.

Aconitum spp.
(monkshood, wolf's bane) page 12.

Ajuga reptans 'Burgundy Glow'
(ajuga, creeping bugleweed) page 16.

Alchemilla mollis
(alchemilla, lady's mantle) page 18.

Allium aflatunense 'Purple Sensation'
(allium, Persian onion) page 20.

Amelanchier alnifolia 'Northline'
(saskatoon, western serviceberry) page 22.

Antennaria rosea
(pussytoes, early everlasting) page 24.

Antirrhinum majus Floral Showers Series
(snapdragon, lion's mouth) page 26.

Aquilegia canadensis
(columbine, granny's bonnet) page 28.

Artemisia ludoviciana 'Valerie Finnis'
(artemisia, wormwood) page 30.

Aster novi-belgii 'Audrey' (Michaelmas daisy,
New York aster) page 32.

Astilbe x *arendsii* 'Fanal'
(astilbe, false spirea) page 34.

Bergenia spp. (bergenia,
elephant ears) page 36.

Campanula persicifolia 'Chettle Charm'
(peach-leaved bellflower) page 40.

Caragana arborescens 'Lorbergii' (fern-leaved
caragana, Siberian pea tree) page 42.

Chrysanthemum x *rubellum* 'Clara Curtis'
(hardy mum) page 44.

Clematis viticella 'Purpurea Plena Elegans'
(Italian clematis, virgin's bower) page 46.

Consolida ajacis 'Dwarf Hyacinth
Flowered' (larkspur) page 48.

Coreopsis verticillata 'Zagreb' (coreopsis, thread-leaved tickseed) page 50.

Cornus alba 'Sibirica' (Siberian coral dogwood) page 52.

Top: *Corydalis lutea*, page 54. Bottom: *Impatiens walleriana* Super Elfin Series (impatiens, busy Lizzie) page 106.

Crocus chrysanthus 'Cream Beauty' (snow crocus) page 56.

Delphinium x *elatum* 'Magic Fountain
Hybrids' (delphinium, bee delphinium) page 58.

Dianthus gratianopolitanus 'Tiny Rubies'
(Cheddar pink, mountain pink) page 60.

Dicentra x 'Luxuriant' (fernleaf
bleeding heart) page 62.

Doronicum columnae 'Miss Mason'
(leopard's bane) page 64.

Echinacea purpurea 'Magnus'
(purple coneflower) page 66.

LESLEY REYNOLDS

Echinops ritro
(globe thistle) page 68.

LESLEY REYNOLDS

Eschscholzia californica 'Thai Silk Mixed'
(California poppy) page 70.

LIESBETH LEATHERBARROW

Fraxinus nigra
(black ash) page 72.

LIESBETH LEATHERBARROW

disease free; however, there are a few insect pests that may occasionally trouble ash trees, particularly green ash. Fortunately, the damage caused by these insects is rarely enough to seriously compromise the health of any vigorous ash tree and will usually not merit chemical intervention.

Prune 'Fallgold' and other ash trees during winter dormancy, removing dead, damaged, or crossing branches.

Perfect Partners

Like all ash trees, 'Fallgold' leafs out later than most other deciduous trees, so does not cast shade as early in the growing season. Plant a selection of spring-flowering bulbs and early-blooming shrubs and perennials near the trees to take advantage of the extended spring sunshine. Choose plants that will be happy in light shade during the summer, such as dogwood (*Cornus* spp.), pulmonaria, primulas, coral bells (*Heuchera* spp.), and globeflowers (*Trollius* x *cultorum*).

Collectors' Choice

Several other hardy, fast-growing ash trees are adaptable to alkaline soil and hot, dry conditions, making them useful trees for the prairie gardener.

- *Fraxinus americana* 'Northern Blaze' is a Manitoba-bred selection of white ash (12 m, 40 ft.) that has proven hardier than others of the species. A pest-resistant tree, it has an upright, oval crown that becomes more open as the tree matures. The large, dark green leaves make this an outstanding shade tree.
- *Fraxinus mandshurica* (12 m, 40 ft.), Manchurian ash, is smaller and more rounded than the green ash. 'Mancana' is a seedless Morden introduction with an attractive, compact form and featherlike leaves. It will tolerate wet or dry conditions.

"I use ash trees as a last-frost warning. The leaves only emerge after the final severe spring frost. They are also the first to change color in the fall."

EDZARD TEUBERT
MILLARVILLE, ALBERTA

- *Fraxinus* x 'Northern Gem' and 'Northern Treasure' (11 to 12 m, 35 to 40 ft.) are hardy hybrids of black ash (*F. nigra*) and Manchurian ash (*F. mandshurica*) developed in Morden, Manitoba. Although only recently released, they appear to be excellent choices for prairie gardeners. 'Northern Gem' has a globe-shaped crown; 'Northern Treasure' is more oval in form.
- *Fraxinus pennsylvanica* var. *subintegerrima* (18 m, 60 ft.), green ash, is a prairie native and the largest species. Green ash has an oval crown and a dense canopy of bright green, pinnate leaves that turn yellow in autumn. It has gray-brown, furrowed bark and displays prominent brown buds in winter. This long-lived tree is useful in shelterbelt and street plantings, although it may be attacked by ash bark beetles, lygus bugs, cankerworms, and ash flower-gall mites. 'Rugby', also sold as Prairie Spire™, is seedless and originates in North Dakota; it is the best-shaped, upright green ash and has excellent winter hardiness. Other available cultivars include 'Patmore' and 'Summit'.

Gaillardia x grandiflora 'Goblin'

(gah-*lar*-dee-ah x gran-di-*flor*-ah)

Gaillardia, Blanket flower

The bright orange and yellow, daisylike flowers of gaillardia (*Gaillardia aristata*), or blanket flower, are a familiar sight swaying amidst prairie grasses in the warm summer breezes. This cheerful and drought-tolerant native plant has also been welcomed into our gardens. One of those useful perennials that keeps blooming until hard frost, it is a staple of the fall garden, with a color selection that is now expanded to include rich shades of red, bronze, and burgundy. Like many plants derived from native species, gaillardia is a food source for bees and butterflies.

Gaillardia derives its generic name from Gaillard de Charentonneau, an eighteenth-century French magistrate and enthusiastic patron of the science of botany. It is said that the flowers inspired the colors used in blankets created by Native women in the American southwest, hence, the common name "blanket flower."

In Belgium in 1857, two native North American species—the perennial *Gaillardia aristata* and the annual *G. pulchella*—were hybridized to produce *G.* x *grandiflora*. Most of the gaillardia cultivars we grow today are bred from this hybrid, and feature multicolored flowers of yellow, orange, maroon, and red.

Portrait

The compact cultivar *Gaillardia* x *grandiflora* 'Goblin' (also sold as 'Kobold') has orange-red petals tipped with yellow, arranged around a dense, rounded, dark red and yellow center. The flowers are held well above the mounds of lance-shaped leaves to make a brilliant show. 'Golden Goblin' is a yellow-flowered cultivar of the same size and growth habit. 'Baby Cole' is only 20 cm (8 in.), with bicolored yellow and red flowers.

Taller *Gaillardia* x *grandiflora* cultivars reach 90 cm (36 in.). These include 'Burgundy' and the mixed-color 'Monarch' strain.

Where to Grow

Use 'Goblin' in rockeries, sunny perennial or mixed borders, or even in containers for the summer, planting them in the garden before winter.

How to Grow

'Goblin' loves full sun and is an excellent choice for hot, dry locations. Avoid planting this and other gaillardias in overly rich soil as it causes them to become floppy

Plant at a Glance

TYPE: perennial
HEIGHT: 30 cm (12 in.)
WIDTH: 45 cm (18 in.)
SOIL: average, well drained
LIGHT: full sun
FLOWERING TIME: mid-summer
to fall

PHOTO – PAGE 121

and may even hasten their demise. Make sure the soil drains adequately; this cultivar will not survive boggy conditions.

Deadhead spent blooms regularly by cutting them off at the base of the flowering stem, unless you wish to leave some to self-seed. Keep in mind that the resultant seedlings may be variable in color and size; however, this could prove charming, especially in naturalized settings.

Since gaillardias are short-lived perennials, rejuvenate 'Goblin' by division every two years, discarding old portions of the plant. It may also be propagated by stem or root cuttings and by seed. If seeds are planted indoors in February, the plants should bloom the first year. Do not cover the seeds as they require light for optimum germination.

Perfect Partners
Plant 'Goblin' with ornamental grasses, including bulbous oat grass (*Arrhenatherum elatius* var. *bulbosum* 'Variegatum'), blue-eyed grass (*Sisyrinchium montanum*), and little bluestem grass (*Schizachyrium scoparium*). The warm colors of the flowers contrast beautifully with the silvery foliage of artemisia and lambs' ears (*Stachys byzantina*), and the deep blue blooms of annual *Salvia farinacea* 'Victoria' or the perennial *S. x sylvestris* 'May Night'. Other excellent choices are yarrow (*Achillea* spp.), coreopsis, coneflowers (*Rudbeckia* spp.), and purple coneflowers (*Echinacea purpurea*), all fellow late-summer bloomers.

Collectors' Choice
Plant a prairie garden with these sun-loving native gaillardia species.
- *Gaillardia aristata* (76 cm, 30 in.), the native perennial species, has yellow petals around reddish orange centers.
- *Gaillardia pulchella* (60 cm, 24 in.), the

"*Gaillardia is a ray of sunshine in my garden. It blooms for a long time and seeds itself. I have a nostalgic attachment to it as it is one of the perennials that my mother grew. It also grows wild in our fields.*"

TENA KILMURY
BRANDON, MANITOBA

native annual species, has yellow petals with red at the base, around a maroon central disk. Look for the cultivars 'Double Mixed' (cream, gold, crimson, and bicolors) and 'Red Plume'.

Other prairie natives are also tough and beautiful plants.
- *Liatris punctata* (30 cm, 12 in.), also called dotted gayfeather or dotted blazing star, bears bottle-brush wands crowded with tiny, rose-lavender flowers. Accustomed to dry, open habitat, this pretty perennial blooms in late summer.
- *Monarda fistulosa* (76 cm, 30 in.), wild bee balm, has loose heads of small, tubular, lilac purple flowers and aromatic leaves. Wild bee balm is attractive to hummingbirds, as well as bees and other beneficial insects.
- *Ratibida columnifera* (60 cm, 24 in.), also known as yellow prairie coneflower, has a large central disk and reflexed, yellow petals. It blooms from early summer until frost.
- *Solidago missouriensis* (30 cm, 12 in.), prairie or low goldenrod, produces showy clusters of tiny, yellow flowers on erect or arching branches.
- *Thermopsis rhombifolia* (60 cm, 24 in.), also called golden bean or false lupine, has lupinelike spikes of small, yellow flowers and leaves divided into three lance-shaped leaflets.

Geranium x magnificum
(jer-*ane*-ee-um x mag-*niff*-ih-cum)

Showy cranesbill

Versatile cranesbills, commonly known as hardy or perennial geraniums, have become an indispensable addition to many prairie gardens. However, the botanical name *Geranium* is often confusing to new gardeners. Cranesbills belong to the geranium family, *Geraniaceae*, as do the brightly colored, popular container and bedding plants also called geraniums by many. These annual geraniums are more properly referred to by their own genus name, *Pelargonium*.

The botanical name *Geranium* comes from the Greek *geranos*, meaning "crane," and refers to the resemblance of the long, pointy seed pod to a crane's bill. There are about 400 species of cranesbills, several of which are native to the prairies. Campers and hikers may be familiar with the bright pinkish purple flowers of the purple sticky geranium (*G. viscosissimum*), found in open woods and meadows.

There are cranesbills to suit most garden locations. They are also terrific to share with gardening buddies, since cranesbills will often self-seed or spread by rhizomes to form a large clump. Add to that their long bloom period, drought tolerance, and pest resistance, and what more could you ask for in a perennial?

Portrait
Geranium x *magnificum* lives up to its name, forming magnificent mounds of soft, hairy, deeply divided leaves, up to 15 cm (6 in.) across. The handsome foliage starts out a velvety, medium green and turns a deep burgundy red in the fall, forming large clumps as it spreads by underground stolons. Its sterile, saucer-shaped, rich purple flowers are prominently veined in dark purple, and shimmer with iridescence in one prolonged early summer flush.

Where to Grow
Showy cranesbill performs superbly in the middle of mixed borders. The plant's attractive leaf form and color are appealing even when it is not in bloom.

How to Grow
Plant showy cranesbill in full or part sun, in average, well-drained soil. Fertilize once a season with a balanced fertilizer, just as new growth is emerging. Too much fertilizer can lead to the formation of lush growth at the expense of flowers, and can also produce weak stems that have a tendency to flop.

Plant at a Glance

TYPE: perennial
HEIGHT: 60 cm (24 in.)
WIDTH: 60 cm (24 in.)
SOIL: average, well drained
LIGHT: full to part sun
FLOWERING TIME: early summer

PHOTO – PAGE 121

The flowering stems should be cut back after blooming has finished; this may encourage further blooms, although *Geranium x magnificum* usually will not flower a second time. Trim the foliage in the fall after it has died back or leave it until early spring to provide protection for the plant in areas of your garden where snow cover is unreliable.

Showy cranesbill may be easily propagated by division; it is sterile so does not self-seed.

Perfect Partners
Yellow-flowered perennials, such as leopard's bane (*Doronicum columnae*), primula, or even the chartreuse sprays of lady's mantle (*Alchemilla mollis*) look striking with the intensely blue blooms of *Geranium x magnificum*. Bellflower (*Campanula* spp.), delphinium, pinks (*Dianthus* spp.), phlox, and ornamental grasses are all excellent partners. Showy cranesbill also paints a pretty picture in combination with hardy shrub roses, sage (*Artemisia* spp.), and catmint (*Nepeta* spp.).

Collectors' Choice
As the popularity of this undemanding perennial continues to increase, so does the number of varieties available at local garden centers. Check plant labels for mature size before you purchase, as some require lots of space.

- *Geranium* x 'Ann Folkard' (45 cm, 18 in.) produces bright magenta flowers in abundance all summer; it is ideal for sun or light shade.
- *Geranium cinereum* 'Ballerina' (15 cm, 6 in.) has lilac-pink, crimson-veined flowers with dark crimson centers and finely cut leaves; it is suitable for alpine gardens.
- *Geranium dalmaticum* (15 cm, 6 in.) has mounds of small, glossy leaves and rose pink or white flowers; it prefers light shade.
- *Geranium endressii* (30 cm, 12 in.) produces pale pink flowers veined with red for most of the summer. Plant this cranesbill in light shade or in sun, but do not allow the soil dry out.
- *Geranium* x 'Johnson's Blue' (60 cm, 24 in.) has lovely bright blue flowers with darker veins; it prefers light shade.
- *Geranium macrorrhizum* (30 cm, 12 in.) has pink-lilac or white flowers and five-lobed, fragrant leaves. It will spread to form a hardy groundcover and even survives in dry shade.
- *Geranium phaeum* (60 cm, 24 in.) has clusters of flat flowers that are usually a dark maroon, but some are almost black. It does well in most locations and even tolerates shade well.
- *Geranium pratense* (90 cm, 36 in.) has light blue flowers, veined in pink, on long stems; give it lots of room. There are also double-blue, white, and double-white flowering cultivars.
- *Geranium sanguineum prostratum* (10 cm, 4 in.) has pale pink flowers and low-growing mats of foliage.

"I think that geraniums are a group of plants with something to offer just about every gardener and every garden location. Geranium x magnificum bears large flowers of deep violet-blue and, as a bonus, its fall foliage is red."

ROSEMARY McNARY
MEDICINE HAT, ALBERTA

Geum triflorum

(*gay*-um try-*flor*-um)

Three-flowered avens,
Prairie smoke

Increasingly, prairie gardeners are recognizing the benefits of growing native plant species. These tough and fascinating plants do not clamor for our attention as do showier cultivars, but instead reward the observant gardener who appreciates their subtle beauty.

One such treasure is the prairie native three-flowered avens (*Geum triflorum*), also known as old man's whiskers or, more poetically, prairie smoke, because of its silken-haired seed pods. The genus *Geum* is represented by species native to North and South America, Europe, and Asia and is rich in folklore and history. The generic name is from the Greek and has been variably translated as meaning "giving perfume" or "giving an agreeable flavor," in reference to the sweetly spicy scent of the roots.

Common in medieval herb gardens, avens was used to treat medical problems, to flavor wine and beer, and to repel evil spirits. The plants were brought indoors or painted on the walls of homes and churches. *Geum urbanum* was commonly called Herb Bennet, a corruption of *Herbe benedicta*, blessed herb or St. Benedict's herb, after the founder of the Benedictine order of monks. In medieval times, the three leaves of the avens signified the Holy Trinity, and the five golden petals of the flowers symbolized the five wounds of Christ.

In North America, the roots of three-flowered avens were boiled to make a drink that tasted like weak sassafras tea. Water avens (*Geum rivale*) was known as Indian chocolate because of a beverage concocted from its roots and leaves. This mixture was used as a cure for dysentery, colic, and stomach problems.

Portrait

Three-flowered avens has finely cut leaves growing in basal rosettes, above which rise long, reddish, branched stems. The top of each stem curves downward and supports three bell-shaped, pink to purple flowers individually measuring about 1.5 cm (0.5 in.).

After the flowers are fertilized they begin to turn upward and feathery plumes grow from the maturing seed pods. In the open grasslands these are borne away in the wind, but in sheltered gardens they give a lovely smoky texture to the plant, which persists long after blooming has finished.

Plant at a Glance

TYPE: perennial
HEIGHT: 30 cm (12 in.)
WIDTH: 30 cm (12 in.)
SOIL: average, well drained
LIGHT: full sun to light shade
FLOWERING TIME: spring to early summer

PHOTO – PAGE 121

Where to Grow

Plant three-flowered avens in natural areas, at the front of perennial gardens, in rock gardens, or in a woodland garden.

How to Grow

Three-flowered avens prefers a sunny location, although it will tolerate shade, and well-drained soil. Like most native prairie plants, it requires little, if any, additional feeding when planted in soil of average fertility.

A well-behaved, non-aggressive little plant, three-flowered avens may be divided in early summer after blooming has finished, or propagated from cuttings. Do not dig them up from the wild unless they are threatened by development. Many native plant nurseries are now offering the species for sale.

Perfect Partners

If you wish to grow three-flowered avens in a natural setting, team it with other easygoing native plants such as alumroot (*Heuchera richardsonii*) and wild blue lupines (*Lupinus argenteus*). Plant it at the front of a border with blue grape hyacinth (*Muscari armeniacum*), Jacob's ladder (*Polemonium* spp.), dwarf purple irises, and *Primula auricula*. The bright yellow daylily species *Hemerocallis lilioasphodelus* blooms at the same time and is a striking backdrop to all these smaller plants. Three-flowered avens also pairs well with *Fragaria* 'Pink Panda', a strawberry with lovely clear pink blossoms that mature to produce small berries.

Collectors' Choice

Several other species of avens deserve to be welcomed into prairie gardens.

- *Geum coccineum* (syn. *Geum* x *borisii*) (45 cm, 18 in.) is the most common avens in prairie gardens. This hardy, reliable plant produces long stems

topped with bright orange flowers from mid-May to early July. The attractive toothed leaves grow in low clumps, spreading about 45 cm (18 in.).

- *Geum chiloense* 'Mrs. Bradshaw' (double, orange-red flowers) and 'Lady Stratheden' (double, golden yellow flowers) (76 cm, 30 in.) are showy cultivars often found in prairie nurseries. They tend to wax and wane according to the vicissitudes of the particular year; however, try them in a protected location in rich, moist soil, and they may prove to be rewarding additions to your garden.

- *Geum rivale* (30 cm, 12 in.), also known as water avens, is a species native to moist meadows or stream banks. It has pink-petalled, bell-shaped flowers with purple sepals. 'Album' has greenish white blooms.

- *Geum urbanum* var. *sibiricum* (30 cm, 12 in.), Siberian avens, is a variety of the old Herb Bennet that has proven hardy in prairie gardens. It produces bright orange-red flowers above basal clumps of dark green leaves.

> "*There are few sights more lovely than the purple haze of beautiful three-flowered avens growing in Grasslands National Park near Val Marie.*"
>
> GRACE KUSHNER
> SWIFT CURRENT, SASKATCHEWAN

Gladiolus callianthus
(gla-dee-*oh*-luss kal-ee-*an*-thus)

Peacock orchid,
Sweet scented gladiolus

If you crave something completely different and exotic for your prairie garden, you can't go wrong with the splendid peacock orchid. Native from Eritrea to Mozambique, peacock orchids are understandably not hardy on the prairies, but their prolonged period of bloom late in the growing season and their wonderful fragrance make them worthy of including in any planting scheme. What's more, as with all tender corms and bulbs, they are easy to grow both in flowerbeds and containers, and are virtually trouble-free.

Portrait

Peacock orchids are related to common gladioli, so their foliage is distinctly spearlike, a dead ringer for the strappy, sword-shaped leaves of the gladiolus. Flower spikes develop by early August, each of which ends in a single, elongated bud that eventually opens to reveal star-shaped blossoms and an astonishingly lovely perfume. The exotic blossoms of peacock orchids definitely weave their magic in the summer air with one fragrant blossom after another opening in sequence from the bottom up, on ever-lengthening flower spikes. The splendid show of beauty and fragrance finally comes to an end on frosty nights in late September. The most common peacock orchids in cultivation grow to 90 cm (36 in.) and produce large, 10-cm (4-in.), creamy white blossoms with throats of the deepest mahogany.

The peacock orchid's botanical name was changed recently to *Gladiolus callianthus* from *Acidanthera bicolor* var. *murieliae* or *A. murieliae*; it may still be found listed and sold by its former names.

Where to Grow

Be sure to plant peacock orchids where you can enjoy their magnificent fragrance: at the front of a flowerbed, along a pathway, under a window, or in large pots on the deck or patio.

How to Grow

Peacock orchids prefer a sheltered, sunny site, with fertile, moist, well-drained soil.

Either plant corms outdoors in the spring a few weeks prior to the last expected frost or give them a head start indoors, and then move them to the patio or transplant them into flowerbeds when all danger of frost has passed. Plant them 15 cm (6 in.) deep, with a similar spacing,

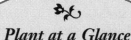

Plant at a Glance

TYPE: tender bulb
HEIGHT: 90 cm (36 in.)
WIDTH: 30 cm (12 in.)
SOIL: fertile, moist, well drained
LIGHT: full sun
FLOWERING TIME: late summer

PHOTO – PAGE 121

dust the soil with a balanced, all-purpose, slow-release fertilizer when the leaves first appear and then again four weeks later. Water well, gradually withholding water as the growing season comes to an end. You may wish to stake them when they are about 30 cm (12 in.) high, to protect them from prairie breezes. Remove faded flowers to encourage spikes to produce more blossoms and thus extend the flowering season.

When peacock orchids finally finish blooming you have two choices: treat them as annuals and replace the inexpensive corms the following growing season, or lift them as you would other tender bulbs, store them in a cool, dry place, and replant them the following spring.

Perfect Partners

In a flowerbed, peacock orchids look lovely interplanted with hardy shrub roses or with blue phlox, asters, and lady's mantle (*Alchemilla mollis*) at their feet. 'Husker Red' penstemon is also a good companion; its burgundy-bronze leaves and white flowers mimic the coloring of peacock orchid flowers.

Collectors' Choice

If you like peacock orchids, then you might be tempted to try some other gladioli.

- *Gladiolus* (30 to 90 cm, 12 to 36 in.) produces tall, flamboyant spikes smothered with funnel-shaped flowers that come in every conceivable color and color combination except true blue. A plant collector's delight, glads may be early- or late-blooming, short or tall, but they are all undeniably spectacular both in the garden and as cut flowers. Over 10,000 cultivars have been developed for cutting, exhibition, and garden use—the possibilities are endless, so take your pick.

> *"If you take the challenge of growing peacock orchids, you'll be happy with the results. I love the fragrant blossoms for their exotic look—they really are outstanding and unique in my garden."*
>
> MICHELLE KEENAN
> FORT MCMURRAY, ALBERTA

- *Gladiolus byzantinus* (90 cm, 36 in.) bears spikes of up to 20 funnel-shaped, deep magenta flowers, 5 cm (2 in.) across, in early summer. The lips of the flowers are marked with thin, white lines. *G. byzantinus* is characterized by the narrow, linear foliage typical of glads.

Crocosomia and *Tritonia* are similar in appearance to peacock orchids; they are also not hardy here, so must be lifted, stored, and replanted, or simply replaced the following year.

- *Crocosomia* (90 cm, 36 in.), montbretia, produces ribbed, sometimes pleated, medium green, strappy foliage and branching spikes of brightly colored, funnel-shaped flowers in late summer. Flower spikes are excellent for cutting. Several named varieties are available including 'Emberglow' (dark red), 'Golden Fleece' (lemon yellow), 'Jackanapes' (bicolor orange-red and yellow), 'Lucifer' (bright red), and 'Spitfire' (orange-red).
- *Tritonia crocata* (50 cm, 20 in.) is related to *Crocosomia* and sometimes mistakenly called montbretia. A spring-bloomer, it is known for long, lance-shaped foliage and slender, arching spikes of orange to pinky-red, cup-shaped flowers.

Helianthus annuus 'Floristan'

(hay-lee-*anth*-us *ann*-you-us)

Sunflower

Few annuals are more at home under the big blue prairie sky than *Helianthus*, the sunflower, its cheerful countenance a welcome symbol of the climax of summer and the start of harvest. Not only decorative, the heavy seed heads of some large sunflowers can be packed with 2,000 to 3,000 seeds.

Sunflowers have a fascinating history. They were grown by the Incas in South America, and were important symbols in the Inca sun-worshipping religion, often reproduced in pure gold. Archaeologists have found sunflower remains in sites in western North America that date to 3000 BC.

Although the towering golden giants are still spectacular, gone are the days when all sunflowers were tall and yellow. There are now dwarf and medium-height cultivars with flowers in warm shades of cream, orange, bronze, and mahogany red; some are even bicolored or double. As a result, sunflowers are more versatile than ever.

Portrait

'Floristan' is a medium-sized, branching sunflower with heart-shaped, toothed leaves. The 15-cm (6-in.) blooms have striking burgundy petals tipped with creamy yellow and dark reddish brown central disks.

Where to Grow

Grow 'Floristan' as an accent plant in mixed or annual borders, or to fill in gaps in perennial plantings. It may also be planted in rows as a screen or hedge.

'Floristan' and other sunflowers always look appropriate as sentinels over a vegetable garden and, unlike scarecrows, will attract birds once the seeds develop. Of course, no child's garden would be complete without a few of these fast-growing plants, and the bright colors of 'Floristan' are sure to please the budding gardener.

How to Grow

Sunflowers tolerate part sun or light shade, but perform best in full sun in a sheltered location. Plant seeds directly into the garden once the soil has warmed; thin seedlings to about 45 cm (18 in.) apart. Average, well-drained garden soil is perfectly acceptable, although added compost, well-rotted manure, or an occasional application of balanced fertilizer will benefit the plants. Keep an eye open for slugs

Plant at a Glance

TYPE: annual
HEIGHT: 1 m (3.3 ft.)
WIDTH: 30 cm (12 in.)
SOIL: average, well drained
LIGHT: full sun
FLOWERING TIME: mid to late summer

PHOTO – PAGE 122

while the plants are young. Aphids may congregate under the leaves and should be washed off with a gentle spray of water.

Perfect Partners
'Floristan' looks striking with dark chocolate-maroon colored 'Nigra' hollyhocks (*Alcea rosea*), 'Gardenview Scarlet' monarda, dark blue or purple monkshood (such as *Aconitum carmichaelii* 'Arendsii'), and sea holly (*Eryngium* spp.).

Collectors' Choice
There are many other spectacular sunflowers to brighten the prairie garden.
- 'Italian White' (1.5 m, 5 ft.) has 10-cm (4-in.) cream-colored flowers with dark centers.
- 'Mammoth Russian' (1.8 m, 6 ft.) is a giant sunflower with huge 25-cm (10-in.) golden yellow flowers.
- 'Music Box' (70 cm, 28 in.) is a well-branched cultivar with cream through yellow, mahogany, and bicolored 12-cm (5-in.) flowers.
- 'Teddy Bear' (90 cm, 36 in.) is a bushy and compact cultivar bearing 13-cm (5-in.) double, golden yellow flowers with greenish yellow central disks.
- 'Velvet Queen' (1.5 m, 5 ft.) has 15-cm (6-in.), rich burgundy red blooms on branching stems.

Sunflowers belong to the large *Asteraceae* family, which includes all daisies and many other sun-loving plants. Here are a few terrific annuals belonging to this family.
- *Calendula officinalis*, also known as pot marigold, is a sturdy, daisylike annual with single or double flowers in shades of cream, yellow, orange, and bronze. There are many cultivars of this cold-tolerant favorite; look for 'Pacific Beauty' (45 cm, 18 in.), 'Art Shades' (60 cm, 24 in.), and the early blooming 'Bon Bon' (40 cm, 16 in.).
- *Dimorphotheca* spp. and *Osteospermum*

spp. (45 cm, 18 in.), both commonly known as African daisies or Cape marigolds, are excellent annuals for containers or mass-plantings, producing showy flowers in creamy white, yellow, and orange, often with chalky blue undersides. 'Whirligig' is a conversation piece with spoon-shaped, white petals with blue undersides around a blue central disk.
- *Tagetes* spp., marigolds, are one of the most popular annuals grown on the prairies. There are dainty French marigolds (15 cm, 6 in.), and huge, round, double-African types (90 cm, 36 in.). Two of many excellent choices are the dependable double-flowered Inca Series (30 cm, 12 in.), and 'Paprika' (15 cm, 6 in.) with bright red, single flowers edged with golden yellow centers.
- *Zinnia elegans* is a versatile drought-tolerant annual with long-lasting flowers in many sizes, colors, and bloom forms. Try the Thumbelina Series (15 cm, 6 in.); 'Peppermint Stick Mixed' (60 cm, 24 in.), which features streaks and splotches of scarlet, vermilion, orange, or purple on a cream background; and 'Envy' (76 cm, 30 in.), a striking chartreuse-green cultivar with slightly quilled petals.

Helichrysum petiolare
(hee-lih-*kriss*-um pet-ee-oh-*lah*-ray)

Licorice plant

Growing annuals is an exciting business these days. With the introduction of dozens of new and unusual plants every year, gardeners have increasingly difficult but wonderful choices to make. Nowhere is this trend more evident than when it comes to choosing among the many trailing and semi-trailing plants now available for container gardening. One newcomer in particular, the silver-leaved licorice plant, was an instant hit when it made its first appearance a few short years ago, and it continues to grow in popularity as gardeners discover its considerable charms.

Portrait
The elegant licorice plant, a native of South Africa, has a mound-forming or trailing habit, depending on whether it is pruned or left to ramble. Its slender, fuzzy stems are smothered in soft, velvety leaves of pure silver-gray on top and lighter gray below; the leaves are delicate, oval or heart-shaped, and up to 4 cm (1.5 in.) long. Mature plants produce small clusters of off-white flowers that must be viewed up close to be appreciated. 'Licorice' is a cultivar with soft, silvery gray foliage; 'Petite' is similar but has much smaller leaves that form tight clusters on slender branches. 'Variegatum' sports gray leaves with creamy white variegations; 'Rondello' (also sold as 'Roundhouse'), a miniature version of 'Variegatum', produces a profusion of creamy yellow flowers with gray-green centers. 'Limelight' is a gold-leaf form that requires protection from strong light and heat to maintain its unique leaf color.

Where to Grow
In recent years licorice plant has made its mark in containers, window boxes, and hanging baskets. However, it can also be grown as a groundcover; its trailing stems of soft gray weave a beautiful tapestry when left to entwine with groundcovers of contrasting greens.

How to Grow
Licorice plant is a sun-loving annual that grows best in fertile, moist, well-drained soil. It is quite drought tolerant in the ground, but it should not be allowed to wilt in containers. Although most gardeners grow it for its trailing habit, it can also be pruned to promote bushier growth. Regular fertilizing benefits all container-grown plants, including this one.

Perfect Partners
In containers and hanging baskets, the

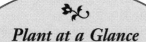

Plant at a Glance

TYPE: annual
HEIGHT: 20 cm (8 in.)
WIDTH: 90 cm (36 in.)
SOIL: fertile, moist, well drained
LIGHT: full sun to light shade
FLOWERING TIME: mid-summer
to frost

PHOTO – PAGE 122

silver leaves of licorice plant are the perfect foil for all blossoms of vibrant color, especially blues, purples, yellows, and pinks. It is also exquisite in an all-white container planted with an assortment of sweet alyssum, bacopa, lobelia, pelargonium, viola, and variegated periwinkle (*Vinca minor* 'Variegata').

Collectors' Choice

For spectacular containers and hanging baskets, choose from the following trailing annuals. Note that the measurement given describes the length of the flowering stems.

- *Anagallis monellii* (30 cm, 12 in.), pimpernel, produces small, lance-shaped, medium green leaves on somewhat pendulous stems. The stunning gentian blue flowers are saucer-shaped and dabbed with rosy red at the base of the petals. A popular cultivar is 'Skylover'.
- *Bacopa* (30 cm, 12 in.) produces attractive small, medium green leaves on trailing stems, smothered in tiny, white, star-shaped flowers all summer long. 'Snowflake' is a common white cultivar; 'Snowstorm' is similar but has larger flowers; 'Pink Domino', also sold as 'Mauve Mist', has lavender-mauve flowers. Bacopa appreciates some protection from midday sun.
- *Bidens ferulifolia* (30 cm, 12 in.) is a heat-loving annual that produces long, trailing stems covered with ferny foliage. Large, bright yellow, star-shaped flowers bloom from mid-summer to frost. Bidens prefers full sun.
- *Lobelia erinus* trailing cultivars (45 cm, 18 in.) are valued for their bright colors and small, narrow, green or bronze leaves. They produce two-lipped, tubular flowers with five petals in shades of blue, carmine red, lilac, pink, and white; the two upper petals are usually erect and the lower three are fan-shaped. Popular trailing cultivars include the

Cascade Series, 'Lilac Fountain', the Regatta Series, 'Sapphire', and 'White Cascade'. They prefer light shade to part sun.

- *Sanvitalia procumbens* (25 cm, 10 in.), creeping zinnia, has a low, creeping or cascading habit. It produces medium green, oval foliage that is covered all summer long with lovely black-centered, yellow, zinnialike flowers. Attractive cultivars include 'Gold Braid' (golden yellow), 'Golden Carpet' (lemon yellow), 'Irish Eyes' (yellow with green center), and 'Mandarin Orange' (semi-double, orange).
- *Scaevola aemula* (30 cm, 12 in.), blue fan flower, produces stiff, semi-trailing, curved stems covered with small, spoon-shaped leaves and unusual blue flowers whose petals all emerge on one side, giving them a fanlike appearance. It thrives in heat but does not like dry soil.
- *Verbena* x *hybrida* trailing cultivars (20 cm, 8 in.) produce delightful 5-cm (2-in.), globular clusters of usually fragrant, primroselike flowers, each with a colored "eye." The best cultivars in the Tapien Series are 'Pink' and 'Purple'. The Temari Series consists of extra large flower clusters in 'Pink' (rose, yellow eye), 'Bright Red' (scarlet), 'Burgundy' (wine red), or 'Violet' (purple, yellow eye).

"I am attracted more and more by foliage plants. Flowers are almost secondary to me, and many plants are lovely without them. Helichrysum is especially lovely, with arching sprays of silvery gray or lime green leaves."

GRACE BERG
SASKATOON, SASKATCHEWAN

Hemerocallis 'Catherine Woodbury'

(hem-er-oh-*cal*-iss)

Daylily

The elegant trumpetlike flowers and grassy foliage of daylilies (*Hemerocallis* spp.) are a common sight in gardens across North America. These well-loved plants are beautiful, hardy, easy to grow, drought tolerant, and almost completely pest free.

Daylilies boast a great range in flower color, form, and size. The only colors that have eluded growers to date are blue and pure white. Bicolor and tricolor forms are common and display bold stripes, bands, and "eyes." Their shape may be tubular, saucer, or spiderlike; petals may be thick or thin; and petal margins may be smooth, wavy, or frilly. Some hybrid flowers are as big as 20 cm (8 in.) across; others are less than 5 cm (2 in.) across.

Individual daylily plants have an extended bloom period, providing continuous color for several weeks. With many early- and late-blooming varieties avail-able, a collection of daylilies can put on a reliable show throughout the entire growing season.

As their name suggests, flowers of species daylilies and many hybrids last for only one day. However, a well-branched flower stem may host about three dozen blossoms. With a well-established, mature clump of daylilies comprising about 10 stems, a single plant can produce as many as 360 blossoms.

Species daylilies first appeared in Europe in the mid-sixteenth century, where they naturalized easily. *Hemerocallis lilioasphodelus* (syn. *H. flava*), the lemon or yellow daylily, is native to Siberia and northern China; *H. fulva*, the tawny daylily, is from China and Japan. In North America, the tawny daylily may be seen along roadsides, in meadows, and around abandoned homesteads. It has earned the name "outhouse lily" because it was frequently planted with phlox and hollyhocks around outhouse foundations. Tawny daylilies are also known as "ditch lilies" because they are invariably found naturalized in roadside ditches.

Portrait

'Catherine Woodbury' bears exquisitely fragrant, pale orchid flowers with green throats. The flowers are composed of three large petals that overlap with three slightly smaller, petal-like sepals, arranged trumpet-fashion. Like all daylilies, the foliage is long and straplike, with a central vein running the entire length that gives a

Plant at a Glance

TYPE: perennial
HEIGHT: 76 cm (30 in.)
WIDTH: 76 cm (30 in.)
SOIL: average to fertile, well drained
LIGHT: full to part sun
FLOWERING TIME: mid to late summer

PHOTO – PAGE 122

keel-like cross-section. In mature plants, leaves emerge from a substantial cluster of crowns that produces numerous flower stems every year.

Where to Grow

'Catherine Woodbury' is effective used in mass-plantings for groundcover in tough spots such as embankments, or in foundation plantings with small trees and shrubs. It is also a fine choice for the middle or back of the perennial border, where it is very adept at hiding dying bulb foliage.

How to Grow

Plant 'Catherine Woodbury' in average to fertile, well-drained soil, in full to part sun; the sunnier the location, the more flowers produced.

Set plants into the ground with their crowns just below soil level. Deadhead daily to keep them looking their best. Remove the entire flower stalk after the last blossom is spent; do not let seed pods develop as this depletes the plant of valuable energy. Use a sharp tug to remove the occasional yellowing leaf as it appears.

'Catherine Woodbury' will bloom untouched for several years. Divide plants if they become too crowded and flower less profusely. Like most daylilies, this one is relatively pest free, although aphids are sometimes a problem. Remove these with a strong blast of water from the garden hose.

Perfect Partners

'Catherine Woodbury' is striking planted in front of tall blue delphiniums. As a bonus, the daylily foliage hides the often ratty lower stems of the delphiniums. Alternatively, try planting it with deep purple salvia, such as 'May Night', ornamental grasses, phlox, and monarda.

"I like cheerful daylilies because they're carefree, bloom most of the summer, and come in a wide range of lovely colors. Some are even repeat bloomers."

PATSY BECK
PORTAGE LA PRAIRIE, MANITOBA

Collectors' Choice

There are over 29,000 named daylily cultivars registered with the American Hemerocallis Society. Of course, only a small percentage of cultivars are available commercially, but local garden centers carry dozens of them, and literally hundreds are available to the serious collector through mail order catalogues. The following daylilies are sure to satisfy.

- 'Charles Johnston' (60 cm, 24 in.), cherry red with yellow-green throat.
- 'Happy Returns' (45 cm, 18 in.), a lemon yellow, repeat bloomer.
- 'Joan Senior' (60 cm, 24 in.), ivory white with lime green throat.
- 'Little Grapette' (30 cm, 12 in.), purple with peach throat.
- 'Prairie Blue Eyes' (70 cm, 28 in.), lavender blue with green throat.
- 'Siloam Fair' (30 cm, 12 in.), peach and purple with rust throat.
- 'Stella de Oro' (60 cm, 24 in.), one of the most common and best-loved daylilies, bears small, golden yellow blooms for several weeks in summer.
- 'Super Purple' (60 cm, 24 in.), deep purple with lime green and yellow throat.

Heuchera x *brizoides* 'Brandon Pink'
(*hue*-kerr-ah x briz-*oi*-deez)

Coral bells, Alumroot

And now, for something completely different, try one of the many recently introduced coral bells cultivars, each one blessed with a winning combination of showy foliage and lovely blossoms. Imagine low-growing mounds of silvery metallic leaves ('Checkers'), silvery leaves with purple veining ('Ring of Fire'), smokey bronze foliage with a ruffled edge ('Smokey Rose'), or blackish leaves overlaid with metallic purple-gray ('Velvet Night'), all topped with airy sprays of pink or white, bell-shaped flowers! Who could refuse such an outstanding display of color and texture in perennial or mixed borders? Even the equally lovely but less exotic-looking coral bells cultivars, more vigorous than their fancy hybrid cousins, are captivating in prairie landscapes.

Portrait

Developed by the late Dr. Henry Marshall at the Agriculture Canada research stations in Manitoba, 'Brandon Pink' is the hardiest of the coral bells hybrids listed in the catch-all group of *Heuchera* x *brizoides*. It produces low, dense mounds of green, lobed foliage with slightly scalloped edges. Tiny, coral pink, bell-shaped flowers paint sprays of color on otherwise naked stems that are inclined to wave elegantly on prairie breezes.

Two other extremely hardy coral bells hybrids are 'Northern Fire', with its scarlet flowers and mottled, deep green foliage, and 'Ruby Mist', which has pinkish red flowers.

Where to Grow

Plant 'Brandon Pink' in large drifts at the sunny margins of woodland gardens or as edging along pathways and at the front of perennial and mixed borders. Although quite tall when in bloom, its see-through sprays of tiny flowers will not obscure its neighbors. 'Brandon Pink' also makes a delicate groundcover beneath deciduous shrubs and trees.

How to Grow

Like all coral bells, 'Brandon Pink' prefers a spot in light shade or part sun, in soil that is fertile, moist, and well drained. A generous organic mulch helps conserve essential soil moisture. If it is planted in full sun without adequate moisture, its leaves will wither and turn brown.

Plant at a Glance

TYPE: perennial
HEIGHT: 60 cm (24 in.)
WIDTH: 30 cm (12 in.)
SOIL: fertile, moist, well drained
LIGHT: light shade to full sun
FLOWERING TIME: early to mid-summer

PHOTO – PAGE 122

Shallow-rooted 'Brandon Pink' eventually produces woody crowns exposed at the soil's surface; this causes plant centers to die out and makes them susceptible to frost heaving. To solve the problem, either fill in around the exposed woody crown with a generous layer of soil and compost, or lift the whole plant and reset it deeper in the ground. You can also divide an aging clump into several sections to rejuvenate or propagate the plant, removing the woody portions before replanting.

'Brandon Pink' can be propagated by taking leaf cuttings attached to a small piece of crown at the base of the plant.

Perfect Partners
'Brandon Pink' goes hand-in-hand with other inhabitants of the light shade garden—geraniums, pulmonaria, bleeding heart (*Dicentra* spp.), ferns, and hostas.

Collectors' Choice
Hybrids of *Heuchera micrantha*, *H. americana*, and *H. sanguinea* have overtaken the species in popularity, although the species still have merit in the prairie garden.

- *Heuchera americana* (60 cm, 24 in.) is grown for its spectacular foliage, which comes in a wide range of dark colors, shapes, and sizes; the flowers are usually greenish white. Although they tolerate heat and humidity, they dislike hot afternoon sun. 'Chocolate Ruffles' is the hardiest *H. americana* cultivar; other outstanding but less hardy cultivars include 'Pewter Veil', 'Ruby Ruffles', and 'Velvet Night'.
- *Heuchera cylindrica* (76 cm, 30 in.), poker alumroot, produces mounds of deeply lobed, dark green leaves and creamy green flowers on thin, hairy stems in early summer. 'Greenfinch' (greenish white flowers) and 'Green Ivory' (white flowers with a green throat) are excellent choices.

"Of all the coral bells cultivars I have tried, those developed on the prairies, such as 'Brandon Pink' and 'Northern Fire', are the hardiest. Coral bells make lovely tidy clumps at the front of perennial borders and in rockeries."

ALBERTHA VAN WAGENINGEN
VERMILION, ALBERTA

- *Heuchera micrantha* 'Palace Purple' (45 cm, 18 in.), small-flowered alumroot, has reddish purple foliage that varies in color because plants are grown from seed; leaves fade to bronze in summer's heat.
- *Heuchera sanguinea* (45 cm, 18 in.) is a red-flowered species, parent to most of the hybrids listed under *H.* x *brizoides*.

Two other delightful perennials similar to coral bells are foamy bells and Allegheny foamflower. Both prosper in light shade, in fertile, moist, well-drained soil.

- x *Heucherella* (45 cm, 18 in.), foamy bells, are hybrids of coral bells and foamflower; they produce compact, non-spreading mounds of heart-shaped foliage combined with showy flower spikes. Try 'Bridget Bloom' (shell pink) or 'Rosalie' (rose pink).
- *Tiarella cordifolia* (30 cm, 12 in.), Allegheny foamflower, forms low, spreading mounds of hairy, heart-shaped leaves, topped by spikes of delicate, white flowers that carpet the ground in early spring. The foliage turns a lovely russet in the fall. *T. wheryii* (*T. cordifolia* var. *collina*) is clump-forming rather than spreading; interesting hybrids include 'Inkblot' and 'Oakleaf'.

Hosta sieboldiana 'Elegans'

(*hoss*-tah see-bold-ee-*ahn*-ah)

Hosta, Plantain lily

When designing colorful, eye-catching landscapes, gardeners often forget the potential of cool green foliage plants for creating a soothing atmosphere of understated elegance. Foremost among foliage plants and made for the shade, hostas are one of the most popular perennials in North America. Their universal appeal lies in their exotic beauty, simple care requirements, and amazing diversity. These qualities were not lost on the tenacious European botanists of old, who brought back the first hostas from the Orient three centuries ago.

The newly discovered genus was first named *Funkia*, after the German botanist Henry Funk. However, unbeknownst to most, it had previously been named *Hosta*, after the Austrian emperor's physician of the day, Nicholaus Host. When this was discovered, the official name changed, and *Funkia* became *Hosta*.

At first, hostas were considered an idle curiosity and were largely ignored. It wasn't until 1830 that the "hosta bug" bit, when German botanist Philipp Franz von Siebold returned from Japan with a remarkable new species. Gardeners raved over *Hosta sieboldiana*, distinguished by its magnificent puckered, blue-gray leaves. Since then, it and its relatives have been a mainstay of gardens the world over.

Portrait

Hosta sieboldiana 'Elegans' is recognized by its distinctive heart-shaped, powdery blue-gray foliage. Individual leaves rising from a central crown have a very crinkled, seersucker aspect and can be over 30 cm (12 in.) long and 23 cm (9 in.) wide. Together, the leaves form an elegant mound that measures a substantial 90 cm (36 in.) at maturity.

Dainty, faintly fragrant, lilylike flowers grow to 5 cm (2 in.) and range in color from white to pale lilac. They are produced in profusion in mid-summer, appearing in loose clusters held on erect stalks just above the foliage.

Where to Grow

'Elegans' makes a spectacular accent or background plant in dedicated hosta beds, in shaded mixed borders, or beside a pond. Massed, they make an excellent groundcover that is tough for weeds to penetrate. They are also perfect for hard-to-manage shady strips between closely spaced houses and for disguising faded bulb foliage.

Plant at a Glance

TYPE: perennial
HEIGHT: 90 cm (36 in.)
WIDTH: 1.2 m (4 ft.)
SOIL: fertile, moist, well drained
LIGHT: light to full shade
FLOWERING TIME: mid-summer

PHOTO – PAGE 123

How to Grow

Choose a shady spot for 'Elegans', sheltered from the wind and hail—under a deciduous tree is perfect. Shade is critical for maintaining the intense color of blue-leaved hostas. The blue coloring derives from a powdery coating that protects hosta leaves from extreme, early spring sunlight. This coating deteriorates in bright light, heat, and rain, and as the coating disappears, so does the blue hue.

Plant 'Elegans' in fertile, moist soil amended with a handful of bone meal and plenty of organic material, placing the crown just below soil level. Apply summer mulch to keep the soil moist and the leaves clean, and water regularly to encourage lush, bushy plants.

Since hostas, including this variety, are some of the last perennials to emerge in the spring, mark their location well to avoid inadvertent damage.

'Elegans', once established, requires little maintenance. In a suitable location, it will thrive for decades, gradually increasing in size without becoming invasive. Although it is easy to divide in early spring or fall, it will not disappoint when left to its own devices. Like peonies, all hostas improve with age.

Unfortunately, slugs love hostas as much as gardeners do; it pays to watch for telltale signs and to take appropriate action.

Perfect Partners

'Elegans' puts on a fine display combined with fellow shade-lovers such as monkshood (*Aconitum* spp.), astilbe, ferns, pulmonaria, spiderwort (*Tradescantia andersoniana*), Jacob's ladder (*Polemonium* spp.), and bleeding heart (*Dicentra* spp.). The shade-loving grasses *Hakonechloa macra* and snowy wood rush (*Luzula nivea*), spreading wild ginger (*Asarum* spp.), creeping phlox (*Phlox divaricata*), and

"Hostas grow in texture, color, and character as they mature over the years. They become more interesting as they age, as we hope we will, too!"

GRACE BERG
SASKATOON, SASKATCHEWAN

sweet woodruff (*Galium odoratum*) are also excellent companions.

Collectors' Choice

The hardest thing about growing hostas is choosing which of the 70 species and hundreds of cultivars to include in your collection. Here are a few suggestions.

- *Hosta fortunei* 'Aureo-marginata' (55 cm, 22 in.) makes a mound of graceful green foliage edged in yellow.
- *Hosta* 'Ginko Craig' (25 cm, 10 in.) has lance-shaped, white-edged, dark green leaves and is a fast grower.
- *Hosta* 'Krossa Regal' (76 cm, 30 in.) forms a distinctive vase-shaped mound of large, glaucous, blue-gray leaves that lose their blue hues as the season advances.
- *Hosta plantaginea* (60 cm, 24 in.) has shiny green foliage and highly fragrant flowers in late summer. Try the cultivars 'Honeybells' and 'Aphrodite'.
- *Hosta venusta* (8 cm, 3 in.) is a vigorous little hosta with dark green, heart-shaped leaves. Try 'Tiny Tears', 'Tee Tiny', or 'Thumb Nail'.

Humulus lupulus

(*hew*-mew-luss *loo*-pew-luss)

Hops

Prairie gardeners, always on the lookout for new and exciting ways to make use of their limited growing space, have been embracing the concept of vertical gardening in unprecedented numbers. This means that reliable perennial vines are becoming popular items at garden centers. Hops, a vigorous, twining climber, is a favorite among gardeners; it is attractive to look at, easy to grow, and spreads quickly to fill its allotted space.

Native to both North America and Europe, hops was a popular food item among the Romans, who served its young shoots boiled or steamed, much like asparagus. It wasn't until the vine became widely cultivated in Europe from the tenth century onward that hops bitters, found in the ripe, conelike fruits of the female plant, were used to flavor and preserve beer, and to increase its alcoholic content. The Dutch and Germans, in particular, were quick to embrace the use of hops in their breweries. However, the British were prohibited from brewing hops until the seventeenth century because it reputedly was the source of melancholy, disease, and a short life.

Portrait

This vine climbs by twining shoots, producing large, broadly lobed, coarsely toothed leaves that bear a resemblance to grape leaves. Male and female flowers are borne on separate plants. The tiny male flowers are greenish yellow and hang in 25-cm (10-in.) clusters, whereas the female flowers form pale green, conelike spikes in early summer that later turn an attractive papery beige; they both make excellent additions to dried flower arrangements.

Although hops dies back to the snow line in winter, it is a fast-growing, vigorous climber that can achieve a height of 6 m (20 ft.) or more in one growing season.

'Aureus' is a very showy, golden-leaved variety that should be planted in full sun for best color.

Where to Grow

Supported on lattice-work, trellises, or netting, hops is an attractive covering for walls and fences. It also looks lovely clambering over arbors, pergolas, and similar sheltering garden structures. Left to its own devices, this creeper rambles freely, forming an open groundcover.

❦

Plant at a Glance

TYPE: perennial vine
HEIGHT: 6 m (20 ft.)
WIDTH: 1 m (3.3 ft.)
SOIL: fertile, moist, well drained
LIGHT: full sun to light shade
FLOWERING TIME: mid to
late summer

PHOTO – PAGE 123

How to Grow

Hops is a heat-loving plant, thriving on neglect and asking for no more than a means of support and average to fertile, well-drained soil, in sun or light shade. Hops will tolerate short periods of drought, but prefers regular watering.

Try to provide for good air circulation in shady spots to prevent powdery mildew.

Propagate hops by dividing young shoots or by cuttings in late summer.

Perfect Partners

Hops makes a charming, understated background to all inhabitants of mixed and perennial borders, showing them off to advantage regardless of blossom color. It also performs admirably on its own.

Collectors' Choice

Several other perennial vines are well suited to prairie gardens; they are all enthusiastic climbers, requiring support in the form of a trellis, arbor, tree, or shrub, and are drought tolerant once established.

- *Lonicera* x *brownii* 'Dropmore Scarlet' (5 m, 16 ft.), climbing honeysuckle, with its paired, blue-green leaves, produces a profusion of scarlet, two-lipped, tubular flowers on woody stems. The scarlet blossoms, borne in terminal clusters all summer long, are magnets for hummingbirds. 'Mandarin', a recent honeysuckle introduction, is similar to 'Dropmore Scarlet' but it produces bigger, more fragrant flowers. It blooms from May to August and tolerates light shade.
- *Parthenocissus quinquefolia* (15 m, 50 ft.), Virginia creeper, is worth growing for its fall color alone—deep green leaves consisting of five oval, sharply toothed leaflets turn a fabulous burgundy red in September. Its greenish white flowers are inconspicuous and eventually become grapelike clusters of round,

"This is a very fast-growing vine for sun or partial shade, and is useful for all kinds of screening situations. It should be cut back in spring or fall and needs a trellis for support."

DONNA DAWSON
EDMONTON, ALBERTA

blue fruit. The vine climbs by tendrils that wrap around whatever support is provided. Engelmann ivy (*Parthenocissus quinquefolia* 'Engelmannii') is slightly smaller than the species and is self-supporting—small, disklike pads at the ends of tendrils adhere directly to brick and painted surfaces. On the prairies, this ivy is not quite as hardy as Virginia creeper.

- *Vitis riparia* (5.5 m, 18 ft.), riverbank or Manitoba grape, is a prairie native that prefers a sheltered, sunny spot, and even moisture until established. It produces shiny, light green, three-lobed foliage and small, inconspicuous flowers in late spring. The clusters of small, dark blue grapes that follow are perfect for making wine, jam, and jelly. Because riverbank grapes are very vigorous growers, they require regular pruning to maintain control and to ensure bountiful harvests. 'Beta' is a hybrid similar to the 'Concord' grape, but smaller. 'Valiant' is a relatively new cultivar that is much hardier than 'Beta', with fruit that matures much earlier. 'Valiant' grapes ripen in August.

Hydrangea arborescens 'Annabelle'

(hie-*drain*-jee-ah ar-bo-*res*-kens)

Smooth hydrangea

Most prairie gardeners associate hydrangeas with the somewhat gaudy pink and blue mopheads of florist's, or bigleaf, hydrangeas (*Hydrangea macrophylla*) that we see in supermarkets or on visits to the west coast. These floral chameleons may have blue or pink flowers, depending on the soil in which they are growing. The blue color is caused by the presence of aluminium in the soil, but since aluminium is only available to the plant in acidic soils—basic (alkaline) soils do not release aluminium ions—it is commonly believed that bloom color depends on soil pH.

Not at all hardy on the prairies, these showy plants, originally woodland natives, may still be grown in part sun or light shade outdoors as annuals. You may wish to think twice about bringing them in for the winter—according to superstition, potted hydrangeas are unlucky if brought into the house, the blue ones reputedly being the unluckier of the two.

The *Hydrangea* genus is named for the Greek words for "water vessel," and likely refers to the plant's cup-shaped fruit, rather than its considerable thirst. The genus comprises 23 species of deciduous shrubs and climbers from North and South America and eastern Asia, 2 of which are tough enough to be recommended for prairie gardens. In cold climates the plants are killed back almost to the ground each winter and are treated as herbaceous perennials.

Portrait

Hydrangea arborescens 'Annabelle' is undoubtedly the best flowering shrub for the late-summer garden. The spectacular rounded, white blossoms are composed of many individual flowers and can measure up to 30 cm (12 in.) across. Borne on stiff stems, the sterile, long-lasting blooms change from creamy white to green as they age and are ideal for cutting and drying. 'Annabelle' has large, bright green, oval leaves that are pointed with serrated edges.

'Grandiflora', often called hills-of-snow or Snow Hills hydrangea, is similar but less floriferous, with flower clusters up to 20 cm (8 in.) across. It blooms slightly earlier than 'Annabelle'.

Where to Grow

'Annabelle' is a lovely specimen plant for partly shaded perennial or shrub beds and

Plant at a Glance

TYPE: deciduous shrub
HEIGHT: 1.5 m (5 ft.)
WIDTH: 1.5 m (5 ft.)
SOIL: fertile, moist, well drained
LIGHT: part sun to light shade
FLOWERING TIME: mid-summer to fall

PHOTO – PAGE 123

woodland gardens. If space allows, plant several for a truly impressive display. Given adequate moisture, it is a suitable foundation shrub for north- or east-facing walls.

How to Grow
'Annabelle' prefers a sheltered location, in part sun or light shade. It requires fertile, well-drained soil and ample water throughout the growing season until freeze-up. Although tolerant of alkaline soil, it will benefit from the regular addition of compost or well-rotted manure to the soil to moderate the high pH levels prevalent in many prairie gardens, as well as to increase soil fertility. Mulch around this shrub year-round to conserve moisture and protect the roots from temperature fluctuations.

It may be necessary to provide support for the large flower heads—peony cages and linking stakes both work well. Cut flowers for fresh bouquets when they are fully open and place them in a vase of water. Allow the water to gradually evaporate and the flowers will dry in the vase. To collect flowers for drying, wait until they have started to turn pale green, then cut and hang them in bunches in a warm, dry place. Left outside, the flower heads will turn beige but retain their shape to add a unique touch to the winter garden.

In late winter or early spring, cut 'Annabelle' back to about 10 cm (4 in.). Flower buds are formed on new wood, so this will not sacrifice bloom. Propagate by division in the spring or from stem cuttings taken in early summer.

Perfect Partners
Even though 'Annabelle' is a fine solo performer, it may be combined with perennial companions that prefer partly shaded, moist locations, including ferns, large hostas like 'Elegans' (*Hosta*

sieboldiana), later-blooming astilbes (*Astilbe chinensis* 'Purpurkerze', or *A. thunbergii* 'Professor van der Wielen'), and 'Luxuriant' fernleaf bleeding heart (*Dicentra* hybrid).

Collectors' Choice
Only one other species of hydrangea is appropriate for prairie gardens, but it is quite different in appearance from 'Annabelle' and well worth a try.

❦ *Hydrangea paniculata* 'Grandiflora' (3 m, 10 ft.), Pee Gee hydrangea, is a Japanese introduction that has been in cultivation since about 1867. It bears loose, conical panicles of creamy white, sterile flowers in late summer and early fall. The large flower heads grow from 15 to 30 cm (6 to 12 in.) long and wide, and turn pink, bronze-pink, then beige, as they age. This hydrangea appreciates similar growing conditions to 'Annabelle'. Cut back the stems to live wood, and then thin to about six stems or new shoots per plant to increase flower size. 'Unique' (3 m, 10 ft.) is similar to 'Grandiflora' but has larger flower heads and may not be as hardy.

"I've grown my hydrangea on the north side of my house for eight or nine years, and it produces masses of huge, round blooms that look lovely right until late fall. I've had many total strangers stop and ask what it is."

DIANE FIDLER
SELKIRK, MANITOBA

Iberis sempervirens 'Snowflake'

(eye-*beer*-iss sem-purr-*veer*-ens)

Perennial candytuft, Evergreen candytuft

*I*beris sempervirens, or perennial candytuft, is a modest and inconspicuous little plant for 11 months of the year. But in spring, this Clark Kent of the plant world explodes with white blooms of such startling purity that all other white flowers cower in comparison.

The genus name *Iberis* indicates the plant is native to the Iberian peninsula, while *sempervirens* is from two Latin words meaning "always alive," a reference to the plant's evergreen foliage.

The common name "candytuft" comes from Candia, or Crete. The plant was called "Cretan cress" when Lord Edward Zouche first brought it from the Greek island to England in Elizabethan times. This nobleman reportedly spent so much money on his garden that he could no longer afford to live in England, travelling instead to Europe, where the cost of living was less.

Portrait

Every spring *Iberis sempervirens* 'Snowflake' bursts forth with masses of dazzling white flowers that make a striking contrast to its dark green leaves. Each flat-topped flower cluster is composed of many tiny, four-petalled flowers, a characteristic of members of the mustard (*Brassicaceae*) family. Even after the snowy blooms have faded, the mounded, low-growing foliage is a handsome counterpoint to later-blooming perennials. Like other perennial candytufts, 'Snowflake' is considered a subshrub due to its woody stems and evergreen leaves.

Some perennial candytufts, such as *Iberis sempervirens* 'Autumn Beauty' and 'Autumn Snow', bloom in the fall as well as the spring. 'Little Gem' is a dwarf cultivar growing to only 13 cm (5 in.). Other notable cultivars include 'Purity' and 'Dick Self', a large-flowered, long-blooming selection.

Where to Grow

Plant 'Snowflake' in rock gardens, or where it can spread to overhang terrace walls. It is an eye-catching perennial for the front of borders, or used as an edging along pathways.

How to Grow

'Snowflake' will reward the gardener with prolific bloom when planted in full sun, in average to fertile, well-drained soil. Untroubled by pests or disease, it is easy to maintain, requiring only a light trim-

Plant at a Glance

TYPE: perennial
HEIGHT: 30 cm (12 in.)
WIDTH: 60 cm (24 in.)
SOIL: average to fertile, well drained
LIGHT: full sun
FLOWERING TIME: spring

PHOTO – PAGE 123

ming to remove spent blooms. Further pruning may be undertaken at this time if plants are straggly.

'Snowflake' can be divided after flowering to propagate new plants, although it is not a rampant spreader and does not require frequent division. Stems will often root where they touch the ground, and such rooted sections may be cut off and transplanted elsewhere. In addition, tip cuttings may be taken in spring or summer.

To prevent winter desiccation, the evergreen foliage of this plant requires a protective blanket of snow. If snow cover is minimal, protect the plants with organic mulch or evergreen boughs.

Perfect Partners

In rock gardens, combine 'Snowflake' with basket-of-gold alyssum (*Aurinia saxatilis*), moss phlox (*Phlox subulata*), rock jasmine (*Androsace sarmentosa*), and *Primula auricula*. Leopard's bane (*Doronicum columnae*), pasqueflower (*Pulsatilla vulgaris* var. *rubra*), ajuga, and deep blue grape hyacinth (*Muscari armeniacum*) all complement 'Snowflake' at the front of the perennial border. The white flowers of this plant also look glorious beneath the pink clouds of an ornamental crabapple tree in bloom.

Collectors' Choice

Two other species of candytuft, one perennial and one annual, are frequently available at prairie nurseries.

- *Iberis saxatilis* (10 cm, 4 in.), rock candytuft, is a spring-blooming perennial with twisted stems clad with small leaves, and tipped with clusters of tiny, white flowers. Use it as edging or in rock gardens.
- *Iberis umbellata* (38 cm, 15 in.), annual candytuft, is ideal for edging or filling in gaps in rock gardens. The fragrant, flat-topped flower clusters are usually

> *"It wouldn't be spring in my garden without* Iberis. *On a sunny day, masses of pure white flowers are so brilliant they almost hurt the eyes. The evergreen foliage looks great after the blossoms are spent—perfect for rock gardens, edging, and mixed borders."*
>
> ROSEMARY MCNARY
> MEDICINE HAT, ALBERTA

available in mixed shades of white, pink, lilac, maroon, and purple. Many other stalwart small perennials bloom in spring, combining to create a tapestry of white, pink, and purple.

- *Arabis caucasica* (20 cm, 8 in.), commonly called rock or wall cress, produces pink or white flowers above mats of gray-green leaves. The evergreen foliage requires winter protection. Good cultivars include 'Compinkie' (rose), 'Snowball' (white), and 'Variegata' (white, cream, and green variegated leaves). *A. ferdinandi-coburgi* is a very low-growing, white-flowered alpine species with variegated leaves; cultivars include 'Old Gold' (yellow and green variegation) and 'Variegata' (white and green variegation).
- *Aubrieta deltoidea* (15 cm, 6 in.), also known as purple or false rock cress, has spreading gray-green foliage covered with masses of purple flowers. *Aubrieta* hybrids include 'Blue Carpet' (blue shades), 'Red Carpet' (rose-red), and 'Dr. Mules' (violet-purple).
- *Cerastium tomentosum* (15 cm, 6 in.), popularly known as snow-in-summer, is a quickly spreading, gray-leaved perennial with many tiny, white flowers. An excellent groundcover for hot, dry areas, snow-in-summer can be invasive and is best avoided in rock gardens.

Impatiens walleriana Super Elfin Series

(im-*pay*-shuns wall-er-ee-*a*-na)

Impatiens, Busy Lizzie

There are many good reasons why impatiens has become the most popular annual in North America. This versatile plant is easy to grow, blooms all summer long, and thrives in dappled shade.

The genus name comes from the Latin word for "impatient" and refers to the plant's readiness to eject its seeds when the seed pods are touched. The common names "busy Lizzie" and "touch-me-not" also refer to this impulsive habit.

First brought to England from Africa in 1865, *Impatiens walleriana* was originally called *Impatiens sultani*, after the Sultan of Zanzibar. It was later renamed in honor of Horace Waller, an English missionary and plant collector.

Impatiens species have been extensively hybridized; the flowers may be white, red, orange, salmon, pink, violet, orchid, lavender-blue, and many shades between. There are also bicolors, some with white star patterns, and others with picotee edges.

Plant at a Glance

TYPE: annual
HEIGHT: 20 cm (8 in.)
WIDTH: 20 cm (8 in.)
SOIL: average to fertile, moist, well drained
LIGHT: part sun to full shade
FLOWERING TIME: early summer to fall

PHOTO – PAGE 78

Portrait

Super Elfin Series flower profusely all summer on low-growing, compact plants. The succulent stems branch near the base, and plants quickly spread to fill in beds or planters.

Perhaps the most exquisite color of the series is 'Blue Pearl', a shimmering lilac-blue shade. Other colors include 'Lavender', 'Lipstick', 'Melon', 'Raspberry', 'Sunrise' (salmon-orange with purple edges), 'Picotee Swirl' (rose with fuchsia-pink edges), and 'Picotee Swirl Mixed' (shades of pink and apricot).

Where to Grow

Super Elfin Series create an enchanting carpet of color beneath deciduous trees, at the front of a partly shaded border, or beside pathways. They are superb annuals for containers, and look striking when massed in low planter boxes.

How to Grow

Super Elfin Series are at their best in light or dappled shade; avoid planting them in deep shade. Locations receiving morning sun are also acceptable, but they will not thrive in full afternoon sun.

Impatiens are tender annuals that should not be planted outside until all danger of frost has passed. Before planting, enrich the soil with organic matter. Compost or a slow-release fertilizer worked into the soil at this time should provide sufficient nutrition for the summer. Water regularly to keep the soil moist.

Plant container-grown impatiens in a

soil-less mix, rather than garden soil, and give them a supplemental feeding with a water-soluble, balanced fertilizer.

Perfect Partners

Use Super Elfin Series with ferns and hostas in dappled shade. Combine them with pansies and mounding forms of lobelia, such as the double-flowering 'Kathleen Mallard' or the Riviera or Palace Series. In containers, complement them with Regatta Series trailing lobelia and nemesia.

Collectors' Choice

There are many superb varieties of impatiens, and each year brings new introductions.

- Accent Series (25 cm, 10 in.) are an exceptional choice with many individual colors and designer mixes.
- Fiesta Series (25 cm, 10 in.) has fully double blooms resembling miniature roses. Colors include 'White', 'Burgundy Rose', 'Lavender Orchid', 'Pink Ruffles', 'Salmon Sunrise', 'Salsa Red', 'Sparkler Red', 'Sparkler Rose', and 'Sparkler Salmon'.
- *Impatiens hawkeri* (35 cm, 14 in.), New Guinea impatiens, prefers sun to part sun. The Celebration Series is available in white and varying shades of pink, purple, and orange. 'Tango' is an All-American Selection with bronze-green leaves and orange flowers.
- 'Mosaic Lilac' and 'Mosaic Rose' (25 cm, 10 in.) have 4-cm (1.5-in.) flowers streaked with white.

Brighten up cool spots in the garden with the vibrant colors of other shade-loving annuals.

- *Begonia semperflorens* (20 cm, 8 in.), also called wax begonia, grows from fibrous roots. These compact plants have shiny bronze, green, or variegated leaves.

The small flowers are available in white and many shades of pink and red.

- *Begonia* x *tuberhybrida* (30 cm, 12 in.), tuberous begonia, produces large blossoms in many colors and forms, including picotee, ruffled, and rose-form. Pendula varieties are suitable for hanging containers. The reliable Non-Stop Series offers a rainbow of shades, including white, pink, yellow, scarlet, orange, and apricot.
- *Fuchsia* x *hybrida* (60 cm, 24 in.), fuchsia, is an outstanding plant for sheltered and shaded locations. Although there are also upright varieties, most prairie gardeners choose hanging fuchsias for their elegant dangling blooms. There is a multitude of hybrids with small or large, single or double flowers in soft pastel pinks to hot corals and reds.
- *Viola* x *wittrockiana* (15 cm, 6 in.), the beloved pansy, is a cold-tolerant little plant that is an ideal choice to put outside in spring containers. Pansies prefer cool temperatures and moist soil that is rich in organic matter. There are pansies to suit every taste—from ruffled pastel blooms to striking nearly black varieties.

Iris pumila hybrids
(*eye*-riss pew-*mill*-ah)

Miniature dwarf bearded iris,
Standard dwarf bearded iris

Few sights are more spectacular than a stand of bearded irises in full bloom. The southern belles of the early summer garden, they hold court in their fragrant and ruffled splendor like Scarlet O'Hara amidst her beaux.

In Greek mythology, Iris carried messages across a rainbow from the gods to mortals. Surely no flowers have ever been more appropriately named than this genus, with over 300 species and thousands of cultivars in every hue of the rainbow.

Non-bulbous irises are divided into three categories: beardless, such as *Iris sibirica* (see page 110); bearded, which are hybrids of many species; and crested. The flowers of bearded irises are composed of six tepals—the three petals that point upward are called standards; the three downward-curving sepals are called falls. The beard is a fuzzy strip near the base of the falls.

Bearded irises are classified according to size and blooming time. Miniature dwarf (20 cm, 8 in.) are the first to bloom. Following them in order of bloom are: standard dwarf (20 to 30 cm, 8 to 12 in.); intermediate (40 to 76 cm, 16 to 30 in.); miniature tall (40 to 76 cm, 16 to 30 in.); border (40 to 76 cm, 16 to 30 in.); and tall (76 to 120 cm, 30 to 48 in.). Tall bearded irises are generally less hardy on the prairies than their shorter counterparts.

Portrait
Iris pumila hybrids include miniature dwarf and standard dwarf bearded irises. They are the hardiest and earliest blooming of all bearded irises, quickly spreading to form substantial clumps of sword-shaped leaves. Although these irises are available in a wide range of colors, there are fewer named cultivars than for the larger irises.

Many selections have proved their worth in prairie gardens. Among them are 'Alpine Lake' (white and powder blue), 'Blue Neon' (dusky blue), 'Cherry Garden' (purple/red), 'Cup and Saucer' (wine red), 'Ditto' (cream with purple splotches), 'Grandma's Hat' (purple and mauve), 'Lemon Puff' (yellow), 'Little Dutch Girl' (violet-blue, dark purple beard), 'Red at Last' (burgundy-bronze, gold beard), 'Ritz' (lemon yellow, copper beard), 'Sarah Taylor' (creamy yellow, blue beard), 'Sleepytime' (powder blue), and 'Spring Violets' (violet blue).

Plant at a Glance

TYPE: perennial
HEIGHT: 20 to 30 cm (8 to 12 in.)
WIDTH: 20 to 30 cm (8 to 12 in.)
SOIL: average to fertile, well drained
LIGHT: full sun
FLOWERING TIME: early summer

PHOTO – PAGE 124

Where to Grow

Use *Iris pumila* hybrids in groups near the front of sunny perennial borders where the swordlike foliage adds a spiky texture all summer long. They are also an excellent choice for a sunny rock garden.

How to Grow

Like all bearded irises, *Iris pumila* hybrids grow from rhizomes — fleshy, horizontal stems from which both foliage and roots grow. Plant the rhizomes in average to fertile, well-drained soil so that the top of the rhizome is slightly exposed. Irises planted too deeply are subject to rot or may not bloom. Fertilize in late spring with bonemeal or a low-nitrogen fertilizer (15–30–15).

Deadhead spent blooms and remove dead foliage throughout the growing season; otherwise, do not cut off any foliage.

Iris clumps frequently die out in the centers after three or four years and require division. Four to six weeks after flowering has finished, dig up the clumps and trim leaves back by one-third to a fan shape. Cut off healthy, young portions of rhizomes from the outer edges of the clump, each with a foliage fan attached, and sprinkle the cut ends with bulb dust to prevent disease. It is advisable to leave the rhizomes to dry overnight before planting them about 30 cm (12 in.) apart.

Perfect Partners

Choose perennials that bloom in early summer and offer contrasting foliage texture as iris accompaniments. Lady's mantle (*Alchemilla mollis*), cranesbill (*Geranium* spp.), coral bells (*Heuchera* spp.), and Oriental poppy (*Papaver orientale*) will all fill the bill. In the rock garden, team these small irises with fan columbine (*Aquilegia flabellata*), maiden pink (*Dianthus deltoides*), candytuft (*Iberis sempervirens*), and *Primula auricula*.

> ❧
>
> *"I boarded with a lady 60 years ago who gave me yellow dwarf irises. I grew descendants of those irises as well as mauve and white dwarf irises for many, many years. They are very hardy."*
>
> EDITH WADDELL
> NEWDALE, MANITOBA

Collectors' Choice

Choosing bearded irises for your garden comes down to a matter of personal taste and the selection available at local garden centers. Those who get hooked on these frilly beauties will want to order from a specialty iris nursery. It should be noted that hybrid bearded irises may be of varying hardiness; many are bred for beauty rather than endurance. This is particularly true of tall bearded irises. Other species of iris also offer exquisite blooms for the prairie garden.

- *Iris cristata* (15 cm, 6 in.), crested iris, is a delightful blue- or white-flowered, woodland iris that prefers dappled shade.
- *Iris pallida* 'Variegata' (60 cm, 24 in.), sweet iris, is a bearded iris chiefly grown for its striking green and white striped foliage, although it also boasts pretty lavender-blue flowers. 'Aureomarginata' has striped gold and green leaves.

Iris sibirica 'Silver Edge'
(eye-riss sy-*bee*-ri-kah)*

Siberian iris

The elegant Siberian iris (*Iris sibirica*) has steadily increased in popularity over the last decade — and no wonder! Not only does it produce enchanting blooms, this hardy perennial is also untroubled by pests and disease, and requires very little maintenance.

Although daintier than its flamboyant bearded iris cousins, the Siberian iris also bears flowers composed of three downward-facing sepals (falls) and three upward-facing petals (standards). Most cultivars are in shades of blue and purple, but there are also white, yellow, wine red, and pink blooming selections.

Hybridizers have developed tetraploid forms of Siberian iris that carry twice the usual number of chromosomes. These usually bear larger flowers and have more upright foliage than diploids, those with a normal complement of chromosomes. However, tetraploids are no hardier than diploids, and many gardeners prefer the more delicate irises to these super-plants.

Portrait
'Silver Edge' is a charming cultivar with sky blue flowers marked with yellow and white at the base of the petals and a fine, silver, wirelike edge to each petal. Vigorous and heavy blooming, it will produce up to five 10-cm (4-in.) blooms on each slim, erect stem. The flowers mature into three-chambered seed pods that make attractive additions to dried flower arrangements.

Like all Siberian irises, 'Silver Edge' is prized for its vase-shaped clusters of tall, grassy leaves, which remain green and upright long after blooming has ceased, adding pleasing vertical accents to the border.

Where to Grow
'Silver Edge' is a valuable addition to a sunny perennial border, either as a specimen plant or grouped for greater impact. Plant it beside a pond, or even in a large container for the summer, sinking it into the ground for the winter.

How to Grow
Plant 'Silver Edge' in fertile, well-drained soil. Add plenty of organic material, such as shredded leaves, peat moss, compost, or aged manure, to increase soil fertility and acidity and to improve soil tilth. Apply a layer of organic mulch around the plant and keep the soil evenly moist throughout

❧

Plant at a Glance

TYPE: perennial
HEIGHT: 76 cm (30 in.)
WIDTH: 60 cm (24 in.)
SOIL: fertile, moist, well drained
LIGHT: full to part sun
FLOWERING TIME: early summer

PHOTO – PAGE 124

the growing season. This perennial excels in full sun, but will also produce adequate bloom in part sun. Staking is not required if plants receive enough sunlight.

Plant 'Silver Edge' in spring, spacing plants 45 cm (18 in.) apart, with the fibrous rhizomes just beneath the soil surface. Siberian irises should be split only when the number and quality of flowers diminish, or plants begin to die out in the middle, usually after 6 to 10 years. Divide them in mid to late August to avoid losing a year's bloom. Cut foliage back to about 30 cm (12 in.) and split the plants into sections, each with at least six growths and a healthy clump of roots.

Fertilize 'Silver Edge' with compost or aged manure each spring; you may also work a little bone meal into the soil around each plant. Deadhead flower stalks as they finish blooming. In late fall, once the foliage has been killed by frost, cut plants back to about 8 cm (3 in.) and mulch with shredded leaves or straw.

Perfect Partners
Versatile 'Silver Edge' is a graceful foil for many hardy perennials. Try it with columbine (*Aquilegia* spp.), artemisia, oriental poppy (*Papaver orientale*), cranesbill, roses, peonies, veronica, lady's mantle (*Alchemilla mollis*), campanula, and *Sedum* 'Autumn Joy'.

Collectors' Choice
There are over 1,500 Siberian iris cultivars. A limited number are generally available at garden centers, but once you get hooked on these trouble-free beauties, you'll want to check out specialty iris catalogues that offer a greater selection. Start with the following outstanding performers.
- 'Butter and Sugar' (70 cm, 28 in.), white and yellow.
- 'Caesar's Brother' (1 m, 3.3 ft.), dark violet.

"Siberian irises are on my list of plants to take to heaven with me. They look wonderful from spring to fall."

BRENDA WINNY
ROSETOWN, SASKATCHEWAN

- 'Chilled Wine' (76 cm, 30 in.), wine-red.
- 'Dreaming Yellow' (76 cm, 30 in.), white and yellow.
- 'Fourfold White' (80 cm, 32 in.), with 15-cm (6-in.), white blooms.
- 'Ruffled Velvet' (60 cm, 24 in.), velvety purple.
- 'Super Ego' (76 cm, 30 in.), light blue.
- 'Welcome Return' (60 cm, 24 in.), lilac.
- 'Wing on Wing' (95 cm, 38 in.), white, ruffled.

Other beardless irises also thrive in prairie gardens.
- *Iris pseudacorus* (90 cm, 36 in.), yellow flag iris, is native to wet areas and is ideal for pond-side plantings. However, it will also readily adapt to life in the perennial border. *I. versicolor*, blue flag iris, is similar in form and growing requirements.
- *Iris setosa* (15 to 30 cm, 6 to 12 in.), arctic iris, has blue or purple flowers and is a good choice for rock gardens.

Juniperus scopulorum 'Medora'

(you-*nip*-er-us skop-ew-*lo*-rum)

Rocky Mountain juniper

Junipers are drought-tolerant evergreens, made to measure for prairie gardens. Common junipers (*Juniperus communis*) are also the source of those little, aromatic juniper berries that flavor gin, an alcoholic beverage developed by the Dutch in the seventeenth century.

Juniper fruit is unique—although it looks like a berry, it is actually a cone. Female flowers consist of scales that eventually become fleshy and coalesce to form sweet, berrylike fruit, an attractive food source for birds.

Some junipers are prairie natives; others, such as the lovely Rocky Mountain juniper (*Juniperus scopulorum*), originate on rocky slopes. Rocky Mountain juniper is commonly known as western red cedar because of its shaggy bark and intensely fragrant wood and foliage. In fact, many so-called cedar chests are actually constructed of Rocky Mountain juniper, every bit as red and aromatic as real cedar.

Plant at a Glance

TYPE: evergreen shrub
HEIGHT: 4 m (13 ft.)
WIDTH: 90 cm (36 in.)
SOIL: average, well drained
LIGHT: full sun

PHOTO – PAGE 124

Portrait

'Medora' is a striking, tall Rocky Mountain juniper with a narrow, pyramidal, almost columnar form. Its main trunk is short and divided near the ground; vertical branches are covered in a red-brown, aromatic, furrowed or shredded bark and bluish green, needlelike foliage.

Other popular cultivars of *Juniperus scopulorum* include 'Moonglow' (silver-blue, broad pyramid, no pruning required); 'Sky Rocket' (blue-green, narrow, and upright); and 'Wichita Blue' (light blue, pyramidal, requires some pruning). An unusual-looking cultivar of *J. scopulorum* is 'Tolleson's Weeping', with its shaggy, silver-blue foliage festooning uniquely drooping branches.

Where to Grow

'Medora' makes an excellent vertical, somewhat formal, foundation planting, but also serves well in a hedge or as a feature shrub toward the back of mixed and shrub borders.

How to Grow

Plant 'Medora' in average, well-drained soil; choose a sunny spot to help maintain its dense habit and blue color. All junipers, including this one, are very drought tolerant once established and will prosper even in hot, dry locations. In fact, most junipers decline in vigor when exposed to high humidity.

'Medora' requires very little pruning to maintain its pyramidal form. However, should you wish to give it a trim, do so during active summer growth. Keep in mind that juniper foliage is very prickly and irritating to the skin; protect yourself accordingly. Watering juniper shrubs before pruning helps soften the foliage.

Most cultivars of *Juniperus scopulorum* are alternate hosts for saskatoon-juniper rust; remove infected branches upon discovery.

Perfect Partners

'Medora' is attractive surrounded by low, contrasting junipers such as *Juniperus communis* 'Depressa Aurea'; *J. horizontalis* 'Mother Lode'; and *J. sabina* 'Arcadia'. A combination of colorful spireas and shrub roses at its base also paints a pretty picture.

Collectors' Choice

In addition to the columnar varieties, there are also creeping and shrub-style junipers well suited to prairie gardens and readily available.

- *Juniperus communis* (0.5 to 6 m, 1.5 to 20 ft.), common juniper, is a native North American spreading shrub or small columnar tree. Sharply pointed foliage is deep green to blue-green with a white band running down the middle. Spherical, blue-black fruit takes three years to ripen. 'Depressa Aurea' has golden yellow foliage that turns bronze in winter, and it is much hardier than the similar *J.* x *pfitzeriana* 'Aurea'.
- *Juniperus horizontalis* (30 cm, 12 in.), spreading or creeping juniper, is native to the Canadian prairies and makes an excellent groundcover. It is a low, prostrate shrub with young, needlelike, gray-green foliage that matures into a flatter, scalelike form. The berrylike fruit is dark blue. Some of the best cultivars include: 'Blue Chip' (silver-blue, branches radiate from center, perfect for draping over walls); 'Blue Prince' (intense powder blue, compact, prefers

winter snow cover); 'Dunvegan Blue' (silver-blue, ground hugging); 'Hughes' (silver-blue, fast-growing); 'Mother Lode' (gold changing to deep orange in the fall); 'Plumosa Compacta' (light green changing to plum in fall); 'Prince of Wales' (green, purple tinge in winter, very low, fast growing); 'Wiltonii' or 'Wilton's Blue Rug' (silver-blue, purple tinge in winter, trailing, fast growing).

- *Juniperus* x *pfitzeriana* (also sold as *Juniperus* x *media*) (1.2 m, 4 ft.) is a spreading, flat-topped, vase-shaped shrub. Its gray-green leaves are scaly and flat-lying; its fruit is dark purple. Try 'Armstrongii' (compact), 'Aurea' (golden-tipped branches, susceptible to some die-back), or 'Glauca' (silver-blue, very prickly foliage).
- *Juniperus sabina* cultivars (2 to 4.5 m, 6.5 to 15 ft.), Savin juniper cultivars, are spreading shrubs of variable height, perfectly suited for foundation plantings and for mixed and shrub borders. They have flaking, red-brown bark and spherical, flattened fruit that ripen over the first winter. Good choices are 'Arcadia' (bright green, arching stems), 'Broadmoor' (low, spreading, dull blue-green), 'Calgary Carpet' (light green, horizontal branching), and 'Skandia' (bright green, compact).

"Medora juniper keeps my yard looking attractive all year round. I prune the branches lightly each June to maintain a dense, columnar look. The silvery blue foliage contrasts well with most shrubs, and waxwings search out the berries in late winter."

RICK DURAND
PORTAGE LA PRAIRIE,
MANITOBA

Larix sibirica
(*lair*-ix sy-*bee*-ri-kah)

Siberian larch

When autumn frosts nip the high mountain valleys from the Rocky Mountains to the Pacific northwest, the western larches (*Larix occidentalis*) shine like golden spires amidst their evergreen neighbors. Another glorious native species, *Larix laricina*, the tamarack, inhabits swampy locations from the Yukon to Newfoundland.

Larches are deciduous conifers that end the growing season in a blaze of glory every fall when the needles transform from green to fiery shades of yellow and orange. More airy and graceful than the solid evergreens many prairie gardeners are accustomed to, their shapely branches and persistent cones create winter interest even though foliage is lacking.

It is interesting, but perhaps not surprising, that the larch species best adapted to dry prairie conditions is not native to North America at all, but from faraway Siberia, a source of many hardy favorites.

Portrait
Larix sibirica, the Siberian larch, is a large, pyramidal tree with lower branches that descend slightly downward from the trunk, then arch up at the tips. The flexible needles are a lovely soft green shade as they emerge in the spring. Needles on new growth are arranged singly around the branch; those on older branches appear in clusters on short spurs. In the fall, these needles turn a bright golden yellow before they drop. Young trees have yellow bark; the bark of older trees is light brown.

The Siberian larch produces both male and female cones; the catkinlike male cones drop off after pollen is released, while the 3-cm (1.25-in.), seed-bearing female cones are scattered all along the branches and remain in place throughout the winter.

Where to Grow
Because the Siberian larch is a tree of large proportions, it is best planted as a specimen tree in large yards or on country properties. It is also suitable for shelterbelts.

How to Grow
Siberian larch is hardy and easy to grow. Give it plenty of space in a location with full sun, and average to fertile, well-drained soil. Although this larch adapts well to dry conditions, the use of an

Plant at a Glance

TYPE: deciduous tree
HEIGHT: 18 m (60 ft.)
WIDTH: 5 m (16 ft.)
SOIL: average to fertile, well drained
LIGHT: full sun

PHOTO – PAGE 73

114

organic mulch around its base can prove beneficial in retaining soil moisture and adding nutrients to the soil. Although some gardeners prune larches into hedges, pruning of specimen trees is unnecessary. In fact, the tree's graceful natural growth habit is one of its best features.

Perfect Partners

The spectacular golden fall color of the Siberian larch is best displayed against a background of tall evergreens. Colorado spruce (*Picea pungens*), including Colorado blue spruce (*P. p.* f. *glauca*) and the narrower Hoopsii blue spruce (*P. p.* f. *glauca* 'Hoopsii'), are admirable choices, as are Scotch pine (*Pinus sylvestris*) or Swiss stone pine (*P. cembra*).

Collectors' Choice

Other hardy larches exhibit the same fresh spring debut and fabulous fall finale as the Siberian larch, although they prefer moister locations.

🌱 *Larix decidua* (18 m, 60 ft.) is also known as European or common larch. It grows in a pyramidal form with drooping branches, scaly bark, and grass green needles that turn yellow in the fall. The European larch should be grown in full sun, in moist, well-drained soil. There is an upright, columnar form, 'Fastigiata', and also a weeping variety, 'Pendula', that sometimes requires staking to keep it erect; 'Pendula' can be used for trailing over walls or rockeries.

🌱 *Larix laricina* (15 m, 50 ft.), also called tamarack or American larch, is a large tree with a pyramidal form and reddish, scaly bark when mature. The name tamarack comes from the Abenaki people of Quebec and Maine and means "wood for snowshoes." The roots were also used to sew birchbark. Although adapted to boggy soil, these

"The Siberian larch is beautiful when it leafs out with new green needles. It's a good shade tree in summer, but lets light through in winter when you need it. Don't plant it in front of your living room window, though—it's just too big."

GORDON MCCOY
PILOT MOUND, MANITOBA

trees will grow well on dry land in well-drained soil, provided they are adequately irrigated. 'Newport Beauty' (30 cm, 12 in.) is a dwarf cultivar that has blue-green needles and is suitable for rockeries.

If you lack the space for a larch tree but admire the fine, soft green foliage, try a shrub that gives a similar effect.

🌱 *Tamarix ramosissima* (2.5 m, 8 ft.), five-stamen tamarisk, is a graceful shrub that is worth incorporating at the back of a border; rated to Zone 3, it may not be fully hardy in the coldest parts of the prairies. Tamarisk has needlelike, deciduous leaves and tiny, pink flowers borne on feathery plumes. It flowers on new growth and should be cut back close to the ground in the spring to encourage the formation of new shoots. This shrub is salt, drought, and wind tolerant. Cultivars include 'Pink Cascade', with shell pink flowers, and 'Summerglow', with dark pink flowers.

Lathyrus odoratus 'Old Fashioned Mixed'

(lah-thi-russ o-doh-rah-tus)

Sweet pea

Affectionately known as "Queen of the Annuals," sweet pea blossoms consistently fulfil gardeners' cravings for exquisite form, vibrant color, and delicious scent in the landscape. In fact, most prairie gardeners have, at one time or another, devoted a few meters of bare fence to a sumptuous display of their favorite sweet peas.

To date, over a thousand different varieties of sweet peas have been developed, in every shade imaginable, except true yellow. Unfortunately, plant breeders have sacrificed bloom perfume in their quest for bigger, frillier, and more abundant sweet pea blossoms. Luckily, conservationists are coming to the rescue by locating and reintroducing original, fragrant, heirloom varieties.

Portrait

'Old Fashioned Mixed' is a collection of sweet pea climbers that were popular at the turn of the century. Their flowers are smaller but more strongly scented than their modern counterparts. Showy sweet pea blossoms consist of a large top petal (standard), two narrow side petals (wings), and two lower petals (keel); to some people they look like old-fashioned sunbonnets. The blossoms are borne on winged stems, covered with alternating, compound, blue-green leaves and twining tendrils that help the vine climb. They make excellent cut flowers from June to frost.

Named varieties of old-fashioned, strongly scented sweet peas are worth looking for; they include 'Black Knight' (deep maroon), 'Bushby' (two-toned pink), 'Captain of the Blues' (deep mauve), 'Cupani' (mauve-and-maroon bicolor), 'Fairy Queen' (white, tinged pink), 'Original' (maroon-and-blue bicolor), 'Painted Lady' (red-and-white bicolor), and 'Prima Donna' (pink).

Where to Grow

Grow 'Old Fashioned Mixed' and other tall sweet peas on a trellis—along fences as a backdrop to perennial and mixed borders, as a screen for private seating areas, or as a divider between garden rooms. You can also grow them on an arbor, pergola, or tripod constructed from long tree branches and set in the middle of a flowerbed or vegetable patch.

How to Grow

Although 'Old Fashioned Mixed' and other sweet peas can be started from seed indoors, they do not transplant well; it's

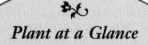

Plant at a Glance

TYPE: annual vine
HEIGHT: 2.5 m (8 ft.)
WIDTH: 30 cm (12 in.)
SOIL: fertile, moist, well drained
LIGHT: full sun
FLOWERING TIME: early summer
to fall

PHOTO – PAGE 124

best to plant seed directly into the ground as soon as it can be worked in the spring. Don't worry about the uncertainties of typical prairie spring weather as sweet peas thrive in cool temperatures and can tolerate some frost.

Soak seeds overnight in lukewarm water, and then plant 'Old Fashioned Mixed' in full sun and well-drained soil, liberally amended with compost. Some gardeners recommend first tossing the seeds with a soil inoculant, available at garden centers; this helps sweet peas use available nitrogen more readily, which accelerates the production of bigger, better flowers. Apply a mulch around them to keep their roots cool.

When the plants are 15 cm (6 in.) tall, pinch them back to encourage branching. Water regularly and apply a balanced fertilizer biweekly. Deadhead or cut a bouquet regularly to encourage continuous flowering from early summer to frost.

All sweet pea parts are poisonous.

Perfect Partners
Plant 'Old Fashioned Mixed' in mixed borders behind low-growing, evergreen or deciduous shrubs, as a background to perennials with large, bold flowers such as daylilies (*Hemerocallis* spp.), lilies (*Lilium* spp.), or delphinium, or interplanted with leafy green vegetables in the kitchen garden.

Collectors' Choice
In addition to old-fashioned heirlooms, sweet peas are also available as Spencer or bush types.

- Spencer cultivars and series (2.5 m, 8 ft.), the most commonly grown sweet peas, produce large, show-quality blossoms with wavy petals and varying degrees of fragrance. Among the most floriferous are the Galaxy, Early Multiflora, and Multiflora groups, the Cuthbertson Floribunda Series, and 'Royal' varieties.
- Bush sweet peas (45 to 90 cm, 18 to 36 in.) are shorter than the Spencer and old-fashioned kinds. Hedge varieties grow to 90 cm (36 in.) and require little support; they include 'Knee High', 'Jet Set', 'Snoopea', and 'Supersnoop' groups. Dwarf varieties such as 'Bijou', 'Little Sweetheart', and 'Patio' grow to 45 cm (18 in.) and are self-supporting. 'Cupid' is a low, carpeting sweet pea, 15 cm (6 in.) tall.

Several other annual vines enjoy popularity in prairie gardens.
- *Cobaea scandens* (10 m, 33 ft.), cup-and-saucer vine, produces fragrant, double, bell-shaped flowers that open pale green and mature to deep violet.
- *Rhodochiton atrosanguineum* (3 m, 10 ft.), purple bell vine, produces deep purple, double, bell-shaped flowers and small, heart-shaped leaves.
- *Solanum jasminoides* (6 m, 20 ft.), potato vine, produces fragrant, white, star-shaped flowers in terminal clusters.
- *Tropaeolum peregrinum* (4 m, 13 ft.), canarybird vine or canary creeper, produces bright yellow, spurred flowers all summer long; its upper petals are fringed and resemble tiny bird wings.

"Sweet peas were the flowers of choice when I was a kid. I always associate them with youth, friendship, and first sweethearts."

BARRY NOWELL
REGINA, SASKATCHEWAN

Liatris spicata 'Kobold'

(lee-*ah*-tris spih-*kah*-tah)

Liatris, Gayfeather

It's hard to believe that the magenta and white fuzzy spires of *Liatris spicata*, a plant native to eastern North America, are kin to ever-popular daisies. Liatris' strong vertical lines and tight, tidy growth habit belie its derivation, although today it is as welcome in gardens as its daisy relatives. In full bloom, a mature clump of liatris presents a singular profile on the prairie, that of an elegant leafy candelabrum burning the biggest, shaggiest candles you ever did see.

Liatris' value in the garden was long overlooked by North Americans. It wasn't until it became a hit with nineteenth-century English gardeners and florists that North Americans realized the worth of this lovely plant, growing right in their own backyards.

Portrait

'Kobold' liatris, also sold as 'Goblin' and 'Gnome', is the most popular cultivar of *Liatris spicata*. Smooth, bright green, linear leaves are up to 30 cm (12 in.) long and form a mound at the plant base; the leaves shorten upward and eventually overlap with unusual flower clusters, which are arranged along the upper end of the bloom stalk in a dense spike. The small, deep purple flower heads consist entirely of button-shaped clusters of seed-producing disk florets; petal-like ray florets are absent. The flower heads open from the top of the spike downward, a habit opposite to that of similar spiky plants, to reveal the inner filamentous florets that give liatris its furry look.

Birds, bees, and butterflies are attracted to 'Kobold' as are florists, who covet the cheerful, wandlike spikes for fresh and dried flower arrangements.

Other cultivars of *Liatris spicata* worth looking for are 'Blue Bird' (blue-violet), 'Floristan White' (creamy white), 'Alba' (off white), 'Floristan Violet' (lustrous violet), 'Silver Tip' (lavender), and 'Snow Queen' (white).

Where to Grow

Compact clumps of 'Kobold' serve well in the front or middle of formal perennial borders, informal mixed borders, and cottage gardens. They are also at home sprinkled across natural prairie gardens and wildflower meadows.

Plant at a Glance

TYPE: perennial
HEIGHT: 50 cm (20 in.)
WIDTH: 30 cm (12 in.)
SOIL: average to fertile, moist, well drained
LIGHT: full to part sun
FLOWERING TIME: late summer

PHOTO – PAGE 125

How to Grow

'Kobold' liatris is happiest when planted in fertile, moist, well-drained soil, although once established it is quite drought tolerant. It also prefers a spot in full sun, but won't complain about a few hours of dappled shade.

Clumps of 'Kobold' can remain undisturbed for years and rarely need dividing. However, if necessary, clumps can be divided in early fall. You can also sow seed outdoors in autumn for germination the following spring; sown from seed, it will take from two to four years to bloom.

Because 'Kobold' spikes produce blooms from the top down, they can be deadheaded by trimming spike ends as flowers fade. This type of deadheading does not encourage reblooming; it merely tidies the plant. Alternatively, consider leaving the flower stalks intact so that the birds can enjoy a generous seed supply in autumn and winter.

Perfect Partners

'Kobold' makes a pleasing companion for other late-blooming perennials, among them goldenrod (*Solidago* spp.), black-eyed Susan (*Rudbeckia* spp.), purple coneflower (*Echinacea purpurea*), monarda, and garden phlox. Its bold magenta flowers and grassy foliage also combine well with ornamental grasses, German statice (*Goniolimon tataricum*), pearly everlasting (*Anaphalis* spp.), and a variety of sedums.

Collectors' Choice

The liatris most commonly available in nurseries is *Liatris spicata*, but there are others worth looking for. They are all late bloomers and prefer full sun and average to fertile, well-drained soil.

- *Liatris punctata* (80 cm, 32 in.), also called snakeroot and dotted blazing star, produces crowded 30-cm (12-in.) spikes of deep rosy purple flowers.

"Instead of the usual petals that make up flowers, liatris has tufts of slender, spikelike petals. The unusual thing about liatris is that it flowers from the top and opens progressively downward on the stem."

IRENE SUNDBY
SWIFT CURRENT, SASKATCHEWAN

- *Liatris pycnostachya* (1.5 m, 5 ft.), also called Kansas gayfeather, produces dense, 45-cm (18-in.) spikes of bright purple flower heads, each 1.5 cm (0.5 in.) across.

For a purple, spiky look in the border you can also plant betony (*Stachys* spp.), popular cottage garden plants that prefer full sun, and average, well-drained soil. They are summer bloomers.

- *Stachys byzantina* (45 cm, 18 in.), also called lambs' ears, forms a dense mat of soft, woolly, gray-green, elliptical leaves. Equally woolly, spiky bloom stalks support whorls of small, pink-purple flowers. 'Silver Carpet' is a non-flowering cultivar grown purely for its felted, silvery leaves.
- *Stachys grandiflora* (*S. macrantha*) (60 cm, 24 in.), also called big betony, forms clumps of dark green, wrinkled, hairy leaves that are heart-shaped at the base, and lovely spikes of hooded violet-pink flowers.
- *Stachys officinalis* (60 cm, 24 in.), also called bishop's wort or wood betony, is similar to *S. grandiflora*, but has denser clusters of smaller, reddish purple, pink, or white flowers.

Ligularia dentata 'Othello'
(lig-ew-*lah*-ree-ah den-*tah*-tah)

Ligularia, Rayflower

Bold, colorful, and dramatic, ligularias never fail to impress with their ornamental leaves and bright yellow or orange blooms. Although not suited to hot, dry, open gardens, these magnificent perennials are undemanding and generally pest free when properly located.

Native to China and Japan, ligularias derive their botanical name from the Latin word for strap, *ligula*, in reference to the straplike ray florets of the flowers. Also known as rayflower, ragwort, and golden groundsel, ligularias are becoming increasingly popular in gardens where "big impact" plants and striking foliage are desired. Most prairie nurseries stock two or three species; others may need to be ordered from specialty perennial catalogues.

Portrait
In the spring, the leaves of *Ligularia dentata* 'Othello' emerge a deep mahogany red, intensifying to dark purple as they grow. The large, heart-shaped leaves are toothed and borne on long stems. Rising well above the glossy leaves are rounded clusters of yellow-orange, daisylike flowers. The flowers are composed of ray florets around a dark brown disk.

'Othello' has a companion, 'Desdemona', which is, not surprisingly, very similar in appearance. 'Moorblut' is another purple-leaved cultivar.

Where to Grow
Grow 'Othello' near the back of a partly shaded perennial border or as a striking feature plant in a woodland garden. This moisture-loving plant is at home in low-lying areas and around pond margins. Although these plants expand slowly, they will eventually become large, so allow adequate growing room.

Like most impressive large-leaved plants, all ligularias are quickly damaged by hail, so a sheltered location is preferable.

How to Grow
'Othello' prefers fertile soil high in organic matter. Some gardeners claim that ligularias grow well in full sun, provided the soil is kept moist, but adequate watering is not usually enough to keep the large leaves from flagging when exposed to the full heat of the prairie sun. Although the wilted

Plant at a Glance

TYPE: perennial
HEIGHT: 1.2 m (4 ft.)
WIDTH: 1.0 m (3.3 ft.)
SOIL: fertile, moist
LIGHT: light shade to part sun
FLOWERING TIME: mid to late summer

PHOTO – PAGE 125

Gaillardia x *grandiflora* 'Goblin'
(gaillardia, blanket flower) page 82.

LESLEY REYNOLDSS

Geranium x *magnificum*
(showy cranesbill) page 84.

LIESBETH LEATHERBARROW

Geum triflorum (three-flowered avens,
prairie smoke) page 86.

LIESBETH LEATHERBARROW

Gladiolus callianthus (peacock orchid,
sweet scented gladiolus) page 88.

LIESBETH LEATHERBARROW

Helianthus annuus 'Floristan'
(sunflower) page 90.

Gray: *Helichrysum petiolare*, page 92. Magenta:
Petunia 'Purple Wave' (petunia) page 156.

Hemerocallis 'Catherine Woodbury'
(daylily) page 94.

Heuchera x *brizoides*
(coral bells, alumroot) page 96.

122

Hosta sieboldiana 'Elegans'
(hosta, plantain lily) page 98.

Humulus lupulus
(hops) page 100.

Hydrangea arborescens 'Annabelle'
(smooth hydrangea) page 102.

Iberis spp. (perennial candytuft, evergreen
candytuft) page 104.

Iris x *pumila* 'Red at Last'
(dwarf bearded iris) page 108.

Iris sibirica 'Silver Edge'
(Siberian iris) page 110.

Juniperus scopulorum 'Medora'
(Rocky Mountain juniper) page 112.

Lathyrus odoratus 'Old Fashioned Mixed'
(sweet pea) page 116.

Liatris spicata (liatris, gayfeather) page 118.

LIESBETH LEATHERBARROW

Top: Ligularia dentata 'Othello' (rayflower) page 120. Bottom right: Rudbeckia fulgida var. sullivantii 'Goldsturm', page 192. LESLEY REYNOLDS

Lilium x Orientpets 'Northern Carillon' (lily) page 130.

LIESBETH LEATHERBARROW

Lysimachia punctata (lysimachia, yellow loosestrife) page 132.

LIESBETH LEATHERBARROW

Malus x *adstringens* 'Thunderchild'
(rosybloom crabapple) page 134.

Molinia caerulea 'Moorhexe'
(purple moor grass) page 136.

Monarda didyma 'Gardenview Scarlet'
(monarda, bee balm) page 138.

Top: *Narcissus* 'Minnow' (miniature daffodil)
page 140. Bottom: *Muscari armeniacum* (grape
hyacinth).

Nepeta x *faassenii* 'Dropmore'
(catmint, blue catmint) page 142.

LIESBETH LEATHERBARROW

Nicotiana sylvestris (flowering tobacco,
woodland tobacco) page 144.

LIESBETH LEATHERBARROW

Osmunda regalis
(royal fern) page 146.

LIESBETH LEATHERBARROW

Paeonia lactiflora
'Festiva Maxima' (peony) page 148.

LIESBETH LEATHERBARROW

Papaver orientale 'Prince of Orange'
(oriental poppy) page 150.

Pelargonium x *hortorum* (zonal pelargonium,
zonal geranium) page 152.

Penstemon digitalis 'Husker Red' (foxglove
penstemon, white beardtongue) page 154.

Philadelphus lewisii (mock orange,
orange flower bush) page 158.

leaves quickly recover once the sun has passed, try planting it in dappled or light shade to avoid the problem. A layer of deep organic mulch around the plant will help keep the roots cool, conserve moisture, and add nutrients to the soil.

If slugs frequent your garden, check the leaves of all ligularias regularly or use your favorite slug barrier methods in the neighborhood of the plant.

'Othello' does not require frequent division, but should you wish to do so, plants may be split or moved in the spring. All ligularia can be propagated from seed; even purple-leaved forms will come true.

Perfect Partners

Plants that thrive in moist soil and light shade are good companions for 'Othello', particularly those with delicate or airy foliage and blooms that contrast with the large, solid-looking leaves. Astilbe, meadow rue (*Thalictrum aquilegifolium*), ferns, spiderwort (*Tradescantia* hybrids), 'Flore Pleno' meadowsweet (*Filipendula ulmaria*), and goose-necked loosestrife (*Lysimachia clethroides*) will all work well.

Collectors' Choice

Several other splendid ligularias are worthy of trial:

- *Ligularia* 'Gregynog Gold' (1.8 m, 6 ft.), a hybrid between *L. dentata* and *L. veitchiana*, has round, toothed foliage and rich orange-yellow conical clusters of flowers. This beauty can grow as wide as 2 m (6.5 ft.).
- *Ligularia hodgsonii* (90 cm, 36 in.) resembles *L. dentata* and is a good choice for a small garden.
- *Ligularia przewalskii* (1.5 m, 5 ft.) bears tall, yellow flower spikes above deeply toothed and lobed, dark green leaves on purple-black stems.
- *Ligularia stenocephala* 'The Rocket' (1.5 m, 5 ft.) is frequently seen in

> "*Ligularia has beautiful leaves and striking flowers. It's easy to grow, prefers a bit of shade during the hot days of summer, and winters very well.*"
>
> HELEN FLAVELL
> YORKTON, SASKATCHEWAN

prairie gardens, and no wonder. This notable perennial has large clumps of finely toothed, triangular leaves and tall, bright yellow flower spikes borne on contrasting black stems.

If you want to impress the neighbors with your green thumb, the following giants will give your garden a lush, tropical appearance. They all require rich, moist soil to nourish their considerable bulk.

- *Cimicifuga racemosa* (2 m, 6.5 ft.), also known as snakeroot or bugbane, is a late-blooming perennial with racemes of white flowers on black stems above dark green foliage divided into many small leaflets. Snakeroot spreads to 1.5 m (5 ft.).
- *Macleaya cordata* (1.8 m, 6 ft.), the plume poppy, is named for its tall, feathery plumes of small, white flowers. The large, gray-green, lobed leaves have silver undersides. This decorative perennial can spread 1.2 m (4 ft.).
- *Rheum palmatum* (1.5 m, 5 ft.), commonly known as ornamental rhubarb, has lavish flower plumes and lobed, toothed leaves that are red or purple when young. The leaves can grow 1 m (3.3 ft.), while the entire plant can spread 1.8 m (6 ft.). 'Atrosanguineum' has red flowers.

Lilium x Orientpets
(*lil*-ee-um)

Lily

Showy and spectacular lilies are among the most popular flowers in the world. Over 200 species and a phenomenal number of hybrids are available in an artist's palette of colors, some bright and hot, others soft and subdued. Lilies produce six-petalled flowers that may be upfacing, out-facing or sidefacing, or downfacing. Flower form varies from bowl- to trumpet- or star-shaped, and many types have recurved petals. The flowers have prominent, pollen-laden stamens, attractive to bees and butterflies, and are generally clustered atop sturdy stems clad with medium to dark green, lance-shaped leaves.

Early-blooming and dependable, Asiatic lilies (*Lilium* x *hybridum*) are undoubtedly the easiest lilies to grow and obtain. However, new hybrids developed on the prairies are also outstanding choices for both the beginning gardener and the lily connoisseur.

Plant at a Glance

TYPE: perennial
HEIGHT: 0.9 to 1.5 m (3 to 5 ft.)
WIDTH: 30 cm (12 in.)
SOIL: fertile, moist, well drained
LIGHT: full to part sun
FLOWERING TIME: mid to late summer

PHOTO – PAGE 125

Portrait

Orientpets are an exciting group of four lily cultivars hybridized from Aurelian trumpet lilies and Oriental lilies. Bred at the Morden Research Center in Manitoba, these fragrant lilies bloom three to five weeks after Asiatic lilies and have proven hardy in Zone 3 without special winter protection.

'Starburst Sensation' (90 cm, 36 in.) bears outfacing, bowl-shaped, pink flowers with dark pink throats, producing up to a dozen flowers per stem.

'Northern Carillon' (1.2 m, 4 ft.) is a vigorous lily with trumpet-shaped, fragrant, pink flowers with dark red throats.

'Northern Sensation' (1.2 m, 4 ft.) is a hardier sister to 'Northern Carillon' with a more bowl-shaped flower and a lighter red throat.

'Northern Beauty' (1.5 m, 5 ft.) bears downfacing, recurved dark red flowers with yellow throats.

Where to Grow

For a striking display, plant Orientpets in mixed or perennial borders. They also look elegant planted in large pots, but must be moved to the garden in the fall.

How to Grow

Orientpets prefer a sunny, sheltered location, although some shade during hot afternoons prolongs bloom life.

Like all true lilies, Orientpets grow from fleshy bulbs made of overlapping scales. Purchase and plant bulbs in late summer or early fall, handling them with care as they bruise easily. Plant bulbs nose side up at a depth of four times the bulb height, in fertile, well-drained soil amended with compost, adding a little bone meal to the planting hole. Apply organic mulch around the plant to keep the soil cool and moist. Plant container-ized lilies at any time during the growing season.

Check leaves regularly for aphids, which may carry mosaic virus. Remove them with a strong stream of water or spray with insecticidal soap. Twisted leaves and buds are symptoms of virus infection and affected plants should be removed. Botrytis, a fungal disease, can affect lilies and is indicated by browning leaves or leaf spots. This may be treated with fungicide and by improving air circulation.

Deadhead spent blooms and allow foliage to die back naturally before cutting stems to the ground in the fall. Add mulch for winter protection, and mark bulb loca-tions to avoid accidental damage in early spring. Top dress Orientpets with compost in the spring; in addition, a balanced fertil-izer can be applied monthly until flower-ing has finished.

Divide Orientpets every few years when clumps become crowded.

Perfect Partners

Combine Orientpets with delphiniums, Galaxy Series achillea, coreopsis, monarda, garden phlox, peach-leaved bellflowers (*Campanula persicifolia*), or Canterbury bells (*Campanula medium*). Roses and lilies are a classic combination, and the foun-tains of Siberian iris (*Iris sibirica*) and daylily (*Hemerocallis* spp.) foliage disguise lily stems once blooming has finished.

Collectors' Choice

Choose an assortment of hardy lilies with varying bloom times and enjoy these floral

"Lilies are hardy, beautiful, showy, stately, and disease resistant, and they multiply into large clumps. What more could you want? If you plan it well, you can have them blooming from early June to early September."

ANNE-MARIE KURBIS
SELKIRK, MANITOBA

aristocrats all summer. Make sure you include this new Canadian lily series.

- Canadian Belles Series are hybrids of Aurelian trumpet lilies with Asiatic lilies. 'Ivory Belles', 'Silky Belles', 'Fiery Belles', and 'Creamy Belles' are now available, with three more to come.

There are an astonishing number of Asiatic lily cultivars. Here are a few tried and true favorites.

- 'Bold Knight' (114 cm, 45 in.), bright red, outfacing.
- 'Connecticut King' (90 cm, 36 in.), copper-yellow, upfacing.
- 'Enchantment' (90 cm, 36 in.), the classic orange, speckled Asiatic lily, upfacing.
- 'Roma' (105 cm, 42 in.), creamy white to yellow, upfacing.
- 'Sorbet' (120 cm, 48 in.), white with pink-red edges, upfacing.
- 'Tiger Babies' (76 cm, 30 in.), peach pink with chocolate spots, downfacing.

Gardeners enamored of lilies should try this hardy species that prefers light shade.

- *Lilium martagon* (1.5 m, 5 ft.), Turk's-cap lily, produces numerous purplish rose, nodding flowers in early to mid-summer. *Album* is a white variety. The hybrid 'Mrs. R. O. Backhouse' (1.2 m, 4 ft.) has recurved, yellow flowers spotted with red.

Lysimachia punctata

(li-si-*mak*-ee-ah punk-*tah*-tah)

Lysimachia, Yellow loosestrife

Some gardeners might avoid a plant described by many as a vigorous grower and by some as being downright invasive. However, it's easy to be impressed by the sunny blooms of yellow loosestrife (*Lysimachia punctata*), which is not to be confused with the extremely invasive and noxious purple loosestrife, with which it shares a common name. Yellow, or whorled, loosestrife belongs to the primrose family (*Primulaceae*) and is unrelated to purple loosestrife (*Lythrum*), a member of the loosestrife family (*Lythraceae*).

Lysimachias comprise a group of rather wild and weedy perennials, but a few among them make wonderful additions to the garden. They were named by Dioscorides, a Greek botanist and physician, after King Lysimachos of Thrace (c. 360–281 BC), one of Alexander the Great's generals who was said to have discovered them. The name Lysimachos is derived from the Greek *lusi*, from *luein*, "to loose," and *mache*, "strife," and can be loosely translated as "causing strife to cease." During Roman times, loosestrife was placed under the yokes of oxen to prevent them from fighting with each other; it was also used to staunch the bloody wounds of war.

Portrait

The starry, bright yellow flowers of yellow loosestrife nestle in the leaf axils, hugging erect stems, and gazing out cheekily in all directions, opening gradually from the bottom up for a long season of bloom. The deep green, lance-shaped leaves, up to 10 cm (4 in.) in length, are crinkled and opposite each other or in tiered whorls around the stem.

Lysimachia punctata 'Alexander' (50 cm, 20 in.) is a handsome cultivar with green leaves edged with cream, which have a pink tinge in spring. It also bears golden yellow flower spikes.

Where to Grow

Yellow loosestrife is at home beside a pond or a stream, or at the edge of a woodland garden. Given sufficient moisture, it will also thrive in a sunny perennial border in ordinary soil. However, periods of dryness will slow its growth and extended drought can be fatal.

How to Grow

Plant yellow loosestrife in fertile, evenly moist soil, in full sun, or in part sun where

Plant at a Glance

TYPE: perennial
HEIGHT: 90 cm (36 in.)
WIDTH: 60 cm (24 in.)
SOIL: fertile, moist
LIGHT: full to part sun
FLOWERING TIME: early to late summer

PHOTO – PAGE 125

the climate is hot. Perhaps the warm, dry prairie summers explain, at least in part, why most loosestrifes in this region do not exhibit the rampant and unruly growth habit that is reputedly theirs. They are also not susceptible to insect or disease damage and require minimal attention once established. Best of all, the sturdy plants do not even require staking. All loosestrifes may be propagated by division.

Perfect Partners

In partly shaded areas, surround yellow loosestrife with lush foliage plants such as hostas and ferns. Meadowsweet (*Filipendula* spp.) and astilbe offer feathery blooms to contrast with its stiff flower spikes. In a sunny border, complement it with ornamental grasses, lambs' ears, coral bells, brightly colored annual poppies, monarda, and cranesbill (*Geranium* spp.), particularly deep blue-purple shades like 'Johnson's Blue'. Other blue-flowered companions include peach-leaved bell-flower (*Campanula persicifolia*) and beard-tongue (*Penstemon strictus*).

Collectors' Choice

Look for these other *Lysimachia* species in your favorite garden center.

- *Lysimachia ciliata* 'Firecracker' (also called 'Purpurea') (90 cm, 36 in.), fringed loosestrife, has striking bronze-purple leaves and yellow flowers. It grows in loose, slowly spreading clumps.
- *Lysimachia clethroides* (90 cm, 36 in.), also called gooseneck loosestrife, Japanese loosestrife, and shepherd's crook, is a late-summer bloomer and is also late to emerge in the spring. The plant's graceful, arching, white terminal flower spikes, when viewed in a cluster, bring to mind a friendly gaggle of geese and make a perfect backdrop to a small woodland pool. Like yellow

"Yellow loosestrife is a wonderful middle-of-the-border plant that has a very long bloom period. I grow it in my prairie garden with old-fashioned sweet William and 'Blue Queen' salvia. It also looks great combined with purple flowers."

MICHELLE CARPENTER
PRINCETON, MINNESOTA

loosestrife, it is not usually invasive in prairie gardens.

- *Lysimachia nummularia* (10 cm, 4 in.), commonly known as moneywort or creeping Jenny, is a rambunctious low-lying groundcover that can quickly clothe the ground with a carpet of gold and green. The stems, which are capable of rooting along their entire length, are covered all season long with the same jaunty bright yellow, star-shaped flowers as yellow loosestrife. It is ideal for rock gardens or for trailing over rock walls, but best excluded from the perennial border. 'Aurea' (10 cm, 4 in.), golden creeping Jenny, will light up any shady corner; its leaves are chartreuse in the spring, darkening to lime green in the summer.

Malus x *adstringens* 'Thunderchild'
(*ma*-luss x ad-*strin*-jenz)

Rosybloom crabapple

Prairie gardeners who are seeking the perfect small tree need look no further than the rosybloom crabapple (*Malus* x *adstringens* cultivars). It is decorative, fast growing, and compact, fitting neatly into urban gardens with limited space. This crabapple is notable for its masses of pink to red flowers that sweetly perfume the spring garden. The foliage is often bronze-green or purple, turning an attractive shade of orange in fall.

It produces small red or purple fruit less than 5 cm (2 in.) in diameter; the sour little apples are more ornamental than edible and are best left for the birds.

Portrait

Introduced by Percy Wright of Saskatoon, Saskatchewan, 'Thunderchild' is prized for its striking foliage and lovely blooms. This outstanding rosybloom crabapple has an oval, spreading crown. The pointed leaves are purple-green when they first emerge, later deepening to purple-red. A blanket of single, rose-pink flowers covers the tree before the foliage appears. Later in the growing season, it is adorned with small, dark purple-red fruit.

Where to Grow

'Thunderchild' is a superb feature tree for a small garden. Plant it near pathways so you can appreciate the light but sweet fragrance. Because the falling fruit may be messy, it is best not to plant this or other crabapples directly over a deck or seating area.

'Thunderchild' is an ideal tree to use for espalier, a technique by which small trees are trained and pruned to grow against a fence or wall in two dimensions.

How to Grow

'Thunderchild' prefers deep, well-drained soil of average fertility. Like all crabapples, it is not happy in consistently wet soil; indeed, established trees can tolerate drought very well. It will produce the most flowers if planted in a sunny location.

Prune 'Thunderchild' and other rosybloom crabapples after flowering has finished and leaves have completely emerged. They may be pruned in late winter while they are still dormant, although some of the flower buds formed the previous summer will be sacrificed. Prune young trees lightly to achieve the desired shape. Remove dead or damaged wood, crossing branches, or water sprouts (vigorous, verti-

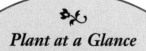

Plant at a Glance

TYPE: deciduous tree
HEIGHT: 5 m (16 ft.)
WIDTH: 5 m (16 ft.)
SOIL: average, well drained
LIGHT: full to part sun
FLOWERING TIME: spring

PHOTO – PAGE 126

cal branches that are unproductive).

'Thunderchild' possesses excellent resistance to fireblight, a serious bacterial disease that attacks members of the *Rosaceae* family, to which the *Malus* genus belongs.

Perfect Partners

Create a romantic spring picture by planting late-blooming tulips or primulas beneath the pink flowering canopy of 'Thunderchild'. Once the tree has leafed out, the protective branches provide the dappled shade beloved by many woodland perennials, including pulmonaria, fernleaf bleeding heart (*Dicentra* hybrids), spiderwort (*Tradescantia* x *andersoniana*), and Jacob's ladder (*Polemonium reptans*).

Collectors' Choice

Since ornamental flowering crabapples may be susceptible to fireblight ('Royalty' is a notable example), it pays to choose cultivars that are moderately to extremely disease resistant. The following crabapples are recommended for prairie gardens.

- 'Kelsey' (6 m, 20 ft.) provides masses of beautiful semi-double, purple-pink flowers each spring. Named after the explorer Henry Kelsey, it was developed at Morden and was introduced in 1969 as Manitoba's centennial tree. 'Kelsey' has bronze-green foliage and small, reddish purple fruit.
- 'Morning Princess' (5 m, 16 ft.) is a hardy, Saskatchewan-bred, weeping ornamental crabapple with a tall central leader, purple leaves, and single, pink flowers.
- 'Rudolph' (5 m, 16 ft.) has a round form and purple-bronze foliage. It blooms lavishly with red buds opening into bright pink flowers, and bears cherrylike fruit that persists into winter. This vigorous and hardy cultivar was introduced in 1954 by Frank

"I've had five 'Thunderchild' crabapples in my garden for over 10 years, and they look great. They are disease resistant, have lovely blossoms, and I like the red leaves in the landscape."

DIANA MCCALLUM
SOURIS, MANITOBA

Skinner; the name 'Rudolph' refers to the resemblance of the bright red buds to the famous reindeer's nose.

- 'Selkirk' (7 m, 23 ft.) has pink flowers and bronze-green foliage. This Morden introduction produces shiny, bright red fruit that is retained during the winter.

Many prairie gardeners love the fall ritual of picking crabapples and making jelly. And who isn't tempted by the crispness and fresh flavor of a just-picked apple while going about late-summer garden chores? If you want ornamental trees with edible fruit, try these varieties.

- 'Dolgo' (8 m, 26 ft.) is a vigorous crabapple tree with spreading branches and fragrant, white flowers. The small, red fruit makes delicious jelly.
- 'Kerr' (6 m, 20 ft.), a white-flowering apple-crab, has tasty, red fruit mid-way in size between an apple and a crabapple. The crisp apples are excellent for eating fresh, for making jelly, and for canning; they also store well.
- 'Rescue' (6 m, 20 ft.) is another white-flowering apple-crab, with green fruit striped with red. 'Rescue' fruit does not store as well as 'Kerr', but is tasty for eating fresh, for cooking, and for canning.

Molinia caerulea 'Moorhexe'

(mo-*lin*-ee-ah kye-*ru*-lee-ah)

Purple moor grass

Grasses, grown since the beginning of recorded time for their food value, have captured the hearts of gardeners for their ornamental worth in mixed borders and as a substitute for traditional lawn grasses. Not only do they add shape and form to most planting schemes, they also introduce sound and motion into the landscape when they rustle and wave in the wind.

Some grasses are grown for their amazing colors—they come in all shades of green, blue-green, gold, cream, red, bronze, and white. Others are grown for their showy and dramatic flower plumes, spikes, or seed heads, which add late summer, fall, and winter interest to the garden. Birds are enticed by their ripe seeds, especially during fall migration.

Warm-season moor grass (*Molinia caerulea*) adapts quite readily to the neutral and alkaline soils that prevail on the prairies. It is treasured for its non-aggressive nature, tall stems of delicate flowers, and fall color. Named for the Chilean natural history writer Juan Ignacio Molina (1740–1829), its swollen stem bases have occasionally doubled as pipe cleaners and toothpicks.

Portrait

'Moorhexe' purple moor grass, sometimes called moor witch or bog witch, forms compact, non-spreading mounds of rigid, grassy foliage. Leaves are flat, linear, and dark green with purple bases, and turn a tawny gold in the fall. During the summer, tall, erect flower stems shoot upward, supporting airy, needlelike sprays of purple-toned flowers high above the compact leaf tussock. Although this grass has a bold, upright presence in the garden, the combination of bare stems and wispy flower panicles gives it a delightful, see-through quality.

In the moor grass family, *Molinia caerulea* 'Variegata' has bright yellow-and-green striped leaves and medium-tall stems of purplish flowers. 'Moorflamme' is similar to 'Moorhexe', but has arching, rather than erect, stems. Several cultivars of the subspecies *M. caerulea* subsp. *arundinacea* are also worth growing. 'Transparent' grows to 1.8 m (6 ft.) and has flower heads that dance in the slightest of breezes; 'Karl Foerster' (2.1 m, 7 ft.) is an erect form with open, delicate flower heads; and at 2.5 m (8 ft.), 'Skyracer' is probably the tallest of the moor grasses.

Plant at a Glance

TYPE: perennial
HEIGHT: 90 cm (36 in.)
WIDTH: 30 cm (12 in.)
SOIL: average, moist, well drained
LIGHT: full sun to light shade
FLOWERING TIME: summer

PHOTO – PAGE 126

Where to Grow

'Moorhexe' is easy to integrate into existing perennial and mixed borders as a specimen plant, or as a transition between highly contrasting plants. It is excellent for interplanting with spring-flowering bulbs to obscure their dying foliage, or with other plants whose foliage deteriorates with time, such as bleeding heart (*Dicentra* spp.), oriental poppies (*Papaver orientale*), and delphinium. This plant may also be massed as a low-maintenance groundcover or added to summer container plantings for textural appeal.

How to Grow

'Moorhexe' prefers a sunny or lightly shaded location, and average, moist, well-drained soil, although it will tolerate some dryness. Leave it standing in the garden for winter interest, and then clip back stems and leaves in early spring before new growth emerges.

This grass may be grown from root divisions or from self-sown seedlings, both of which will take several years to mature.

Perfect Partners

'Moorhexe' looks lovely with such garden standards as purple coneflower (*Echinacea purpurea*), Joe Pye weed (*Eupatorium maculatum*), monarda, salvia, and strappy-leaved plants such as daylilies (*Hemerocallis* spp.) and iris. Dramatic when paired with sages (*Artemisia* spp.) and Russian sage (*Perovskia atriplicifolia*), in autumn it complements yellow-blooming sunflowers (*Helianthus* spp.), false sunflowers (*Heliopsis helianthoides*), sneezeweed (*Helenium autumnale*), and goldenrod (*Solidago* spp.).

Collectors' Choice

The following are only a few of the many other ornamental grasses that do well in prairie gardens. Cool-season grasses begin

"With its dwarf, variegated forms that love boggy conditions to the skyscraping cultivars, purple moor grass deserves a place in every garden. It tolerates a wide variety of growing conditions; its amber fall color and shade tolerance are a bonus."

KEN GIRARD
CALGARY, ALBERTA

growing in early spring and reach maturity before summer's arrival. Warm-season grasses thrive in hot summer weather, reaching maturity in late summer and early fall.

- *Arrhenatherum elatius* var. *bulbosum* 'Variegatum' (60 cm, 24 in.), variegated bulbous oat grass, forms bushy, low clumps of cream-and-green striped leaves, topped by tan-colored spikes in early summer. It is a cool-season grass, drought tolerant once established, and a good substitute for invasive ribbon grass (*Phalaris arundinacea*).

- *Festuca glauca* (30 cm, 12 in.), blue fescue, is a cool-season, clump-forming grass with fine-textured, blue or green foliage and spikelets of blue-green flowers. Try 'Elijah Blue', 'Sea Urchin', 'Solling', or 'Skinner's Blue'.

- *Hakonechloa macra* 'Aureola' (35 cm, 14 in.), hakone grass, is an excellent specimen plant for shady locations. Its leaves are golden yellow with narrow green stripes; they arch to one side like a waterfall and flush red in autumn.

- *Helictotrichon sempervirens* (90 cm, 36 in.), blue oat grass, is a non-spreading, cool-season plant. It forms perfect dome-shaped clumps of spiky, intensely blue leaves.

Monarda didyma 'Gardenview Scarlet'

(moh-*nar*-dah dih-*dih*-mah)

Monarda, Bee balm

No prairie garden is complete without the colorful, shaggy mop-tops of monarda, constantly abuzz with the friendly sounds of bees and birds, especially hummingbirds. Gardeners never feel alone or lonely when their flowerbeds are anchored by monarda; the constant comings and goings of busy winged visitors make monarda's red, pink, purple, or white flowers a study in constant motion.

Named for Nicolas Monardes, a Spanish physician and plant collector, monarda is native to eastern North America where it was brewed into tea by the Oswego Indians of upstate New York, hence, the common name "Oswego tea." When the Boston Tea Party resulted in a shortage of imported tea in the American colonies, the Oswego Indians taught Europeans to use the leaves of monarda as a substitute. Monarda is also called bergamot because its brewed leaves have the distinct aroma of oil of bergamot, an essential ingredient of Earl Grey tea, derived from bergamot oranges, which, in turn, were named after Bergamo, Italy.

Portrait

When 'Gardenview Scarlet' monarda emerges in the spring, it forms bushy clumps of tall, square stems, clad in 15-cm (6-in.), medium green, aromatic leaves. The square stems indicate this plant is closely related to mints; this is confirmed by brushing past a plant or gently rubbing its leaves, which release a delicious, fresh, minty fragrance. At the top of each flowering stem, one or two whorls of very large, shaggy, scarlet red flower clusters are cupped in colorful modified leaves, called bracts. The tubular red flowers are magnets for bees and hummingbirds, and provide an attractive meeting place and cafeteria for every little hummer in the area.

Where to Grow

'Gardenview Scarlet' thrives in the middle of an informal, moist, sunny border or massed in a cottage garden. It is also at home at the edge of a pond, and naturalized in a prairie meadow.

How to Grow

Plant 'Gardenview Scarlet' in average to fertile, moist, well-drained soil, in full sun, giving it enough space to spread into a sizable clump. Fertilize in early spring with a balanced fertilizer and again one month later. Because its root system is very shal-

Plant at a Glance

TYPE: perennial
HEIGHT: 90 cm (36 in.)
WIDTH: 60 cm (24 in.)
SOIL: average to fertile, moist, well drained
LIGHT: full sun to light shade
FLOWERING TIME: mid-summer to fall

PHOTO – PAGE 126

low, take care when cultivating around it.

In satisfactory light conditions, 'Gardenview Scarlet' requires no staking. If it becomes floppy, move it to a sunnier spot.

All monarda must be kept evenly moist at all times; application of organic mulch around the plant helps maintain moisture levels. If it dries out, it will lose leaves, produce fewer flowers, and be susceptible to disease, especially powdery mildew. Too much shade also encourages powdery mildew. Although 'Gardenview Scarlet' is resistant to this disease, it is not immune to its disfiguring effects.

Deadhead this cultivar on a regular basis to ensure the longest period of bloom possible. Then cut the plant back to 10 cm (4 in.) in the fall, disposing of all clippings in the garbage to prevent the spread of powdery mildew.

'Gardenview Scarlet' spreads vigorously by underground stolons; it is not a prolific self-seeder. Propagate it by division or stem cuttings. Except for 'Panorama Mix', named varieties of monarda do not come true from seed.

Perfect Partners

Plant 'Gardenview Scarlet' with other sun-lovers, including yarrow (*Achillea* spp.), lilies (*Lilium* spp.), daylilies (*Hemerocallis* spp.), yellow loosestrife (*Lysimachia punctata*), blue delphinium, purple coneflower (*Echinacea purpurea*), phlox, veronica, and false sunflower (*Heliopsis helianthoides*). In a moist, lightly shaded border, bee balm combines well with astilbe, cranesbill (*Geranium* spp.), and meadowsweet (*Filipendula* spp.).

Collectors' Choice

The named varieties of bee balm grown in gardens today are usually hybrids of *Monarda didyma* and *M. fistulosa*, both of which are lovely to grow in their own right. Many recent monarda introductions

"I've liked monarda ever since I was a child. When I used to pick saskatoons in the bush, the wild monarda was blooming. It had a lovely smell—like sage."

CAROL CLEGG
LAC DU BONNET, MANITOBA

are the result of work done by the late Dr. Henry Marshall when he worked at the Morden and Brandon agricultural research stations in Manitoba.

- *Monarda didyma* (90 cm, 36 in.) forms bushy clumps of square stems. Its medium green leaves are aromatic and slightly hairy underneath; scarlet red or pink flowers grow at the top of each flowering stem.
- *Monarda fistulosa* (1.2 m, 4 ft.) is native to western North America, has pale pink or lilac-purple flowers, and is similar to but less showy than *M. didyma*. It is perfect for wildflower meadows.
- Named varieties of monarda worth trying include 'Beauty of Cobham' (pale pink), 'Blue Stocking' (deep violet-purple), 'Croftway Pink' (rose pink), and 'Mahogany' (wine red). The best mildew-resistant varieties include 'Marshall's Delight' (medium pink), 'Prairie Night' (purple-lilac), 'Twins' (dark pink), and 'Violet Queen' (violet purple). The best dwarf monardas on the market are 'Petite Delight' and 'Petite Wonder'.

Narcissus 'Minnow'
(nar-*siss*-us)

Miniature narcissus,
Miniature daffodil

The delightful displays of cheery yellow narcissus that grace prairie gardens every spring are a welcome sight after long, dark winters. Narcissus, commonly referred to as daffodil or jonquil, is an ancient and storied flower, populating Greek and Roman myth and found in Egyptian tombs.

We have all admired the large, showy trumpet varieties of narcissus. Less familiar are the dwarf and miniature varieties, although they too make exquisite additions to the spring garden. As their name suggests, miniature daffodils are just a petite version of their larger counterparts, growing to a maximum of 25 cm (10 in.). Flowers can be single or double, and consist of a cup or trumpet (corona) and an outer ring of petals (perianth). When established, many miniatures will spread to form ever-larger blankets of spring color, with blossoms often lasting for several weeks.

Plant at a Glance

TYPE: hardy bulb
HEIGHT: 15 cm (6 in.)
WIDTH: 5 cm (2 in.)
SOIL: fertile, moist
LIGHT: full sun to light shade
FLOWERING TIME: spring

PHOTO – PAGE 126

Portrait
Fragrant 'Minnow' has clusters of four or more creamy yellow, single flowers with deep yellow cups. The leafless flower stalks emerge from elongated, strappy foliage in early spring. The leaves remain green until mid-summer, when they turn yellow and die back to the ground.

Other miniatures to try are 'Hawera' (18 cm, 7 in.), which produces up to six lemon-yellow, starlike blooms on each of several flower stalks; 'Tête à Tête' (15 cm, 6 in.), which is also fragrant and produces a multitude of yellow blooms with tiny, soft orange cups; and 'Rip van Winkle' (14 cm, 5.5 in.), which has bright yellow, double flowers with narrow, pointed petals.

Where to Grow
'Minnow' is perfect in gardens where space is limited, or in a spot where it can be enjoyed at close range—at the front of a perennial border or next to a path, deck, or patio. All miniature daffodils are excellent choices for planting in rock gardens or naturalizing under deciduous trees or in the lawn.

How to Grow
Like all daffodils, 'Minnow' grows from bulbs, which are available in garden centers or catalogues in late summer. On the prairies, they should be planted in full sun to light shade before mid-September to give their roots ample time to establish before winter sets in.

Plant 'Minnow' bulbs 10 cm (4 in.)

deep and with a similar spacing; they are most effective when planted in informal groups of 12 or more. Interplanting with annuals, fast-growing perennials, or herbs will disguise their withering foliage after they have finished blooming. Their diminutive stature makes it easier to be successful at this task than for the larger narcissus.

Daffodils reproduce by seed and by forming bulblets, or offsets, at the base of each bulb. After several years, clumps may be divided by separating the small bulblets from the parent bulb. However, miniature daffodils do not require dividing as frequently as their larger relatives, and often bloom prolifically for years if left undisturbed.

Perfect Partners

'Minnow' looks charming planted with other spring-flowering bulbs, particularly deep blue Siberian squill (*Scilla sibirica*) and grape hyacinth (*Muscari armeniacum*). They also coordinate beautifully with yellow and white *Tulipa tarda*, and yellow and red waterlily tulips (*Tulipa kaufmanniana*).

In the rockery, 'Minnow' are pretty companions to rock cress (*Arabis* spp.), purple rock cress (*Aubrieta deltoidea*), draba, and moss phlox (*Phlox subulata*).

Collectors' Choice

With about 50 species and thousands of named varieties, it's not surprising that daffodils come in a myriad of colors, ranging from white through yellow to orange, red, apricot, pink, and even green. There are also dozens of shapes and sizes; in fact, daffodils have been classified into 12 divisions depending on flower shape and origin. Among many others, the following are beautiful choices for prairie gardens.

- 'Actaea' (40 cm, 16 in.) has a white perianth and short, yellow corona rimmed with red. This heirloom

"After a long white winter, the bright yellow narcissus blooms are very welcome—some are even fragrant. I have had success with several varieties, including many miniatures that have bloomed since 1971."

MARCUS OLSEN
BRANDON, MINNESOTA

variety has a spicy fragrance and blooms in mid to late spring.
- 'Ceylon' (45 cm, 18 in.) is bright golden yellow with an orange-red corona and blooms in early to mid spring.
- 'February Gold' (30 cm, 12 in.) is a vigorous, early-blooming daffodil with a golden yellow perianth and darker yellow corona.
- 'Ice Follies' (40 cm, 16 in.) has a creamy white perianth and frilled, pale yellow corona; it flowers in mid-spring.
- 'Salomé' (40 cm, 16 in.) has a creamy white perianth and a corona that is yellow-apricot when it opens, maturing to soft pink. 'Salomé' blooms in mid to late spring.
- 'Tahiti' (35 cm, 14 in.) produces double, yellow blooms with orange centers in mid-spring.
- 'Thalia' (35 cm, 14 in.) is a fragrant, pure white daffodil, blooming in mid to late spring.

Nepeta x *faassenii* 'Dropmore'

(*ne*-peh-tah x fah-*sen*-ee-ee)

Catmint, Blue catmint

Gardeners intent on evoking an image of soft romance in their garden should keep catmint in mind. Its misty clouds of delicate, blue-lavender flowers crown flowing mounds of gray-green, textured foliage, making it a welcome addition to pastel planting schemes and the perfect foil for a Valentine's day favorite—roses.

As its name suggests, catmint foliage contains oils that are attractive to cats. Catnip (*Nepeta cataria*) is the species that stirs felines into a frenzy, but all catmints inevitably beckon to cats for a clandestine roll in the foliage. To discourage feline guests from damaging delicate catmint plants, lay down a piece of chicken wire or some thorny rose branches on the ground where catmints emerge in the spring. They will soon be hidden by foliage and will definitely repel cats who intensely dislike the feel of wire and thorns on their feet.

Although catmint does belong to the mint family, it's not invasive like some of its relatives.

Portrait

'Dropmore' is a sterile nepeta hybrid and forms compact mounds of soft, scalloped, gray-green leaves that have a finely pebbled texture and a minty fragrance when brushed or crushed. Square stems confirm its membership in the mint family. The stems branch and elongate into flower stems that support a few small leaves and spikes of copious large, lavender-blue, tubular, two-lipped flowers, also characteristic of the mint family.

Because it is sterile, 'Dropmore' does not set seed. Instead, it flowers for most of the summer, making it one of the longest-blooming perennials on the prairies.

Other named varieties often listed as *N*. x *faassenii* cultivars include 'Blue Wonder' (deep lavender blue), 'Six Hills Giant' (deep lavender blue), 'Snowflake' (creamy white), and 'White Wonder' (white).

Where to Grow

'Dropmore' and other nepetas make an excellent groundcover, attractive edging for informal flower borders, and unusual but lovely additions to hanging baskets and other summer containers. Some nepetas are more aggressive than others; these are suitable for naturalizing in a cottage garden or for stabilizing slopes.

Plant at a Glance

TYPE: perennial
HEIGHT: 30 cm (12 in.)
WIDTH: 30 cm (12 in.)
SOIL: average, moist, well drained
LIGHT: full sun to light shade
FLOWERING TIME: early summer to fall

PHOTO – PAGE 127

How to Grow

Plant 'Dropmore' in a sunny spot, in average, moist, well-drained soil. Easy to grow, it tolerates dry soils better than many other perennials but also flowers less profusely in that circumstance. Applying organic mulch around the plant in summer helps maintain the moisture levels it prefers. Fertilize lightly in spring, if you wish, though it isn't necessary; too much fertilizer encourages floppy, leggy growth. Some of the taller varieties may need staking.

Deadhead regularly and cut back the plant by at least half after the first big flush of blossoms has faded to encourage the growth of tidy, bushy foliage and a possible second wave of color before season's end. Leave 'Dropmore' foliage in place until spring to protect the plant's center from winter's harmful effects.

'Dropmore' can be left undisturbed for many years. However, if you wish to propagate it, divide or take stem cuttings in spring or early summer.

Perfect Partners

The blue haze of all nepetas, including 'Dropmore', creates a stunning effect when used with pink-flowering plants, whether they are roses, cranesbills (*Geranium* spp.), mallow (*Malva* spp.), penstemons, or pink spike speedwell (*Veronica* spp.). This cultivar also pairs well with like-minded bluish plants, such as sea holly (*Eryngium* spp.) and lavender (*Lavandula* spp.).

Collectors' Choice

There are several nepetas worth growing, although their provenance is not always clear. For example, plants once sold as the species *Nepeta mussinii* are now thought more likely to belong to *N.* x *faassenii*. The details, while interesting, don't matter. In most cases it is safe to assume that named varieties are sterile, hybrid cultivars and

> *" 'Dropmore' nepeta is drought tolerant, low growing, and well mannered, with gray foliage and continuous bloom. What more could you want in a plant?"*
>
> BRENDA WINNY
> ROSETOWN, SASKATCHEWAN

well suited to growing in the garden.

- *Nepeta cataria* (60 cm, 24 in.) is the proverbial catnip; expect frequent feline visitors if you grow it. It produces purple-spotted, white flowers in summer and autumn.
- *Nepeta racemosa* (syn. *N. mussinii*) (30 cm, 12 in.) has a semi-upright habit and produces fragrant, scalloped, finely haired leaves, and deep lilac-blue flowers. It self-sows like mad.
- *Nepeta sibirica* (90 cm, 36 in.), commonly known as Siberian catmint, has fragrant, light green leaves and large, lilac-blue flowers on 30-cm (12-in.) spikes. It has a long bloom period. 'Souvenir d'André Chaudron', also called 'Blue Beauty', is a very popular, more compact version of the species.

Nicotiana sylvestris

(nick-oh-shee-*ah*-na sil-*vess*-triss)

Flowering tobacco, Woodland tobacco

In their quest for perfect combinations of plant color, form, and texture, prairie gardeners often overlook the pleasures of fragrance in the garden. Although searching out fragrant plants is a very personal and sometimes time-consuming task, it's worth the effort. Strong scent is the stuff that memories are made of; more than anything else, it is capable of evoking images, incidents, and emotions from the past.

Among annuals, flowering tobacco is one of the most deliciously perfumed. The South American native is a night bloomer and opens its fragrant blossoms late in the day to attract nocturnal pollinators. It was introduced into European culture in the late-nineteenth century, where it became an instant inhabitant of so-called night gardens; these were frequented by Victorian ladies who wished to avoid exposing their skin to the sun's harsh rays. Really!

Portrait

Nicotiana sylvestris is the giant of flowering tobacco plants, both in stature and fragrance. It forms large rosettes of dark green, oblong, slightly sticky leaves that are up to 90 cm (36 in.) long. By midsummer, a single, thick stalk emerges from the basal rosette and rapidly grows to 1.5 m (5 ft.). A terminal cluster of buds produces flowers continuously, sometimes as many as 50 at a time, from mid-July to frost. The drooping, slender, white, tubular flowers flare into a flat, five-petalled star, and are easily 13 cm (5 in.) long; they remain closed during the day and open at dusk to release a magnificent spicy fragrance. All parts of this and other flowering tobacco species are poisonous.

'Daylight' is a cultivar with blossoms that stay open during the day.

Where to Grow

Nicotiana sylvestris is a striking accent plant at the back of mixed or perennial borders; it also holds its own quite nicely planted in bays between shrubs in a shrub border.

How to Grow

Once established in a lightly shaded location, in fertile, moist, well-drained soil, *Nicotiana sylvestris* looks after itself. However, regular watering is a must, especially during dry spells; deadheading encourages prolonged bloom.

Plant at a Glance

TYPE: annual
HEIGHT: 1.5 m (5 ft.)
WIDTH: 60 cm (24 in.)
SOIL: fertile, moist, well drained
LIGHT: light shade
FLOWERING TIME: mid-summer to fall

PHOTO – PAGE 127

Perfect Partners

Nicotiana sylvestris combines well with other tall, back-of-the-border plants such as veronica, delphinium, *Verbena bonariensis*, sneezeweed (*Helenium autumnale*), and asters. It is also striking against an evergreen backdrop of spruce, pine, or juniper.

Collectors' Choice

Several other species of flowering tobacco make attractive additions to mixed and perennial borders.

- *Nicotiana alata* (syn. *N. affinis*) (1.5 m, 5 ft.), jasmine tobacco, produces a basal clump of oval leaves covered in fine, sticky hairs and racemes of long, trumpetlike flowers that flare into a broad, star-shaped face. The flower of the species is chalk white on the inside, greenish on the outside; it opens in early evening to attract pollinators with its spicy fragrance.

- *Nicotiana* x *sanderae* (60 cm, 24 in.) is a hybrid of *N. alata*, developed for its daytime bloom, compact growth habit, and colors, including red, white, pink, purple, yellow, lime green, and salmon; regretfully, much of the original fragrance of *N. alata* was sacrificed during hybridization. Several series are commonly available, including Domino (45 cm, 18 in.), Havana (30 cm, 12 in.), Merlin (30 cm, 12 in.), fragrant Sensation Mix (76 cm, 30 in.), and Starship (30 cm, 12 in.).

- *Nicotiana langsdorfii* (90 cm, 36 in.) forms a delicate, branched, upright plant smothered in sprays of drooping, tubular, chartreuse flowers from early summer to frost. Despite their height, these plants do not require staking.

If you are smitten by the fragrance bug, as many gardeners are, then you can't go wrong with the following annuals.

- *Heliotropium arborescens* (30 to 90 cm, 12 to 36 in.) forms bushy plants with handsome dark green, slightly pebbled foliage. It bears a multitude of flat clusters of tiny flowers, in all shades of purple. Its sweet fragrance reminds people of scents as variable as vanilla, spiced apples, cinnamon, and honey.

- *Matthiola bicornis* (30 cm, 12 in.), night-scented stock, produces spikes of relatively insignificant four-petalled, pink, mauve, or purple flowers that close by day and open in the evenings to release an exquisite fragrance.

- *Matthiola incana* (45 cm, 18 in.), stock, produces heavy spikes of clove-scented, single or double flowers, in shades of pink, rose, lavender, and white. Lance-shaped leaves are a dull gray-green.

- *Reseda odorata* (30 cm, 12 in.), mignonette, is a spreading plant with many small, yellowish brown flowers that are excellent for cutting. Although inconspicuous, the flowers release a delicious, distinctive fragrance on warm, sunny days. The named cultivars available today are lovely but do not have the same intense fragrance of the unimproved species mignonette.

> *"I like this tall, old-fashioned white nicotiana, because of its incredible fragrance."*
>
> DIANE FIDLER
> SELKIRK, MANITOBA

Osmunda regalis
(oz-*mun*-dah ray-*ga*-lis)

Royal fern

It comes as a surprise to some that many ferns are grown successfully on the prairies. They are magnificent and dependable foliage plants for the shade, and there is considerable variation in foliage color and texture between varieties. One of the loveliest, and also one of the easiest to grow, is the royal fern, one of the osmund or *Osmunda* ferns. They take their name from Osmunder, the Saxon name for Thor, who was the Norse god of thunder, weather, and crops.

Portrait
The royal fern, *Osmunda regalis*, is one of the largest ferns in North America. The divided, feathery leaves form large, vase-shaped clusters. In general, the sterile, or foliage, fronds are different from the fertile, or spore-bearing, fronds, which gives added visual interest to an already pleasing plant.

In spring the royal fern pushes forth tightly curled, wiry, purple fiddleheads, which then rapidly unfurl into elongated, blunt-tipped leaflets, without teeth or divisions, that turn from red to green as they mature. Narrow, fertile (spore-bearing) leaflets can be found clustered at the tips of inner fronds. Spore capsules covering the veins of these leaflets turn brown as they ripen and resemble the dead flowers of an astilbe plant.

Where to Grow
The royal fern loves partly shaded, cool, damp locations and is ideal for planting under trees, on the north side of a fence, beside a pond, or in a woodland garden. Use them in clumps or drifts, or plant them between other ferns and shade-loving wildflowers. Because this fern tolerates a certain amount of direct sunlight (as long as the roots don't dry out), it can be added to most perennial beds as a dramatic accent.

How to Grow
Plant royal ferns in early spring in fertile, moist soil, in full shade to part sun, with the crowns at soil level. Space them 60 to 90 cm (24 to 36 in.) apart to avoid the need for transplanting at a later date.

There is no need to fertilize royal ferns if you enrich the soil regularly with organic matter such as leaves or compost. This also helps maintain the slightly acidic soil conditions that all *Osmunda* ferns love. Surround them with a layer of organic

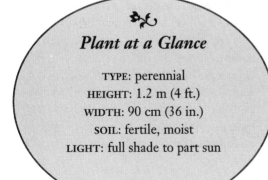

Plant at a Glance

TYPE: perennial
HEIGHT: 1.2 m (4 ft.)
WIDTH: 90 cm (36 in.)
SOIL: fertile, moist
LIGHT: full shade to part sun

PHOTO – PAGE 127

mulch to nourish the soil and maintain the damp conditions vital to healthy fern growth. Some protection from the wind helps prevent dehydration. Finally, even though it is important to keep these ferns well watered, do not overwater them as this may cause plant stress as well as providing an ideal environment for slugs, the only pest that might affect these plants.

Royal ferns may be cultivated from spores, but the spores are viable for only a few days so it is best to divide multi-crowned plants in late spring or early fall.

Perfect Partners

Just about any shade-loving perennial enhances the natural woodland setting beloved by royal ferns. The large, textured leaves of hostas are a pleasing contrast to the delicate fern fronds. Astilbe, masterwort (*Astrantia major*), bugbane (*Cimicifuga racemosa*), and meadowsweet (*Filipendula rubra*) all bear delicate, airy blooms that combine beautifully with ferns. Smaller companions include primula, pulmonaria, and corydalis.

Collectors' Choice

Other *Osmunda* ferns are equally lovely in a woodland garden or any shady nook.

- *Osmunda cinnamomea* (90 cm, 36 in.), the cinnamon fern, forms clusters of dark green fertile (spore-bearing) fronds in the spring that gradually turn from green to bright cinnamon brown, eventually withering and falling after they have shed their spores. Sterile fronds emerge a little later in the spring and maintain their green color until fall, when they turn from russet to gold.
- *Osmunda claytoniana* (60 cm, 24 in.), also called the interrupted fern, has fronds that are divided into many deeply cut segments. Most of the outer leaves are almost exclusively foliage (non-fertile) fronds, but a few pairs of small, brownish leaflets covered with spores are found on some inner leaves toward the center of the frond. Once the spores have been dispersed, these leaflets wither and drop, leaving an empty space or interruption in the middle of the frond. The rest of the fern's leaflets remain green until the first frost.

Once you've tried the outstanding *Osmundas*, you're sure to want more hardy ferns.

- *Adiantum pedatum* (50 cm, 20 in.), maidenhair fern, is a lovely native North American fern with shiny black stems and delicate, light green fronds.
- *Athyrium filix-femina* (60 cm, 24 in.), lady fern, has lacy, bright green fronds divided into many small leaflets.
- *Athyrium niponicum* var. *pictum* (45 cm, 18 in.), the Japanese painted fern, has arching fronds marked with metallic gray and burgundy.

> *"I grow many different ferns in my shade garden and love them all! They are restful, attractive, and take very little care. I can't wait until they grow even bigger."*
>
> HELEN FLAVELL
> YORKTON, SASKATCHEWAN

Paeonia lactiflora 'Festiva Maxima'

(pay-*own*-ee-ah lak-tih-*flor*-ah)

Peony

Peonies, which have been cultivated in the Orient for at least two millennia, are beloved mainstays of perennial gardens the world over. Every spring, their extravagant blossoms unfold to reveal layer upon layer of intricate petals that blaze unrestrainedly in all imaginable shades of red, pink, and white.

Peonies are divided into four groups based on flower shape: single, Japanese, semi-double, and double. Blossoms in each group are distinguished by having more petals than those in the previous one. Typically, single-flowered peonies stand up well to prairie wind and rain, rarely requiring staking. In contrast, other peony types need support for their heavier, showier blossoms.

Most valued in the ornamental garden are the named cultivars and hybrids of the deliciously fragrant *Paeonia lactiflora*, cherished for its willingness to be hybridized into luxurious flowers that reveal more than just a hint of the exotic.

Portrait

'Festiva Maxima' is one of the most dazzling lactifloras. Its asparaguslike shoots emerge burgundy red in early spring, transforming into shrubby clumps of shiny, deeply lobed, dark green foliage that remains showy throughout the summer. Large flower buds develop at or near the stem tips and open into very fragrant, white, double flowers; the petals may be flecked with red. The blossom's center is suffused with a radiance borne of yellow tinting at the base of inner petals.

Of all the gorgeous lactifloras to choose from, most popular are 'Bowl of Beauty' (Japanese, rosy pink with cream-colored center), 'Felix Crousse' (fragrant, double, magenta), 'Karl Rosenfield' (double, crimson red), 'M. Jules Elie' (fragrant, double, rose pink), and 'Sarah Bernhardt' (fragrant, double, shell pink flecked with red).

Where to Grow

Use 'Festiva Maxima' as an accent plant in the middle of mixed or perennial borders, or include it in a collection of favorite peonies interplanted with later-blooming perennials to define a peony walk. These peonies can also be used for hedging.

How to Grow

'Festiva Maxima' prefers to bask in full sun, in fertile, moist, well-drained soil. Planting depth is critical; the crown should

Plant at a Glance

TYPE: perennial
HEIGHT: 90 cm (36 in.)
WIDTH: 90 cm (36 in.)
SOIL: fertile, moist, well drained
LIGHT: full sun
FLOWERING TIME: late spring to early summer

PHOTO – PAGE 127

be no deeper than 5 cm (2 in.) or the plant may not flower. A top dressing of compost in early spring up to, but not covering, the crown ensures healthy growth. When using synthetic fertilizer, make sure it is not too high in nitrogen, or luxuriant foliage will be produced at the expense of blossoms.

Support 'Festiva Maxima' with forked sticks, linking stakes, peony rings, or wide tomato cages to help blossoms withstand wind and rain. Deadhead once blossoms fade.

This peony, like all peonies, may take several years to realize its full potential. Once established it can be left undisturbed indefinitely; it does not need to be divided to maintain vigor. However, to propagate, divide 'Festiva Maxima' in the fall.

Although this cultivar is a robust plant, all peonies are susceptible to botrytis, a fungal disease that causes leaves to wilt and collapse and prevents buds from opening. To control botrytis and prevent its spread, be vigilant; remove infected foliage, immediately disposing of it in the garbage, not the composter. The same applies to disposal of peony foliage during fall clean-up.

Ants are attracted to the sweet nectar of peonies but don't affect blossom development in any way.

Perfect Partners

'Festiva Maxima' is enchanting interplanted with early-blooming perennials such as bleeding heart (*Dicentra* spp.), Siberian iris (*Iris sibirica*), yellow loosestrife (*Lysimachia punctata*), and foxgloves (*Digitalis* spp.). Its attractive leaves are also perfect for filling in gaps left by dying spring bulb foliage.

Collectors' Choice

Although hybrids are the most popular peonies, the species are also worthy garden

"I've grown many peonies during my 86 years. I particularly love the Japanese peonies because they bloom early and have a wonderful fragrance. I like to put one in a rose bowl to enjoy inside the house."

OLGA URBAN
LAC DU BONNET, MANITOBA

inhabitants, requiring the same care as 'Festiva Maxima'.

- *Paeonia lactiflora* (60 cm, 24 in.), common garden peony or Chinese peony, produces deep green, lobed foliage, mottled red stems, and single, bowl-shaped, fragrant, white to pale pink flowers.

- *Paeonia officinalis* (60 cm, 24 in.), common peony, has deep green, lobed leaves and single, cup-shaped, shiny deep red or rose-pink flowers with yellow stamens. 'Alba Plena' (double, white), 'Rosea Plena' (double, pink), 'Rubra Plena' (double, red), and 'China Rose' (single, salmon pink) are reliable cultivars.

- *Paeonia tenuifolia* (45 cm, 18 in.), fernleaf peony, is one of the first peonies to flower. Its delicate, very finely divided foliage forms a compact mound; single, cup-shaped, ruby-red flowers are produced at the tips of stems and nestle in the ferny foliage. 'Plena' is a double. *P. tenuifolia* dies back earlier than other peonies; withering foliage in August is common and does not reflect poorly on the health of the plant.

Papaver orientale 'Prince of Orange'

(pa-*pah*-ver or-ee-en-*tal*-eh)

Oriental poppy

Oriental poppies are flamboyant ladies—the belles of the ball in the early summer garden. Their extravagant, brilliantly colored petals range through shades of deep red, orange, pink, and pure white, forming luminous, chalice-shaped flowers on slender stems. Oriental poppy blossoms shimmer boldly in the sun and reach such generous proportions—up to 15 cm (6 in.) across—that they can't help but add drama to perennial and mixed borders.

Among oriental poppies, the red ones are the most outstanding of all. Despite the plant's relatively short bloom period and regrettable habit of retreating in midsummer dormancy, no garden should be without at least one fleeting but vivid splash of oriental-poppy red.

Portrait

'Prince of Orange' produces basal rosettes of coarse, bristly, deeply divided, gray-green leaves up to 30 cm (12 in.) long. Large, nodding buds at the ends of slightly lax, thin stems transform into magnificent scarlet red, bowl-shaped flowers (10 cm, 4 in.) with overlapping, satiny petals. There is a dark patch at the base of each petal. At the flower's center is a small forest of hairy, black stamens encircling a black central structure that eventually becomes an ornamental seed pod. Dried seed pods are perfect for dried flower bouquets.

Many other oriental poppy cultivars are available in solid and bicolor forms, with single or double blossoms: 'Allegro' (orange-red with black basal marks); 'Black and White' (white with crimson-black basal marks); 'Carnival' (fringed, red with white basal marks); 'Cedric Morris' (soft pink with black basal marks); 'Helen Elizabeth' (salmon pink); 'Maiden's Blush' (ruffled, white with pink edge); and 'Princess Victoria Louise' (salmon pink with black basal marks).

Where to Grow

Plant 'Prince of Orange' as an early-summer focal point in the middle of sunny perennial and mixed borders.

How to Grow

Choose a sheltered site for 'Prince of Orange', in full sun, with average to fertile, well-drained soil. Once established, this cultivar requires very little care; all it

Plant at a Glance

TYPE: perennial
HEIGHT: 90 cm (36 in.)
WIDTH: 60 cm (24 in.)
SOIL: average to fertile, well drained
LIGHT: full sun
FLOWERING TIME: late spring to early summer

PHOTO – PAGE 128

needs to thrive is a reasonable supply of water, some support for stems when they are top-heavy with blossoms, and vigilant deadheading to prolong its bloom period. Flowers may also be left to develop into ornamental seed pods that are eye-catching in the winter garden.

As with all oriental poppies, 'Prince of Orange' lies dormant for part of the summer; its foliage turns yellow and disappears soon after flowering, leaving gaps in the border that can be filled with neighboring plants and foliage. In late summer, small tufts of new basal leaves emerge; these are next year's plants getting a head start. Although this plant is long-lived and rarely needs dividing to maintain health and vigor, it can be propagated by taking cuttings from its long taproot in August, just as the new foliage is emerging.

Because it has a long taproot, 'Prince of Orange' does not transplant well. However, if you must transplant it, do it in August, just as it breaks summer dormancy.

Perfect Partners
'Prince of Orange' is spectacular next to blue-blossomed catmint (*Nepeta* spp.), salvia, Siberian iris, flax (*Linum* spp.), veronica, and cranesbills (*Geranium* spp.). Later-blooming annual baby's breath (*Gypsophila* spp.), Russian sage (*Perovskia atriplicifolia*), daylilies (*Hemerocallis* spp.), and yarrow (*Achillea* spp.) will fill gaps left by this plant when it goes dormant.

Collectors' Choice
Two other poppies—alpine and Iceland— add cheer to the garden. They are short-lived perennials that happily self-sow to ensure their continuity.

- ❧ *Papaver alpinum* (20 cm, 8 in.), alpine poppy, is very similar to the Iceland poppy, only smaller. Its 4-cm (1.5-in.) flowers are white, yellow, orange, or red.

"Oriental poppies are so bright, so showy, so vibrant, they can't help but catch your eye. They are very hardy, and I always let some of them seed around the garden."

IRENE PETERS
PORTAGE LA PRAIRIE, MANITOBA

- ❧ *Papaver croceum* (syn. *P. nudicaule*) (30 cm, 12 in.), Iceland poppy, blooms all summer, producing single, 10-cm (4-in.), cup-shaped flowers in shades of yellow, orange, pink, and white on wiry stems above finely dissected, fernlike, hairy, gray-green foliage. 'Champagne Bubbles' (pastel), 'Garden Gnome' (bright, dwarf), 'Sparkling Bubbles' (pastel), 'Summer Breeze' (bright), and 'Wonderland' (bright, dwarf) are all good choices.

Another plant that puts on a lovely display of satiny, poppylike flowers in spring and early summer is the sundrop, an immediate relative of the evening primrose. Sundrops require full sun and lean, dry soils.

- ❧ *Oenothera fruticosa* subsp. *glauca* (45 cm, 18 in.), common sundrop, is a day-flowering plant that produces oval, dark green leaves tinted red, erect leafy stems, and cup-shaped, bright yellow flowers that emerge from red-tinted buds. The leaves turn a lovely burgundy red in fall.
- ❧ *Oenothera missouriensis* (30 cm, 12 in.), Ozark sundrop, has showy, crepe-textured, yellow blossoms; the solitary flowers open during the day and cling to low, sprawling stems that are often tinted red. It is an excellent edging plant.

Pelargonium x *hortorum*

(pell-are-*go*-nee-um x hor-*tor*-um)

Zonal pelargonium, Zonal geranium

When prairie gardeners think RED they invariably think of pelargoniums—the "Sunday best" of container and bedding plants. More commonly but incorrectly (!) known as geraniums, the perfectly globe-shaped clusters of scarlet flowers announce summer's arrival and serve as a vibrant exclamation mark to the joys of gardening.

For the record, pelargoniums belong to the family *Geraniaceae*, which comprises three main genera. Members of the *Geranium* (cranesbill) genus are native to temperate woodlands and are grown as perennials on the prairies; they are properly called geraniums. Members of the *Pelargonium* (stork's bill) genus are native to South Africa and are grown as annuals on the prairies; the popular bedding "geraniums" fall into this group and are properly called pelargoniums. Members of the *Erodium* (heron's bill) genus are native to calcareous mountains of Europe, northern Africa, and the Americas; these alpines are not readily available on the prairies.

Thanks to the genius of plant hybridizers, thousands of pelargonium cultivars have been developed. They are loosely grouped into four categories: zonal, regal, ivy-leaved, and scented. Of these, the zonal pelargoniums are by far the most popular.

Portrait

Zonal pelargoniums are so named because their pungent, bright green, scalloped leaves are usually marked with a dark bronze-green or maroon, curved band or "zone."

Basic or single zonals form sturdy, well-branched plants that produce large, round clusters of five-petalled, saucer-shaped flowers up to 2.5 cm (1 in.) across, in every imaginable shade of red, pink, purple, white, and orange. Zonal pelargonium flowers also come in semi-double (six to eight petals), double (more than eight petals), and rosebud forms. Rosebud flowers are composed of such a tight mass of petals that they resemble rosebuds.

Dwarf (13 to 20 cm, 5 to 8 in.) and miniature (less than 13 cm, 5 in.) zonal pelargoniums are also available, although they are sometimes hard to come by. They suit tiny gardens, narrow window boxes and windowsills, and small containers.

Several zonal pelargoniums are grown exclusively for their colorful foliage, which comes in combinations of green, gold, and creamy white, overlaid with deep red-black zones.

Because the availability of pelargoniums

Plant at a Glance

TYPE: annual
HEIGHT: 30 to 90 cm (12 to 36 in.)
WIDTH: 30 to 45 cm (12 to 15 in.)
SOIL: fertile, moist, well drained
LIGHT: full to part sun
FLOWERING TIME: early summer to fall

PHOTO – PAGE 128

varies considerably from year to year, no specific cultivar recommendations are made here.

Where to Grow
For a bold splash of color, tuck your favorite zonal pelargoniums into summer containers and window boxes, mass them along walkways, or plant them as filler toward the front of mixed or perennial borders.

How to Grow
Plant zonal pelargoniums in the garden after the last expected frost; they require fertile, moist, well-drained soil, in a sunny location. Pinch back the growing tips occasionally to encourage branching. Plants may stop blooming during hot, humid spells, but usually resume their colorful display when cool weather returns. Deadhead regularly to prolong blooming. Zonal pelargoniums withstand drought well, so let them dry out between waterings; overwatering kills them. Container-grown plants benefit from a routine application of high phosphorus fertilizer (high middle number).

At one time, zonal pelargoniums were propagated from cuttings only. Now a number of single-blossomed hybrids can also be grown from seed. To overwinter these plants indoors, cut them back by three-quarters and store them in a cold room where the temperature remains just above freezing.

Perfect Partners
Bright red pelargonium blossoms perform brilliantly next to vivid blue ones; try catmint (*Nepeta* spp.), heliotrope (*Heliotropium arborescens*), bellflowers (*Campanula* spp.), *Salvia farinacea* 'Victoria', and 'Crystal Palace' lobelia as partners. Silver-leaved plants such as artemisia, licorice plant (*Helichrysum petiolare*), and lambs' ears

> "I grow all kinds of annual geraniums and especially like the fancy-leaved varieties. Geraniums are an old standby and go with any border, any container, any hanging basket, or any window box. You can even save them from year to year."
>
> MITCHELL WLOCK
> YORKTON, SASKATCHEWAN

(*Stachys byzantina*) are also excellent companions.

Collectors' Choice
If you have a penchant for growing pelargoniums, be sure to include some of these plants in your repertoire.

- *Pelargonium* x *domesticum* (30 to 60 cm, 12 to 24 in.) are known as regal, showy, or Martha Washington pelargoniums. They produce large, single or double, azalealike blossoms in shades or combinations of red, pink, purple, and white, often marked with blotches of a darker hue on the two upper petals. They are shade tolerant and only set new flower buds where cool night-time temperatures prevail.
- *Pelargonium peltatum* (90 cm, 36 in.), ivy-leaved or trailing pelargonium, is tolerant of summer heat and ideally suited for containers and hanging baskets. Its foliage is distinctly ivy-shaped and dainty flowers bloom in shades of pink and purple.
- Scented pelargoniums (60 cm, 24 in.) comprise species and hybrids prized for their fragrant and often ornate foliage. Try *Pelargonium crispum* (lemon-scented), *P.* x *citrosum* (orange-scented), *P.* x *fragrans* (nutmeg-scented), *P. graveolens* (rose-scented), *P. odoratissimum* (apple-scented).

Penstemon digitalis 'Husker Red'
(*pen*-ste-mon di-ji-*ta*-liss)

Foxglove penstemon,
White beardtongue

Prairie gardeners who plant penstemons are often rewarded by the enchanting sight of tiny hummingbirds, their iridescent plumage flashing in the sun as they dart from flower to flower. Any perennial that attracts hummingbirds is a winner, but the genus *Penstemon* has much more to recommend it, including pest and disease resistance and a long blooming season.

Many penstemons are native to western North America, thriving in such diverse habitats as tall-grass prairie, barren hills, high mountains, and woodlands. However, not all species are hardy on the prairies, and even the toughest ones are usually short-lived. If you wish to perpetuate a favorite penstemon, it is wise to save seed or take cuttings.

Most penstemons sport racemes of white, pink, scarlet, blue, or purple flowers. The botanical name for the genus is from the Greek *pen*, "missing," and *stemon*, "stamen," referring to the stamens within the tubular blooms. The common name "beardtongue" is from the hairy stamen that sometimes protrudes from the flower.

Portrait
Penstemon digitalis 'Husker Red' is notable for its admirable wine red foliage that retains its rich color all season long. It is also a splendid flowering plant, bearing up to 50 creamy-white blooms on each upright, red flower stalk—a stunning contrast to the lance-shaped, red leaves. The species name *digitalis* refers to its resemblance to the foxglove, also a member of the *Scrophulariaceae* family.

Introduced by the University of Nebraska in 1983, 'Husker Red' was named the 1996 Perennial Plant of the Year by the Perennial Plant Association.

Where to Grow
'Husker Red' is a standout in any perennial border. Planted in groups, it makes a striking focal point, or it may be used singly as a specimen plant. Add it to a natural prairie garden for a touch of dramatic contrast.

How to Grow
'Husker Red' will grow in part sun or light shade, but full sun is preferable to maintain the red foliage color. Average prairie soil enriched with organic matter should prove ideal. Once established, this plant is somewhat drought tolerant, although it will benefit from a moderate amount of

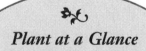

Plant at a Glance

TYPE: perennial
HEIGHT: 76 cm (30 in.)
WIDTH: 30 cm (12 in.)
SOIL: average to fertile, well drained
LIGHT: full sun to light shade
FLOWERING TIME: early to mid-summer

PHOTO – PAGE 128

water. Proper drainage is essential; no penstemon will long endure soggy soil.

Like all penstemons, 'Husker Red' requires little maintenance. Deadhead once blooming has finished, and enjoy the striking foliage for the rest of the summer.

Propagate 'Husker Red' by division in spring, or take basal or stem tip cuttings in summer. If you do attempt to grow this plant from seed, make sure to discard any seedlings with green leaves.

Perfect Partners

One of the few hardy perennials with red foliage, 'Husker Red' looks splendid against blue-flowering perennials. 'Crater Lake Blue' or 'Sunny Border Blue' veronica, 'Butterfly Blue' scabiosa, 'Blue Queen' salvia, or blue delphiniums are all fine companions. Silver-leaved 'Valerie Finnis' artemisia or ornamental grasses are equally effective.

Collectors' Choice

Other *Penstemon* species are spectacular in borders or rock gardens.

- *Penstemon barbatus* (90 cm, 36 in.), common or sharkshead beardtongue, produces slender spikes of 3-cm (1.25-in.), scarlet (*coccineus* form) or pink, tubular flowers. It often requires staking. *P. barbatus* hybrids are more compact: 'Elfin Pink' (45 cm, 18 in.) has pink flowers; 'Hyacinth Flowered' (60 cm, 24 in.) is a mix of rose, pink, blue, purple, and scarlet; 'Prairie Dusk' (60 cm, 24 in.) has purple flowers.
- *Penstemon caespitosus* (5 cm, 2 in.), mat beardtongue, has lavender blue flowers borne above mats of small, shiny leaves.
- *Penstemon fruticosus* 'Purple Haze' (20 cm, 8 in.), bush beardtongue, is an evergreen sub-shrub that forms a mound of dark green foliage, covered in lilac-purple flowers in early summer.

> "*If you need some bright, contrasting foliage color in the garden, this is the plant for you. 'Husker Red' foliage is maroon red—a great contrast in the perennial garden. The flower spikes bearing white flowers are a bonus in early summer!*"
>
> DEBBIE LONNEE
> MINNEAPOLIS, MINNESOTA

An ideal plant for rock gardens, this penstemon benefits from a deep snow cover or winter mulch.

- *Penstemon glaber* (60 cm, 24 in.), smooth beardtongue, is a sun-loving prairie native from South Dakota, Nebraska, and Wyoming. The flowers are an unusual blue and pink combination, giving a lilac hue.
- *Penstemon pinifolius* (25 cm, 10 in.), pineleaf beardtongue, is a low-growing, drought-tolerant species with fine foliage and small, scarlet flowers from early to late summer. Protect it with a winter mulch.
- *Penstemon strictus* (60 cm, 24 in.), stiff beardtongue, has slim, glossy leaves and long-lasting, bright blue-purple flowers.

Another fine perennial with upright flower spikes has an interesting characteristic.

- *Physostegia virginiana* (90 cm, 36 in.) is called the obedient plant because each pink or white flower in a flower spike is individually hinged and may be repositioned. 'Variegata' has cream-edged leaves and lilac flowers.

Petunia Wave Series
(pe-*tewn*-ee-ah)

Petunia

For many prairie gardeners an abiding love of plants began with a few petunias in a planter. The most popular North American annual in the 1950s and 1960s, petunias were ubiquitous in suburban gardens, usually lined up like soldiers in narrow foundation beds. Predictably, some gardeners tired of petunias in the search for more exciting plants, and in the early 1980s, impatiens eclipsed petunias as the continent's favorite annual. But subsequent years have brought about a petunia renaissance of sorts. The profusion of new petunia hybrids offers a multitude of flower forms and colors, improved weather tolerance, and more versatile growth habits.

There are three types of petunias. Grandifloras are tall plants that produce flowers up to 10 cm (4 in.) across. They are very showy but tend to be more easily damaged by rain than other types. Multifloras produce smaller flowers, about 5 cm (2 in.) across, and are more floriferous and compact than grandifloras. Floribundas, the intermediate type, have blooms that are 8 cm (3 in.) across. Double flowers are available in all types.

Many petunias are fragrant; this is especially true of white, purple, and violet-blue flowered cultivars.

Portrait

The Wave Series of petunias caused a great stir among gardeners, and rightly so. They are dense, quickly spreading plants that make an ideal groundcover, producing masses of 8-cm (3-in.) blooms along the entire length of the stems throughout the summer. Wave petunias do not need to be cut back to encourage flowering.

The Wave Series includes the original magenta 'Purple'; 'Pink', bright pink with a paler throat and a slightly more upright and mounded habit than 'Purple'; 'Rose', a deep rose pink; 'Misty Lilac', which has mauve flowers with white splashes; and 'Coral'.

Where to Grow

Grow Wave Series petunias wherever you need fast-growing annuals to fill in gaps. They also look splendid spilling over banks and walls, and tumbling from containers, hanging baskets, and window boxes.

Although all petunias are suitable for annual or mixed borders and containers, the heavy blooms of double-flowering petunias are less tolerant of wind and rain than single-flowered cultivars and are best

Plant at a Glance

TYPE: annual
HEIGHT: 15 cm (6 in.)
WIDTH: 90 cm (36 in.)
SOIL: average to fertile, well drained
LIGHT: full to part sun
FLOWERING TIME: early summer to fall

PHOTO – PAGE 122

planted in sheltered locations. Plant the taller grandiflora types behind shorter, bushier plants as they may become spindly or floppy as the summer progresses. Multiflora or floribunda types are perfect for mass-planting.

How to Grow

Wave Series petunias do best in full to part sun, preferring six or more hours of sun per day (although double-flowering types are slightly more shade tolerant). Like all petunias, they are not fussy and thrive in average to fertile, well-drained soil. They will benefit from weekly fertilizing with a half-strength solution of 20–20–20, alternating with 15–30–15. If they overgrow their allotted space, cut them back and root the cuttings to get even more plants.

Unlike the Wave Series, many petunias become leggy and produce fewer blooms by mid-summer. If this happens, cut them back by half and continue to fertilize. This encourages bushy growth and a new flush of flowers.

Perfect Partners

Plant Wave Series petunias with complementary shades of geraniums, silvery dusty miller (*Centaurea cineraria*), and 'Snowstorm' or 'Lavender Showers' bacopa. Lobelia is a dainty counterpoint; try the trailing Regatta Series, especially 'Lilac' and 'Blue Splash'. 'Kathleen Mallard' lobelia has gorgeous small double, lavender-blue flowers. 'Purple Wave' looks terrific with bright green foliage of 'Limelight' helichrysum or 'Marguerite' sweet potato vine (*Ipomoea batatus*).

Collectors' Choice

There are many outstanding petunia cultivars, and each year brings new developments. Here are just a few of the many excellent choices available to prairie gardeners.

"'Purple Wave' petunia has made such an impact in the Calgary Zoo garden, it has become a mainstay. A gardener who is just over one-and-a-half meters tall held one plant above her head at arm's length and there were still flowers spilling around her feet."

OLIVIA JOHNS
CALGARY, ALBERTA

- Cascadia Series are available in many colors and have a similar growth habit to Wave petunias. They are excellent for groundcover or hanging baskets.
- Double Madness Series (floribunda) (30 cm, 12 in.) have double, 8-cm (3-in.) flowers in several shades including veined and bicolored blooms.
- Fantasy Series (multiflora) (25 cm, 10 in.) are dwarf plants with dainty 4-cm (1.5-in.) flowers in several colors, including a mix.
- Madness Series (floribunda) (30 cm, 12 in.) produce abundant 8-cm (3-in.) blooms on compact, weather-resistant plants in a wonderful variety of individual colors, plus two mixes. 'Just Madness' includes veined flowers; 'Total Madness' is a mix of all colors.
- 'Prism Sunshine' (grandiflora) (35 cm, 14 in.) has 8-cm (3-in.) flowers in pure yellow fading to cream on the edges. This is a striking improvement on previous yellow petunias.
- Storm Series (grandiflora) (30 cm, 12 in.) produces 10-cm (4-in.) blooms in a variety of shades. It is more weather resistant than many other grandifloras.

Philadelphus lewisii 'Blizzard'
(fill-a-*dell*-fuss loo-*wiss*-ee-ee)

Mock orange, Orange flower bush

Every prairie garden should have a mock orange or two tucked into shrub or mixed borders, if only for the spicy, orange-blossom perfume they impart to their surroundings in late spring and early summer. Not only are their blossoms deliciously fragrant, they are also lovely to look at; large, cup- or bowl-shaped flowers of the purest white envelop these showy deciduous shrubs from head to toe. Blossoms are usually four-petalled when single, but also come in semi-double or double forms; some even grow in the shape of a cross.

Although mock oranges rapidly fade from the limelight when the last of their petals have fallen to the ground, they never detract from the landscape. Instead, their tidy but rather nondescript green foliage blends well with shrubs of a fancier bent.

Mock oranges, which are native to North America and parts of eastern Europe and Asia, are assigned the genus name of *Philadelphus*. Philadelphus was an Egyptian pharaoh, and his name was derived from Greek words meaning "brotherly love." Interestingly, these shrubs were at one time designated as the genus *Syringa*. That should have changed forever when *Syringa* became the exclusive domain of lilacs; however, old habits die hard and in eastern North America, some gardeners still speak of *Syringa* when they really mean *Philadelphus*.

Portrait

Philadelphus lewisii 'Blizzard' is the hardiest of the mock oranges. It is a tall deciduous shrub with bright green, oval leaves up to 10 cm (4 in.) long, arranged in opposing pairs on arching branches. It is a dependable bloomer, producing masses of single, white, moderately fragrant blossoms in June, after the shrub has leafed out. The fruits that follow are small, brown capsules.

Another Lewis mock orange, *Philadelphus lewisii* 'Waterton', is native to Waterton Lakes National Park in southwestern Alberta. Every spring it, too, is smothered with moderately fragrant, white blossoms from the ground up; it is almost as hardy as 'Blizzard'.

Where to Grow

'Blizzard' is best grown in a shrub bed or mixed border; plant it so that passersby can enjoy its marvelous scent. It is also a good candidate for tall, unclipped hedges.

Plant at a Glance

TYPE: deciduous shrub
HEIGHT: 2.1 m (7 ft.)
WIDTH: 1.5 m (5 ft.)
SOIL: fertile, moist, well drained
LIGHT: full sun
FLOWERING TIME: late spring to early summer

PHOTO – PAGE 128

How to Grow

'Blizzard' grows in almost any type of garden soil, but prefers a fertile, moist, well-drained spot, in full sun. A regular water supply is important for the first several years while this shrub develops a strong root system; once established, it is quite drought tolerant.

Prune all mock oranges, including 'Blizzard', directly after flowering by cutting back older shoots to the base. Mock orange flowers on second-year wood so do not prune new, first-year branches or you will be robbing yourself of next year's blossoms. Regular pruning encourages flowering and maintains a compact shrub size.

'Blizzard' can be propagated by seed or cuttings.

Perfect Partners

Because 'Blizzard' transforms into a rather ordinary-looking shrub after blooming, plant it directly behind shorter, more distinctive-looking shrubs that can carry the show after 'Blizzard' blossoms fade. 'Dart's Gold' golden ninebark (*Physocarpus opulifolius*), golden variegated dogwood (*Cornus alba* 'Gouchaultii'), or a small grouping of 'Goldflame' spirea (*Spiraea* x *bumalda*) are good companions.

Collectors' Choice

Because mock oranges hybridize easily both in the wild and in cultivation, many cultivars and hybrids are becoming available for the home gardener, although some have yet to be proven hardy on the prairies.

- ❦ *Philadelphus coronarius* 'Aureus' (1.2 m, 4 ft.), golden mock orange, develops into a hardy shrub with golden foliage, smothered in early summer with cup-shaped, single, very fragrant, creamy white flowers. The golden foliage sometimes turns a greenish color toward the end of summer. To preserve

"In early July, mock orange blooms in full, fragrant splendor, attractively grouped with a very tall **Crambe cordifolia**, *several varieties of white hardy roses, and a snowball bush in the Silverdale Garden Adopt-a-Park, which our home faces."*

HELEN PACHOLKO
FORT MCMURRAY, ALBERTA

the golden leaf color, plant this cultivar in light shade, although it might not bloom as profusely as it would if growing in full sun. 'Aureus' is one of the best short, golden-leaved shrubs for landscape use.

- ❦ *Philadelphus* x 'Galahad' (1.5 m, 5 ft.) is a compact, hardy shrub with glossy green foliage, well-suited to shrub beds and mixed borders. Its large, 2.5-cm (1-in.), single, white flowers appear in late June and are extremely fragrant.
- ❦ *Philadelphus* x *virginalis* 'Minnesota Snowflake' (2.5 m, 8 ft.), sometimes listed as 'Snowflake', produces fragrant, double, waterlily-type, white flowers in clusters of 8 to 10.
- ❦ *Philadelphus* hybrids also worth trying in prairie gardens include: 'Audrey' (2.5 m, 8 ft.), which has large, fragrant, white blossoms and was developed at the research station in Morden, Manitoba; 'Marjorie', another Morden introduction that is slightly shorter than 'Audrey'; 'Patricia' (90 cm, 36 in.), which has creamy white blossoms; and 'Sylvia' (2 m, 6.5 ft.), which has semi-double, fragrant, white flowers.

Phlox paniculata 'David'

(flocks pan-ick-you-*lah*-tah)

Garden phlox

A worthy stalwart of gardens everywhere, garden phlox has delighted generations of gardeners with its lofty, ornate flower clusters and divinely decadent scent. Although its roots are in the woodlands of eastern North America, garden phlox was not cultivated in its native land until after it had taken the European gardening scene by storm and was subsequently reintroduced here by European horticulturists.

Garden phlox derives its name from the Greek word for flame, in reference to the hot colors of some cultivars. Despite having a bit of a reputation because of its susceptibility to disfiguring powdery mildew, by choosing disease-resistant cultivars and providing the right growing conditions, all gardeners can have brilliant, healthy garden phlox to showcase in mid-summer borders.

Plant at a Glance

TYPE: perennial
HEIGHT: 90 cm (36 in.)
WIDTH: 90 cm (36 in.)
SOIL: fertile, moist, well drained
LIGHT: full to part sun
FLOWERING TIME: mid-summer to fall

PHOTO – PAGE 169

Portrait

One of the earliest-blooming and most mildew-resistant garden phloxes is the white-flowered cultivar 'David'. Its delicate, five-petalled flowers are tubular at the base and flare into flat, upward-facing disks; these are arranged in large, billowy clouds at the end of tall, sturdy stems that require no staking. The dark green, lance-shaped leaves contrast vividly with the very fragrant, radiant white flowers.

Other beautiful, mildew-resistant cultivars of garden phlox include 'Dusterlohe' (deep neon violet), 'Fujiyama' (snow white), 'Julyfest' (silvery pink with a white center), 'Miss Jo Ellen' (blush pink with a rose pink eye), 'Miss Karen' (strawberry pink with a candy pink eye), and 'Redividus' (carmine pink). 'Norah Leigh' has pink flowers and variegated foliage.

Where to Grow

Give 'David' spacious accommodation in the middle or back of a sunny border, or tucked into the corner of an informal cottage garden.

How to Grow

Plant 'David' in fertile, moist, well-drained soil, in full to part sun. Although it is extremely mildew resistant, as for all phlox, it is important to continuously maintain satisfactory moisture levels, especially during hot, dry weather when powdery mildew usually rears its blighted head. A year-round organic mulch around the plant helps in this regard. Thin the multi-stemmed clumps to about a half-dozen stems to encourage good air circulation, another tool in the fight against powdery mildew.

Restricting the number of flower stems has another benefit; it triggers the production of fewer, but larger, showier flower clusters. If you desire more plentiful but slightly smaller flower clusters, then pinch the growing tips once or twice early in the season to encourage the formation of side shoots. Just take into account that pinching back delays flowering by a few weeks.

Deadhead this cultivar and other phlox on a regular basis to prevent self-seeding. Named phlox cultivars do not come true from seed and the rather ordinary but vigorous pink progeny will eventually crowd out and replace choice parent cultivars.

Propagate 'David' by stem cuttings in the spring, root cuttings in the fall, and division in the spring or fall. Dividing plants every three or four years also invigorates them and gives their flower power a timely boost.

When 'David' is cut back in the spring or fall, deposit stems and leaves in the garbage—not the compost pile—to prevent the spread of powdery mildew.

Perfect Partners

'David' looks splendid paired with late-blooming lilies, asters, liatris, and purple Russian sage (*Perovskia atriplicifolia*). It is also a perfect match for yellow, daisylike, black-eyed Susan (*Rudbeckia* spp.), false sunflower (*Heliopsis helianthoides*), and sneezeweed (*Helenium autumnale*).

Collectors' Choice

In addition to tall, stately garden phlox, two other low-growing forms of phlox are a must for every garden. Moss phlox (*Phlox subulata*) prefers full sun and produces an explosion of color in the spring. Woodland phlox (*P. divaricata*, *P. stolonifera*) prefers

"By growing 'David' phlox, gardeners no longer have to look on helplessly as powdery mildew sets in during the hot, humid days of summer. This is the best recent introduction of tall, white garden phlox—wonderfully fragrant, long blooming, and loved by butterflies!"

MARY ELLEN CONNELLY
SIOUX FALLS, SOUTH
DAKOTA

shade and blooms from spring to midsummer.

- *Phlox divaricata* (30 cm, 12 in.) prefers shade. It produces fragrant, lavender, pink, or white flowers in spring, above semi-evergreen, lance-shaped foliage.
- *Phlox stolonifera* (15 cm, 6 in.) is also a shade-lover and produces broad clumps of deep green foliage topped by loose clusters of pink, purple, or white flowers.
- *Phlox subulata* (15 cm, 6 in.), moss phlox, forms low mats of dense, needlelike foliage smothered with lavender, purple, pink, or white flowers. Shear it back after flowering to refresh it and encourage a second flush of bloom. It is an excellent candidate for the rock garden.

A beloved plant that looks like phlox, only blooms much earlier in the season, is the biennial or short-lived perennial sweet rocket.

- *Hesperis matronalis* (90 cm, 36 in.), also called sweet rocket, has very fragrant, purple, magenta, pink, or white flowers that are produced in open clusters at the end of stout, leafy stems. It perfumes the evening air in spring and early summer, and is a prolific self-sower.

Picea pungens f. glauca 'Globosa'

(pie-see-ah pun-jenz f. glau-kah)

Globe Colorado blue spruce

Countless prairie gardens are graced with the tall, elegant spires, vivid blue-green color, and graceful sweeping skirts of Colorado blue spruce (*Picea pungens* f. *glauca*). These magnificent trees have a powerful presence on spacious properties, but sadly, they eventually outgrow their allotted space in gardens of average size. In the end, many gardeners become dissatisfied with their friendly blue giants and reluctantly conclude they have no choice but to cut them down.

Thankfully, nursery owners and plant developers have taken this dilemma to heart, and now dozens of dwarf spruce cultivars are available for landscape use. Many of the small spruce originate as witches' brooms, spontaneous mutations that frequently occur in conifers.

Dwarf spruce come in all shapes—weeping, globular, columnar, and prostrate—and all sizes, ranging from 30 cm (12 in.) to 3 m (10 ft.) or more. The foliage of dwarf Colorado blue spruce is still as blue as blue can be, but the diminished stature of its many cultivars is much more appropriate for average-sized mixed and shrub borders.

Portrait

Picea pungens f. *glauca* 'Globosa' is an outstanding dwarf, globe-shaped Colorado blue spruce. It is slow growing and compact, maintaining its natural form without shearing. Individual sharp, blue needles are borne on peglike stalks, which look like little warts on the branches; they are short, square in cross-section, and distributed around the circumference of branchlets, more densely on top than below. The glaucous blue foliage coloring is imparted by a powder that is gradually worn away by the elements; fresh spring growth intensifies and renews the blue color.

Other popular *Picea pungens* f. *glauca* cultivars include: 'Bakeri' (4 m, 13 ft.), a conical tree with long, dark blue needles; 'Fastigiata' (3 m, 10 ft.), an upright, columnar blue spruce; 'Hoopsii' (12 m, 40 ft.), a dense, narrow, silvery blue, pyramidal tree; 'Montgomery' (3 m, 10 ft.), a compact, broadly pyramidal, blue evergreen; 'Pendula' (3 m, 10 ft.), a weeping form that requires staking but may also be grown as a groundcover; 'Procumbens' (30 cm, 12 in.), a low shrub with glaucous blue needles on low, spreading branches.

Plant at a Glance

TYPE: evergreen tree
HEIGHT: 1.5 m (5 ft.)
WIDTH: 1.5 m (5 ft.)
SOIL: fertile, moist, well drained
LIGHT: full sun

PHOTO – PAGE 169

Where to Grow

Include 'Globosa' as an accent in mixed or shrub borders, or toward the back of an alpine rock garden. This shrub also makes a striking hedge.

How to Grow

'Globosa' prefers fertile, moist, well-drained soil, and a sunny location. It is reasonably drought tolerant once established, although regular watering ensures a healthier tree. An organic mulch around the base of the tree keeps soil cool and moist.

Like all spruce, 'Globosa' is very hardy and usually withstands the drying effects of winter wind and sun; it may suffer a bit of yellowing in extremely windy or cold locations, but recuperates easily.

Keep an eye out for spruce spider mites, spruce gall aphids, and yellow-headed spruce sawfly larvae. Spider mites (and their silken webs) and sawfly larvae can often be removed successfully with a forceful spray of water. Remove galls by hand before they open.

Perfect Partners

In mixed borders, the blue-green needles of 'Globosa' contrast beautifully with silver-leaved plants such as lambs' ears (*Stachys byzantina*), artemisia, and lavender, or the pure white flowers of shasta daisy (*Leucanthemum* x *superbum*), 'David' phlox, 'Henry Hudson' hardy shrub rose, and 'Husker Red' penstemon. In shrub borders, it is attractive grouped with contrasting, deciduous shrubs such as spirea, potentilla, or any of the variegated dogwoods (*Cornus alba* spp.); it also grows with distinction when paired with purple-leaved shrubs such as redleaf rose (*Rosa glauca*) or the new 'Diablo' ninebark.

"The beautiful blue of the globe spruce makes the other colors in the surrounding landscape brighter and bolder. I use globe spruce in perennial borders to contrast with daylilies, lilies, and irises, and to add permanent structure to the border."

KIMBERLY BROWN
REGINA, SASKATCHEWAN

Collectors' Choice

Two other species of spruce make interesting additions to prairie gardens.

- *Picea abies* (15 m, 50 ft.), Norway spruce, starts out pyramidal in shape and becomes more columnar with maturity. Its gently sweeping branches are covered with dark green, blunt needles; many dwarf forms are extremely slow growing and ideal for rock gardens. Both 'Gregoryana' (76 cm, 30 in.) and 'Little Gem' (45 cm, 18 in.) are slightly flattened, dome-shaped trees. 'Nidiformis' (90 cm, 36 in.), nest spruce, produces semi-erect branches that curve outward, creating a depression that looks like a nest. 'Pendula' (2 m, 6.5 ft.) is a weeping spruce that requires staking to grow upright; it also makes an unusual groundcover when left to ramble. 'Pumila' (90 cm, 36 in.) is dwarf and globe shaped.

- *Picea glauca* (20 m, 65 ft.), white spruce, forms a narrow pyramid with descending branches that curve upward slightly at the tips. The dull, dark green needles sometimes have a bluish cast and produce an unpleasant aroma when bruised. It is very tolerant of wind, drought, and heat. 'Densata', known as Black Hills spruce, is a compact form of the species.

Pinus cembra

(pee-nus or py-nus kem-brah)

Swiss stone pine, Arolla pine

Pines are trees with personality. Many are open and asymmetrical in form, or grow in twisted shapes quite unlike the regular silhouettes of the spruce trees found in most urban prairie landscapes. There are over a hundred *Pinus* species native to the Northern Hemisphere, ranging in size from small shrubs to stately tall trees. They have long been highly valued for timber.

Pines are identified by their long needles arranged in clusters of two, three, or five, each cluster encased in a papery sheath at the base. They often grow in challenging locations—in high mountains, on dry, windswept slopes, or in poor soil.

Portrait

Pinus cembra, the Swiss stone pine, is a splendid tree native to the mountains of central Europe and Asia. A slow-growing, dense pine, it has a columnar to pyramidal shape when young, becoming more open and rounded with age. The flexible, 13-cm (5-in.) needles, grouped in bundles of five, are dark green above and bluish white underneath.

The bark of the Swiss stone pine is smooth and gray. The deep blue-violet cones are up to 8 cm (3 in.) long and remain on the tree for three or four years before dropping. The name "stone" refers to the large edible seeds, relished by both birds and squirrels.

Pinus cembra 'Nana' (3 m, 10 ft.) is a dwarf form that is an ideal addition to rock gardens or shrub beds.

Where to Grow

Swiss stone pine is a lovely feature tree for a small garden. Where space allows, it may be included in a grove of small trees.

How to Grow

Plant Swiss stone pine in a sunny location, in average to fertile, well-drained soil. When planting this and other pines take care that the root ball is not damaged or the fibrous roots exposed to air.

Water well and provide winter protection with organic mulch around the root area until the tree is well established. This tree has good resistance to sunscald.

Swiss stone pine does not require fertilizing or pruning.

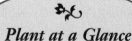

Plant at a Glance

TYPE: evergreen tree
HEIGHT: 12 m (40 ft.)
WIDTH: 4.5 m (15 ft.)
SOIL: average to fertile, well drained
LIGHT: full sun

PHOTO – PAGE 169

Perfect Partners

Although Swiss stone pine is a lovely specimen tree left on its own, those with capacious gardens may wish to combine it with deciduous trees bearing contrasting foliage, or with bright fall color, such as Amur maple (*Acer tataricum* var. *ginnala*) or mountain ash (*Sorbus* spp.).

Collectors' Choice

Most of the 40 *Pinus* species native to North America grow naturally in sandy, well-drained soil. However, gardeners have found several species to be adaptable to prairie growing conditions.

§ *Pinus aristata* (12 m, 40 ft.), the bristle-cone pine, is an extremely slow-growing pine with a fascinating twisted or irregular form. One of the oldest living plants, some bristlecone specimens in the southwestern United States are approximately 4,700 years old. The dark green needles, clustered in groups of five, are flecked with white resin.

§ *Pinus flexilis* (8 m, 26 ft.), limber pine, is a drought-tolerant species native to hot, dry, rocky terrain in British Columbia, Alberta, and North Dakota. Frequently multi-stemmed, the slow-growing limber pine has bluish green needles in bundles of five, gray bark, and light brown cones. 'Extra Blue' is a silvery blue cultivar.

§ *Pinus mugo*, commonly called mugo or Swiss mountain pine, is a popular hardy species frequently used for foundation plantings and rock gardens. Extremely variable in size, these pines are usually multi-stemmed with dense, dark green needles in bundles of two. Gardeners with limited space should select either the dwarf form, *P. m. pumilio*, or one of the dwarf mounding or spreading cultivars, among them 'Mops Mugo', 'Gnom', 'White Bud', and 'Slowmound'. Be aware, however,

> *"Swiss stone pine is a classic representation of a five-needled pine. It typifies the windswept bonsai look that pines can get. The needles are beautiful and soft to the touch. Requiring very little maintenance, it is a great tree for small gardens."*
>
> KEVIN LEE
> CALGARY, ALBERTA

that even small varieties are notorious for growing larger than expected. Keep mugo pines compact by removing half of the new growth on each growing tip, or candle, in late spring, just before the needles have opened. If you yearn for a larger mugo pine, *P. m.* var. *rotundata* grows to 3 m (10 ft.), and *P. m.* var. *rostrata* (syn. *P. m.* var. *uncinata* or *P. uncinata*) is a single-trunked variety growing up to 20 m (65 ft.).

§ *Pinus sylvestris* (15 m, 50 ft.), Scots pine, is pyramidal when young, becoming more open and irregular when mature. The bark on the upper trunk and branches peels to reveal light orange inner bark. It bears twisted, blue-green needles grouped in pairs, and curved cones growing on short stems. Since Scots pine has a deep taproot, it may be successfully underplanted with small shrubs or perennials. Cultivars include: 'Fastigiata', a columnar form; 'Viridis Compacta' and 'Nana', dwarf cultivars; 'Hillside Creeper' (60 cm, 24 in.), a useful groundcover spreading 3 m (10 ft.); and 'French Blue Scotch', a large, blue-needled tree.

Polemonium reptans 'Blue Pearl'
(paw-li-*moh*-nee-um *rep*-tans)

Creeping Jacob's ladder, Greek valerian

Gardeners on the prowl for plants with unusual leaf shapes and textures need look no farther than Jacob's ladder (*Polemonium* spp.). Its pinnate leaves consist of pairs of fine, elongated leaflets, arranged on arching leaf stems. They are a welcome sight each spring and really do resemble the rungs of a ladder, specifically, the ladder to heaven's gate dreamed of by Jacob in the Old Testament. The delicate, mostly lavender blue, cup- or bell-shaped flowers appear early in the season and create the same dreamy effect in shade gardens that the sky blue blossoms of perennial flax (*Linum perenne*) do in sunny borders.

Portrait

'Blue Pearl' forms low mounds of feathery, apple green leaves, up to 25 cm (10 in.) long, in early spring; each leaf consists of 7 to 19 oblong leaflets, each from 2.5 to 5 cm (1 to 2 in.) long and arranged in opposite pairs—the rungs of Jacob's ladder. Short, branching stems rise above the foliage in spring and early summer to be smothered with a succession of relatively large (2.5 cm, 1 in.), bright sky blue, bell-shaped flowers. Intensely yellow stamens contrast beautifully with the blue blossoms.

Similar in habit, other cultivars of *Polemonium reptans* worth looking for include 'Sapphire', 'Pink Beauty', and 'Lambrooke Mauve' (also sold as 'Lambrooke Manor').

Where to Grow

The low-mounding habit of 'Blue Pearl' makes it perfect for creating a sea of hazy blue at the front of mixed borders, naturalizing in woodland gardens, or scattering in wildflower gardens. Equally at home on the damp margins of a pond or the banks of a stream, it also makes a lovely and unusual addition to summer container arrangements.

How to Grow

Plant 'Blue Pearl' in light shade or full sun, in fertile, moist, well-drained soil. The foliage does well all summer, as long as the plant is kept uniformly moist. However, it may get that "tired look" late in the season if allowed to dry out; this is often the case with spring-flowering, moisture-loving perennials.

Take advantage of the tendency of 'Blue Pearl' to self-sow by letting the

Plant at a Glance

TYPE: perennial
HEIGHT: 30 cm (12 in.)
WIDTH: 30 cm (12 in.)
SOIL: fertile, moist, well drained
LIGHT: light shade to full sun
FLOWERING TIME: spring to
early summer

PHOTO – PAGE 169

seedlings be, thus increasing the size of your patch of Jacob's ladder at no effort or cost to you. Alternatively, prevent self-seeding by deadheading blossoms before they set seed. This plant can also be propagated by division or cuttings, in early spring or fall.

Perfect Partners

To create a pleasing effect, plant 'Blue Pearl' with columbine (*Aquilegia* spp.), fernleaf or fringed bleeding heart (*Dicentra formosa* or *D. eximia*), ferns, hostas, and low-growing Siberian bugloss (*Brunnera macrophylla*) and blue-eyed Mary (*Omphalodes verna*). Blue- and yellow-flowered plants always make great partners, so you can also try 'Blue Pearl' with globe-flower (*Trollius* spp.), marsh marigold (*Caltha palustris*), yellow primulas, or yellow corydalis.

Collectors' Choice

There are other attractive species of Jacob's ladder to try. They all require a moist, well-drained soil, thrive in full sun to light shade, and bloom in late spring and early summer.

- *Polemonium caeruleum* (60 cm, 24 in.) forms a mound of 13-cm (5-in.) leaves, each consisting of 27 pairs of elongated leaflets, that develop quickly in spring. Tall flower stems are topped with nodding clusters of dainty, blue, cup-shaped flowers. 'Album' is a white variety, 'Blue Bell' is light blue, and 'Brise d'Anjou' has variegated leaflets that are a deep green, edged in cream.
- *Polemonium pauciflorum* (45 cm, 18 in.) is native to the mountainous American southwest. Its elegant tubular flowers flare into shallow cups and are a lovely creamy yellow, suffused with a hint of red.
- *Polemonium pulcherrimum* (30 cm, 12 in.), also called skunkleaf Jacob's

> *"The arrangement of leaves on the stems of this plant is well described by the name 'ladder.' Its tiny, blue-purple flowers with yellow centers are among the first to open in spring. It even spreads easily from seed."*
>
> IRENE SUNDBY
> SWIFT CURRENT, SASKATCHEWAN

ladder, is smothered in early summer by bell-shaped, purple-blue or white flowers, with a soft yellow interior.

Two other woodland plants with a leaf arrangement similar to Jacob's ladder, though on a larger scale, are Solomon's seal and false Solomon's seal. They both prefer fertile, moist soil, and a spot in light to full shade.

- *Polygonatum biflorum* (90 cm, 36 in.), also called Solomon's seal, forms clumps of graceful arching stems clothed in nearly stemless, alternating, elliptical, veined leaves. Pairs of small, greenish white, bell-shaped flowers sprout from leaf axils in late spring and transform into dark blue berries come fall.
- *Smilacina racemosa* (90 cm, 36 in.), known as false Solomon's seal, forms clumps of arching stems with elongated, pointed, veined leaves. It differs from Solomon's seal by producing feathery, pyramidal clusters of fragrant, creamy white flowers at the end of its stems in spring and summer, and red berries in the fall.

Populus tremula 'Erecta'

(*pop*-ewe-luss *trem*-ewe-lah)

Swedish or European columnar aspen

Poplar trees—the liberty tree of the French Revolution and one of the five official trees of mourning in China—have been cultivated since Roman times. They are a familiar sight on the prairies, where native balsam poplars hug the banks of streams and rivers, and other large poplars form the backbone of thousands of rural shelterbelts. Poplars can also be seen in prairie towns and cities where they were once planted as fast-growing, hardy shade trees.

Many poplars lost their appeal as ornamental trees after people realized most of them are much too big and troublesome for city gardens. The sticky spring bud drop, fluffy seed dispersal from female catkins, and strong suckering habits are messy; what's more, their extensive, shallow, water-seeking root systems damage foundations, as well as sewer and water lines.

Despite the poplar's poor reputation, two columnar versions are rapidly gaining favor among gardeners. The Swedish columnar aspen (*Populus tremula* 'Erecta'), introduced in Sweden in 1911, and the 'Tower' poplar (*P.* x *canescens* 'Tower'), introduced in 1979 at Morden, Manitoba, are perfect for growing in small to average-sized gardens.

Portrait

Swedish columnar aspens are non-suckering, seed-free male trees with a distinctly upright, narrow form and near-vertical branches that spiral toward the top. The small, rounded, toothed leaves emerge a soft rusty maroon color and mature to medium green; they rustle pleasantly in light breezes, thanks to their flat, flexible stems.

Where to Grow

Swedish columnar aspen makes a dramatic, vertical accent tree in mixed or shrub borders; where space permits, a clump of three of them is very eye-catching. These aspens can also be used to form a tall, semi-formal hedge around the perimeter of a property or to separate "garden rooms."

How to Grow

Swedish columnar aspen is tolerant of almost all soil types, but does best in fertile, moist, well-drained soil, in full sun. Other than maintaining adequate moisture levels, they require very little care. Their

---

❧ Plant at a Glance

TYPE: deciduous tree
HEIGHT: 9 m (30 ft.)
WIDTH: 3 m (10 ft.)
SOIL: fertile, moist, well drained
LIGHT: full sun

PHOTO – PAGE 170

Phlox paniculata 'David'
(garden phlox) page 160.

LIESBETH LEATHERBARROW

Picea pungens f. *glauca* 'Globosa'
(globe Colorado blue spruce) page 162.

LIESBETH LEATHERBARROW

Pinus cembra (Swiss stone pine,
Arolla pine) page 164.

LESLEY REYNOLDS

Polemonium reptans 'Blue Pearl' (creeping
Jacob's ladder, Greek valerian) page 166.

KEN GIRARD

Populus tremula 'Erecta' (Swedish or
European columnar aspen) page 168.

LESLEY REYNOLDS

Potentilla fruticosa 'Pink Beauty'
(potentilla, cinquefoil) page 178.

LESLEY REYNOLDS

Primula auricula
(primula, primrose) page 180.

LIESBETH LEATHERBARROW

Prunus tomentosa (Nanking cherry,
Manchu cherry) page 182.

LLYN STRELAU

Pulmonaria longifolia 'Bertram Anderson'
(longleaf lungwort) page 184.

Pulsatilla vulgaris var. *rubra* (red
pasqueflower, prairie crocus) page 186.

Quercus macrocarpa (bur oak,
mossy cup oak) page 188.

Rosa 'Winnipeg Parks'
(hardy shrub rose) page 190.

Salix silicola 'Polar Bear'
(willow) page 194.

LIESBETH LEATHERBARROW

Left: *Sambucus racemosa* 'Plumosa Aurea'.
Right: *Sambucus racemosa* (European red elder)
page 196. LIESBETH LEATHERBARROW

Bottom: *Saxifraga* x *urbium* 'Aureopunctata',
page 198. Top: *Osmunda claytonia* (interrupted
fern). LIESBETH LEATHERBARROW

Scabiosa columbaria 'Butterfly Blue' (scabiosa,
small scabious) page 200.

LIESBETH LEATHERBARROW

Scilla sibirica
(Siberian squill, bluebells) page 202.

Sedum 'Autumn Joy' (showy sedum,
showy stonecrop) page 204.

Shepherdia argentea (silver
buffaloberry) page 206.

Sorbus decora (showy mountain ash,
elder-leaf mountain ash) page 208.

Spiraea japonica 'Little Princess'
(Japanese spirea) page 210.

Syringa meyeri 'Palibin' (dwarf Korean lilac,
Meyer lilac) page 212.

Syringa reticulata (Japanese tree lilac,
giant tree lilac) page 214.

Thalictrum delavayi 'Hewitt's Double' (Yunnan
meadow rue) page 216.

Thuja occidentalis 'Brandon' (eastern or
northern white cedar, arborvitae) page 218.

Thymus serpyllum (mother-of-thyme,
mountain thyme) page 220.

Tilia x *flavescens* 'Dropmore'
(linden, basswood) page 222.

Tradescantia x *andersoniana* 'Osprey'
(spiderwort, widow's tears) page 224.

Tulipa tarda
(tarda tulip) page 226.

Verbascum chaixii 'Album'
(nettle leaved mullein) page 228.

Veronica x 'Sunny Border Blue'
(veronica, speedwell) page 230.

Viburnum trilobum (American highbush
cranberry) page 232.

tidy, columnar growth habit precludes the need for pruning.

Keep an eye out for tent caterpillars, rust, and bacterial cankers, and remove and destroy affected branches immediately.

Propagate Swedish columnar aspen by hardwood cuttings in late fall or winter.

Perfect Partners

Although Swedish columnar aspen does very well as a stand-alone tree, it is also attractive in a shrub border with medium-sized Savin junipers (*Juniperus sabina*), cheerful potentillas (*Potentilla fruticosa* 'Pink Beauty', 'Abbotswood', 'Red Robin'), and elegant spirea clustered at its feet.

Collectors' Choice

Swedish columnar aspen is not the only poplar that is perfect for growing in small spaces.

- *Populus* x *canescens* 'Tower' (12 m, 40 ft.), 'Tower' poplar, is an extremely fast-growing, upright, fluff-free, male tree. Its oval leaves have wavy margins, are glossy green above and fuzzy white underneath, and turn a wonderful yellow in fall. These stately poplars are perfect as specimen trees or for semi-formal screens and hedges, although they do have a tendency to sucker.

The following poplars are suitable for large urban lots, acreages, and rural windbreaks where their shallow, water-seeking root systems and suckering tendencies don't matter.

- *Populus alba* (12 m, 40 ft.), silver poplar, forms a large, spreading tree covered in glossy, maplelike leaves that are dark green on top and fuzzy, silvery white on the underside. The female cultivar, 'Nivea', has a dark, chunky lower trunk and pale creamy gray upper trunk; it produces fluffy seeds in the spring. 'Pyramidalis', the male cultivar, produces no fluff. It has smoky cream-

"The Swedish columnar aspen is a popular tree for the smaller city lot, providing screening from the neighbors or an unsightly view. It also has a great shape for formal designs, adding a stately appearance to the landscape."

WENDY ARIS
LANGDON, ALBERTA

colored bark, is columnar when young, and swells into a globe-shaped canopy when mature. Its leaves are not as maplelike as those of 'Nivea'.

- *Populus* 'Brooks No. 2' (syn. *P.* 'Griffin') (10 m, 33 ft.), the well-known 'Griffin' poplar, is one of the smaller poplars; it is an upright, fluff-free, oval tree with triangular, medium green leaves.

- *Populus* x *jackii* 'Northwest' (20 m, 65 ft.), 'Northwest' poplar, is a fluff-free, male clone with bark that is a light creamy gray. Its leaves are heart shaped at the base, boldly toothed, shiny dark green on top and lighter underneath, and red-stemmed; they turn a brilliant glowing yellow in fall.

- *Populus tremuloides* (12 m, 40 ft.), trembling aspen, has the widest range of any tree species in North America. It is a graceful, slender tree with greenish white bark and glossy, light green, finely toothed, circular leaves that turn a dazzling orange-yellow in the fall. The leaves, attached by flexible, flattened stems, tremble in the slightest of breezes. Aspens grow as colonies, reproducing from an extensive root system; some colonies in Alberta may be more than 6,000 years old.

Potentilla fruticosa 'Pink Beauty'
(po-ten-*till*-ah froo-ti-*co*-sah)

Potentilla, Cinquefoil

Few prairie folk are unfamiliar with the shrubby little potentillas (*Potentilla fruticosa*), also called cinquefoil, that grow across the western North American plains. These wiry, little shrubs bear cheerful yellow, buttercuplike flowers throughout the summer and have gray-green leaves divided into five leaflets, hence, the common name "cinquefoil." The *Potentilla* genus includes about 500 species of deciduous and evergreen shrubs and perennials native to the Northern Hemisphere.

The generic name *Potentilla* derives from the Latin *potens*, meaning "powerful," a reference to the medicinal efficacy of some species. All potentillas have astringent qualities and have been used as a gargle and mouth wash, and to reduce fever. The five-part leaves were said to symbolize the five senses of man, and were emblazoned on the shields of knights. Fishermen also attempted to harness the potency of potentilla by putting it in their nets to ensure an abundant catch.

Hardy and long-blooming, *Potentilla fruticosa* adapts to almost any soil type, and there is now a bevy of beautiful cultivars ranging in color from white to yellow, orange to pink and red.

Portrait

Potentilla fruticosa 'Pink Beauty' was developed by Professor Louis Lenz at the University of Manitoba and introduced in 1995. This vigorous and hardy shrub bears semi-double, medium pink flowers from early summer until fall. Unlike many pink or red potentillas, the blossoms hold their color well, although if subjected to extreme heat they will fade to a light creamy pink. A bushy, mounded shrub, 'Pink Beauty' has dark green, compound leaves composed of small, oval leaflets.

Where to Grow

'Pink Beauty' is an ideal specimen shrub for small gardens, and a superb choice for mixed or shrub borders, foundation plantings, a low hedge, or a mass-planting. It is also a good candidate for topiary.

How to Grow

Like most hardy potentillas, 'Pink Beauty' is a versatile shrub well suited to the prairie climate. Plant it in full to part sun, in average, well-drained soil that has been amended with organic material. Once established, it is drought tolerant, but flowering duration and quality will be better if the plant receives a moderate amount of water. Use an organic mulch around

Plant at a Glance

TYPE: deciduous shrub
HEIGHT: 90 cm (36 in.)
WIDTH: 90 cm (36 in.)
SOIL: average, well drained
LIGHT: full to part sun
FLOWERING TIME: early summer to fall

PHOTO – PAGE 170

178

'Pink Beauty' to retain soil moisture.

Prune in early spring, removing dead or weak growth at ground level. If the plant is crowded, thin out older branches at soil level. Strong growth can be pruned back by one-third.

'Pink Beauty' may be propagated by softwood cuttings.

Perfect Partners

Plant 'Pink Beauty' in the middle of a perennial border with Asiatic lilies, daylilies, blue or white delphinium, and garden phlox. In a shrub border, plant it in front of 'Northline' saskatoon (*Amelanchier alnifolia*), mock orange (*Philadelphus lewisii*), 'Ivory Halo' (*Cornus alba*), dogwood, or silvery-leaved shrubs like 'Polar Bear' willow (*Salix silicola*).

Collectors' Choice

There are many robust and beautiful *Potentilla fruticosa* cultivars that will bloom all summer.

- 'Abbotswood' (90 cm, 36 in.) has a spreading habit, blue-green foliage, and large, pure white flowers.
- 'Coronation Triumph' (90 cm, 36 in.) is a vigorous and early-blooming, upright cultivar that bears bright yellow flowers. It originated in Indian Head, Saskatchewan, in 1950.
- 'Goldfinger' (90 cm, 36 in.) is a compact cultivar with deep green foliage that produces abundant showy, deep yellow flowers up to 4 cm (1.5 in.) in diameter.
- 'Katherine Dykes' (90 cm, 36 in.) has primrose-yellow flowers and gray-green leaves.
- 'McKay's White' (76 cm, 30 in.) has a spreading habit with arching branches, light blue-green foliage, and creamy white flowers.
- 'Orange Whisper' (90 cm, 36 in.) is a University of Manitoba introduction,

"'Pink Beauty' is the best pink-flowering potentilla anywhere. The semi-double flowers present an awesome display from early August to the first killing frost, fading slightly during extremely hot summer days."

RICK DURAND
PORTAGE LA PRAIRIE, MANITOBA

with a mounded form and pale orange flowers.

- 'Red Robin' (60 cm, 24 in.) produces red-orange flowers. It is hardier and retains its flower color better than the familiar 'Red Ace'.
- 'Yellowbird' (90 cm, 36 in.) is an upright cultivar with bright yellow, semi-double flowers and is a good choice for hedges.
- 'Yellow Gem' (60 cm, 24 in.), a University of British Columbia introduction, is a long-blooming, spreading shrub with bright yellow flowers.

Low-growing, creeping potentillas are less familiar than their shrubby relatives, but are useful perennials for the front of borders and rock gardens.

- *Potentilla nepalensis* 'Miss Willmott' (30 cm, 12 in.) bears single, cherry pink flowers with darker centers on spreading, branching stems. Although not invasive, it is capable of spreading 60 cm (24 in.) or more. Try 'Miss Wilmott' in a lightly shaded woodland garden.
- *Potentilla tridentata* (15 cm, 6 in.), the three-toothed cinquefoil, is an evergreen groundcover potentilla with saucer-shaped white flowers. It is also called wineleaf cinquefoil for its red fall foliage color.

Primula auricula
(*prim*-you-lah or-*ik*-kew-lah)

Primula, Primrose

Cultivated in England since the late sixteenth century, primulas are indispensable in traditional English gardens. Among the first flowers to bloom in the spring, they have long been considered a symbol of youth. This early-blooming habit is reflected in the botanical name for the genus *Primula*, derived from the Latin *primus*, meaning "first." The common name "primrose" comes from the Latin *prima rosa*, meaning "first rose." Most primulas are from the Northern Hemisphere, natives of Europe, Asia, or North America, with over 600 species and thousands of hybrids and cultivars.

Primulas may be grouped according to preferred habitat. Some thrive in rock-garden conditions with morning sun and good drainage; some prefer fertile, moist soil and light shade; others like boggy conditions. Unsuited to extremely arid locations, primulas must have adequate moisture, particularly in the spring; a summer mulch around the plants is beneficial to keep roots cool and conserve moisture during the hottest days of the year. Many of these plants will droop in full sun.

Although there are hundreds of rare and specialized varieties of primulas sought out by avid plant collectors, there are also hardy primulas readily available to prairie gardeners.

Portrait
Primula auricula and hybrids thereof are among the hardiest and easiest to grow of the genus, and are available in assorted colors including red, maroon, pink, purple, blue, copper, and yellow. Auriculas have fleshy leaves, usually covered with a powdery substance called farina, single, two-toned flowers, or double flowers. The eye of the single flowers is often yellow or cream.

There are colorful auriculas aplenty at most garden centers, but some of the choicest named single-flowered hybrids, such as 'Rufus' (scarlet) and 'Irish Blue Eyes', may be more difficult to obtain.

Double-flowered auriculas resemble tiny roses. They are not quite as vigorous as single-flowered ones, but pretty enough to be worth a try. Cultivars include 'Camelot' (deep purple) and 'Trouble' (light coffee-color).

Where to Grow
Use auriculas in rock gardens, at the front of perennial borders, or even in an attrac-

---

Plant at a Glance

TYPE: perennial
HEIGHT: 30 cm (12 in.)
WIDTH: 40 cm (14 in.)
SOIL: average to fertile, moist, well drained
LIGHT: part sun to light shade
FLOWERING TIME: spring to early summer

PHOTO – PAGE 170

tive container as a specimen plant for a deck, patio, or balcony. They will also grow well in a lightly shaded woodland garden.

How to Grow

Auriculas prefer part sun to light shade, although they will grow well in full sun if adequate moisture is provided. The ideal soil mixture consists of approximately 40 percent grit, 20 percent loam, 20 percent peat moss, and 20 percent compost or manure. When the leaves unfurl in the spring, begin to feed weekly until mid-summer with a half-strength solution of balanced fertilizer (20–20–20).

Deadhead auriculas to prevent energy going to seed production, and remove dying or dead leaves before winter sets in. Mulch around the plants for winter protection. Since auriculas do not come true from seed, split mature plants for propagation after they have finished blooming.

Perfect Partners

Auriculas pair beautifully with other primulas that enjoy similar growing conditions. In the rockery, combine them with alpine lady's mantle (*Alchemilla alpina*) and alpine columbine (*Aquilegia alpina*). Ferns, hostas, violets, and shooting stars (*Dodecatheon meadia*) are all excellent companions in woodland settings.

Collectors' Choice

Dainty primulas provide an amazing variety of leaf and flower form and color to the garden. Start with a few of the following prairie-hardy species.

- *Primula cortusoides* (30 cm, 12 in.), sometimes labelled *Primula saxatilis*, produces umbels of delicate, pink flowers above bright emerald green foliage. This species may go dormant in hot, dry conditions, but will self-seed profusely if happy with its environment.

"Auricula primulas are glorious in spring. I like the way the showy flowers stand up well above the foliage on long stems. They bloom for six weeks in my garden!"

MARGARET JOHNSTON
CARMAN, MANITOBA

- *Primula denticulata* (30 cm, 12 in.), drumstick primula, features round heads of lilac, pink, or white flowers on upright stems.
- *Primula* x *juliae* (15 cm, 6 in.) is a reliable primula for mixed border plantings, tolerating more sun than many other primulas. 'Wanda', the most commonly available cultivar, has magenta flowers with a yellow eye.
- *Primula marginata* (5 to 20 cm, 2 to 8 in.) has pale blue to mauve flowers and distinctive serrated, heavily powdered, and often silver-edged foliage. Hybrids and cultivars produce cream to yellow through to pink and purple blooms.
- *Primula secundiflora* (30 cm, 12 in.), side-flowering primrose, bears clusters of purple-red bells rising from leaf rosettes. The stems and flowers are often attractively dusted with silvery farina.
- *Primula veris* (20 cm, 8 in.), cowslip, has clustered flowers that are usually golden yellow, but may also be orange, red, or russet.
- *Primula vulgaris* (15 cm, 6 in.), common primrose, has single flowers that are usually pale creamy yellow; double-flowered cultivars exist in several other colors. *P. vulgaris* subsp. *sibthorpii* is a vigorous lavender-pink form.

Prunus tomentosa

(*proo*-nuss toe-men-*toe*-sah)

Nanking cherry, Manchu cherry

Flowering shrubs and trees in full bloom are a welcome sight to prairie gardeners—they are a sure sign that spring is unfolding as it should and that summer is not far behind. One genus that offers up more than its fair share of showy spring finery is *Prunus*, a well-loved group of ornamental trees and shrubs. Although in warmer climates much attention is focussed on the fruit-bearing trees of this genus (apricot, cherry, plum), on the prairies it is the shrubs that are most reliably hardy. Among them, Nanking cherry is a winner. Not only is it beautiful to look at when in full bloom, it also produces delicious edible fruit.

Portrait

Nanking cherry is a delightful open vase-shaped shrub that is enveloped in a delicate haze of bowl-shaped, fragrant, pale pink flowers in early spring. After the flowers fade, dull green, wrinkled, softly hairy, and distinctly toothed leaves emerge on branches covered in peeling, shiny, reddish brown bark. By late summer the shrub is adorned with edible red cherries up to 1.3 cm (0.5 in.) in diameter. These cherries are not just a tasty treat for birds, they also make delicious jelly and wine for humans, if you can beat the birds to them!

Where to Grow

Plant Nanking cherry in shrub or mixed borders, or as a foundation planting. This shrub also makes a very attractive hedge, both in spring, when it is blooming, and afterward.

How to Grow

Nanking cherry thrives in a sunny, sheltered spot, in fertile, moist, well-drained soil. Once established, it is quite drought resistant, although it will always look its best with an adequate supply of moisture.

Nanking cherry maintains its pleasing shape with very little pruning. However, routine removal of dead, diseased, or damaged wood should take place in late winter or early spring when the shrub is still dormant. It flowers on the previous year's growth, so prune it when flowering has finished. The fruit yield increases when the shrub is cross-pollinated by another Nanking cherry in close proximity.

Propagate Nanking cherry by softwood cuttings.

Plant at a Glance

TYPE: deciduous shrub
HEIGHT: 3 m (10 ft.)
WIDTH: 5 m (16 ft.)
SOIL: fertile, moist, well drained
LIGHT: full sun
FLOWERING TIME: spring

PHOTO – PAGE 170

Perfect Partners

Spring-flowering bulbs such as grape hyacinth (*Muscari* spp.), snowdrop (*Galanthus nivalis*), daffodils (*Narcissus* spp.), and tulips always enhance Nanking cherry's spring floral extravaganza. Other shrubs that bloom concurrently with Nanking cherry also make perfect partners, especially purpleleaf sand cherry (*Prunus* x *cistena*), double flowering plum (*Prunus triloba* 'Multiplex'), and Russian almond (*Prunus tenella*). Low-growing, evergreen junipers also contrast beautifully with Nanking cherry.

Collectors' Choice

The following flowering shrubs, all members of the genus *Prunus*, put on a spectacular show of spring color. They prefer fertile, moist, well-drained soil in a sunny spot; prune as for Nanking cherry.

- *Prunus* x *cistena* (2 m, 6.5 ft.), purpleleaf sand cherry, has fabulous red-purple leaf color. In spring, it is covered with bowl-shaped, white flowers; these are sometimes followed by dark purple, cherrylike fruit. After severe winters with little or no snow cover, blossom and fruit set are unreliable; the shrub may also suffer die-back. However, it can achieve up to 90 cm (36 in.) of new growth in one season, making it worth growing for its leaf color alone.
- *Prunus tenella* (1.5 m, 5 ft.), Russian or flowering almond, is a small shrub suitable for mass-planting. It is covered with solitary or clustered, bright pink, bowl-shaped flowers in early spring, just as the shrub starts to leaf out. Flowers are followed by flat, slightly hairy, almond-shaped fruit. This shrub tends to sucker, so plant it where this doesn't matter.
- *Prunus triloba* 'Multiplex' (3 m, 10 ft.), double flowering plum, forms an upright shrub that is smothered every

"Nanking cherry is such a nicely shaped shrub and it blooms very early. I use the attractive foliage in flower arrangements. The fruit makes a delicious, rich, red-colored jelly, if you can get it picked before the birds get to it."

TENA KILMURY
BRANDON, MANITOBA

spring with very showy, fully double flowers. The blossoms, which are red in bud, open to a glorious bright pink and appear in clusters along stems. Distinctive three-lobed foliage only emerges after blossoms begin to fade. This shrub does not set fruit.

- Many fruit-producing *Prunus* trees (cherry, plum, cherry plum, apricot) have now been bred to survive prairie winters. Although always ornamental, they are not always reliable fruit producers. Because they bloom early, they run the risk of being nipped by late killing frosts typical of the prairies, which often results in no blossoms and no fruit. Most fruit trees also rely on cross-pollination from related trees; without relatives close by, there may be no fruit set. If you are prepared for occasional disappointment, then the following *Prunus* cultivars are worth a try: 'Brook Gold', 'Brook Red', and 'Pembina' plums; 'Manor', 'Opata', and 'Sapa' cherry plums; 'Westcot' and 'Manchurian Strain' apricots. 'Evans' cherry is an exciting new self-pollinating introduction that produces big, semi-sweet, bright red cherries.

Pulmonaria longifolia 'Bertram Anderson'

(pull-mon-*air*-ee-ah long-ih-*foe*-lee-ah)

Longleaf pulmonaria, Longleaf lungwort

As in nature itself, a delightful aspect of woodland gardens and lightly shaded borders is the kaleidoscope of foliage shapes, textures, and colors that weave intricate tapestries on garden floors. In this context, the unique bristly, matte green, spotted leaves of pulmonaria stand in bold counterpoint to the pure green, shiny foliage of most other shade-loving plants.

Spotted pulmonaria leaves were once thought to resemble diseased lungs, and in keeping with the practices of the day, were used to cure lung ailments, hence, its descriptive names—the rather unbecoming common name "lungwort," and the botanical name *Pulmonaria*, derived from the Latin *pulmos*, meaning "lung."

Portrait

'Bertram Anderson' flower stems emerge from a small clump of foliage in spring to produce pink flower buds that transform into rich blue, nodding flowers. The flowers are tubular and flare into a small, round, five-petalled face; they are produced in nodding clusters at the ends of short stems, and are a favorite with hummingbirds!

As with all pulmonaria foliage, that of 'Bertram Anderson' emerges when flower stems do, but doesn't expand into its full glory until the flowers have faded. The leaves are very long, narrow, strap-shaped, and speckled a silver-gray. They form a tidy, round clump and put on a lovely show all summer. Stem leaves are slightly smaller than the basal leaves.

Where to Grow

'Bertram Anderson' is a favorite in lightly shaded beds and borders. It also serves well as edging for borders and paths, and looks wonderful massed as a groundcover in woodland gardens.

How to Grow

Plant 'Bertram Anderson' in light shade to part sun, in fertile, moist, well-drained soil. Apply a thick organic mulch up to but not touching the plant's crown to help conserve soil moisture. Once established, this cultivar is quite drought tolerant and will survive in dry shade. However, if left dry for too long, its leaves will turn an unsightly brown; they may even disappear altogether, as this plant protests prolonged dry conditions by going dormant.

Excessively dry conditions also favor

Plant at a Glance

TYPE: perennial
HEIGHT: 30 cm (12 in.)
WIDTH: 60 cm (24 in.)
SOIL: fertile, moist, well drained
LIGHT: light shade to part sun
FLOWERING TIME: spring

PHOTO – PAGE 171

184

the spread of powdery mildew, which occasionally affects 'Bertram Anderson'. Dispose of infected leaves in the garbage, not the composter, to prevent the spread of disease.

Deadhead 'Bertram Anderson' to prevent self-seeding unless you are looking to increase your pulmonaria count and are willing to take potluck; named varieties of pulmonaria do not come true from seed. To propagate, take divisions as soon as they have finished blooming in the spring.

Be vigilant in the spring if you have covered 'Bertram Anderson' with a winter mulch; it blooms very early and can be damaged by mulch left in place too long.

Perfect Partners
Pulmonaria pairs well with other spring bloomers such as bleeding heart (*Dicentra* spp.), primrose (*Primula* spp.), coral bells (*Heuchera* spp.), hostas, creeping phlox, tulips (*Tulipa* spp.), and daffodils (*Narcissus* spp.).

Collectors' Choice
Several species of pulmonaria are available for collectors of shade-loving plants.

- *Pulmonaria angustifolia* (30 cm, 12 in.), blue lungwort, is a vigorous plant that produces narrow, dull green, bristly, unspotted leaves and pink buds that open into vibrant blue, bell-shaped flowers. 'Azurea', 'Johnson's Blue', 'Mawson's Blue', and 'Munstead Blue' are good choices.
- *Pulmonaria officinalis* (30 cm, 12 in.), Jerusalem cowslip, produces greenish white, bristly, heart-shaped leaves; they are heavily spotted in the spring and more subdued in the summer. Pinkish blue flower buds become true blue flowers. 'Sissinghurst White' has white flowers.
- *Pulmonaria saccharata* (30 cm, 12 in.), lungwort, produces small pink flower

buds that change into delightful, blue tubular flowers; the leaves are slightly hairy, medium green, and adorned with white spots. Garden-worthy cultivars and hybrids include 'Argentea' (blue), 'British Sterling' (blue), 'Excalibur' (rosy red), 'Janet Fisk' (blue), and 'Spilled Milk' (rose), which all have predominantly silvery leaves; 'Dora Bielefeld' (clear pink), 'Frühlingshimmel' (light blue, dark purple eye), and 'Mrs. Moon' (blue) have spotted leaves. Two other plants that flower first and then produce lovely foliage for the lightly shaded garden are Siberian bugloss and hepatica.

- *Brunnera macrophylla* (30 cm, 12 in.), Siberian bugloss, has forget-me-not blue flowers that emerge with small, medium green, heart-shaped leaves in spring. After flowering, the leaves continue to grow, providing a lovely display of bold foliage all summer long.
- *Hepatica nobilis* (20 cm, 8 in.), liverleaf, produces small, blue or white, anemonelike flowers just before its heart-shaped, three-lobed, silky leaves emerge in spring. After flowers fade, the foliage expands into a circular mound that looks its best until frost. Mulch it in winter.

Pulsatilla vulgaris var. *rubra*

(pul-sah-*til*-ah vul-*gair*-iss var. *roo*-brah)

Red pasqueflower, Prairie crocus

Have you ever taken a stroll across the prairie in early spring and been greeted by a ground-hugging haze of silvery foliage and nodding, purple flowers? If so, then you have experienced the magic of the prairie crocus (*Pulsatilla patens*), a wildflower that is one of the surest harbingers of spring for prairie-dwelling folk.

Although the wild prairie crocus is off-limits for the garden plant collector (it is protected by law, and doesn't transplant well anyway), there are cultivated varieties that are a must for every prairie garden. The domesticated pasqueflower (*Pulsatilla vulgaris*), which is also purple, is bigger and bolder than its prairie cousin; a red version (*Pulsatilla vulgaris* var. *rubra*) paints a vivid splash of vibrant color early in the spring.

Plant at a Glance

TYPE: perennial
HEIGHT: 30 cm (12 in.)
WIDTH: 35 cm (14 in.)
SOIL: average, well drained
LIGHT: full to part sun
FLOWERING TIME: spring

PHOTO – PAGE 171

Portrait

In the spring, the woody crowns of *Pulsatilla vulgaris* var. *rubra*, the red pasqueflower, are transformed into a mass of silvery shoots that soon develop into plump buds, bursting at the seams. Ferny foliage emerges at a slower pace. The leaves are mostly basal and covered with fine, silvery hairs that shimmer in the sun and offer protection from drying winds and cold temperatures.

The silky buds unfold to produce large, nodding, cup-shaped flowers of purple or ruby-red that surround a small bundle of bright yellow stamens. White, mauve, and rose-colored forms are also available.

As the flowers fade, they are replaced by plumes of long, silky-tailed seeds that provide textural interest in the garden for many weeks, until they are finally dispersed by the wind. Fortunately, the germination rate is not high, and unwanted seedlings are easy to pull.

In addition to red, there is also a white form (*Pulsatilla vulgaris* var. *alba*). A European strain, *P. v.* 'Papageno' (30 cm, 12 in.), has large flowers in spring and in fall. The blooms are semi-double in mixed shades of purple, white, pink, and red.

Where to Grow

The short stature of red pasqueflowers makes them a perfect choice for rock gardens, at the front of perennial borders, between deciduous shrubs, and in wildflower meadows or other wild garden areas.

How to Grow

Red pasqueflowers do best in neutral to slightly alkaline soil of average fertility, in full to part sun; good drainage is essential. If your soil is clay-rich, amend it with large amounts of coarse sand and compost.

For winter protection, apply a mulch of finely shredded leaves up to, but not over, the plant crowns. The insulating properties of this leaf layer will help to regulate the soil temperature, keeping the ground frozen and preventing plants from making a premature appearance during prolonged winter Chinooks.

Pasqueflower patches expand slowly and their woody crowns are difficult to divide, so it is best to leave them undisturbed.

Perfect Partners

Combine red pasqueflowers with spring bulbs such as the yellow-and-white *Tulipa tarda*, dwarf narcissus 'Minnow', blue grape hyacinth (*Muscari armeniacum*), or Siberian squill (*Scilla sibirica*). Complementary small perennials include *Primula auricula* and *P. denticulata*, alpine or dwarf columbines, white rock cress (*Arabis caucasica*), and blue-flowered speedwell (*Veronica pectinata*).

Collectors' Choice

Gardeners should visit nurseries that specialize in native plants for this prairie treasure.

- *Pulsatilla patens* (15 cm, 6 in.), prairie crocus, comes alive with cup-shaped, lavender or purple blooms in early spring. The prairie crocus is the floral emblem of Manitoba and South Dakota.

Anemones are closely related to pasqueflowers (in fact, the genus *Pulsatilla* was once part of the *Anemone* genus). Provide winter mulch for all anemones.

- *Anemone blanda* (15 cm, 6 in.), Grecian

"The prairie crocus is a perfect symbol promising that, no matter what our winter is like, spring is invincible. Pure joy!"

KATHERINE CLAGGETT
CARMAN, MANITOBA

windflower, grows from tubers and has ferny foliage and white, pink, or blue flowers in late spring.

- *Anemone canadensis* (15 cm, 6 in.), meadow anemone, produces white flowers in late spring and early summer. Good for naturalizing, this anemone spreads by rhizomes.

- *Anemone nemerosa* (15 cm, 6 in.), wood anemone, has white, pale pink, or lavender-blue flowers and spreads by rhizomes. Since it will go dormant after flowering in the spring, tuck it among later-blooming small perennials.

- *Anemone sylvestris* (30 cm, 12 in.), snowdrop anemone, has attractive dark green foliage and produces scented, 5-cm (2-in.), white flowers in spring. In addition to spreading by underground stems, it also self-seeds readily.

- *Anemone tomentosa* (sometimes sold as *Anemone vitifolia* 'Robustissima') (90 cm, 36 in.), Japanese anemone, blooms in late summer until frost. The showy pink or white flowers are arranged in clusters. Some prairie gardeners report success with these lovely fall flowers, but they are of borderline hardiness in particularly cold or exposed areas.

Quercus macrocarpa
(*kwair*-kuss ma-crow-*car*-pah)

Bur oak, Mossy cup oak

The genus *Quercus* is named from the Latin word for the cork oak, a European species. It includes approximately 600 deciduous and evergreen species of trees and a few shrubs. Oaks are native to the Northern Hemisphere and are usually characterized by deeply lobed leaves and acorns, once an important food source.

Ancient and venerable trees, oaks are synonymous with strength and can live for centuries. In fact, the word "robust" has its root in the Latin word for a species that provided hard wood, *Quercus rober*, the tree we now call the English or European oak. The noble oak's size and longevity are inspirational, and sacred groves of oak have served as outdoor temples for many peoples; perhaps the best known oak worshippers were the Druids, Celtic priests in Britain and Gaul.

Although common in many parts of North America, oaks have not been planted extensively on the prairies. Undoubtedly this will change as more prairie gardeners discover the fine qualities of the bur oak.

Portrait
The hardiest oak for the prairies is indisputably the majestic bur oak (*Quercus macrocarpa*). With its high, oval shape, sturdy trunk, and strong, twisted branches, bur oak is a splendid sight both summer and winter. The large leaves are lobed and rounded at the tip, glossy green above and lighter gray beneath, turning yellow in fall.

A conspicuous feature of the bur oak is its sizeable acorns, which can be 2.5 cm (1 in.) long. They contribute to both the common and species names of this oak; both "bur" and "mossy-cup" refer to the fringes on the acorn case, while *macrocarpa* means "large fruit." The sweet-tasting acorns are beloved by squirrels and other wildlife, as well as by livestock.

Bur oak is native to much of eastern North America. It is also found on the prairies as far north as Manitoba and south-eastern Saskatchewan.

Where to Grow
Bur oak is a slow-growing tree that will eventually become very large and may live for 400 years. Choose a location with plenty of space; it is an ideal shade tree for rural gardens or for parks. Planting bur oak on your property or in your community is a legacy to gardeners yet unborn.

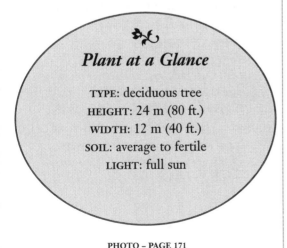

Plant at a Glance

TYPE: deciduous tree
HEIGHT: 24 m (80 ft.)
WIDTH: 12 m (40 ft.)
SOIL: average to fertile
LIGHT: full sun

PHOTO – PAGE 171

How to Grow

A hardy tree, bur oak adapts to a wide range of soils and climates, and even withstands city pollution. Plant it in a sunny location and water regularly until it is established. It has a deep taproot and is drought tolerant. The nature of the root system means that bur oaks should be transplanted as small trees, preferably with a caliper (trunk diameter) of less than 5 cm (2 in.). Container-grown trees purchased from nurseries are root pruned to make them easier to handle and to encourage lateral branching of the roots. Prune this oak in late winter while the tree is still dormant.

These mighty oaks will indeed grow from small acorns when they are sown immediately, but if you wish to relax under the shade of your bur oak tree in your lifetime, it is advised that you buy a larger specimen.

Perfect Partners

Bur oaks are so deep-rooted that they offer little competition to surrounding plants or lawns. They are ideal trees for underplanting with annuals, perennials, or even small shrubs.

Collectors' Choice

Although bur oak is the best choice for prairie gardeners, if you are an adventurous Zone 3 gardener, you may wish to experiment with the red oak.

§ *Quercus rubra* (20 m, 65 ft.), red oak, has pointed, lobed leaves and splendid red fall color. The red oak may be sold as the northern red oak, *Q. borealis*.

Elegant, vase-shaped elms are traditional boulevard and shade trees that have been decimated by Dutch elm disease across much of North America, including parts of the prairies. American elms (*Ulmus americana*) are most affected; Siberian elms (*U. pumila*) are less vulnerable but can still

"The bur oak has great cut leaves and a wonderful texture that distinguishes it in a city landscape full of elms like Regina. It is a beautiful, large shade tree that is extremely long-lived and should have a place in everyone's garden."

KIMBERLY BROWN
REGINA, SASKATCHEWAN

be afflicted. Gardeners with these trees on their properties are encouraged to familiarize themselves with the symptoms of Dutch elm disease. Fortunately, there is a very promising new selection of elm that is resistant to this disease.

§ *Ulmus davidiana* var. *japonica* 'Discovery' is a hardy elm developed by Rick Durand in Portage la Prairie, Manitoba. Approximately 30 percent smaller than the American elm, it is upright with symmetrical branching. Mature trees display the characteristic American elm vase shape. 'Discovery' elm grows in sun or part sun, and adapts to a variety of soil conditions. It has yet to be extensively tested in the Chinook zone, but has performed well elsewhere on the prairies.

Rosa 'Winnipeg Parks'
(*rob*-zah)

Hardy shrub rose

For sheer romance and passion in the garden, roses are the answer; few of us can resist their delicious fragrance and perfect beauty. Roses are undeniably the most popular flowers of the Western world. Legends and rose symbolism abound in mythology, religion, art, and literature, and in Canada alone, over 38 million roses are sold as cut flowers every year!

Gardeners have long succumbed to the myth that roses don't do well on the prairies, and, indeed, familiar tender roses of more moderate climes (hybrid tea, grandiflora, floribunda) require serious attention to survive harsh prairie winters. However, hardy shrub roses are no more difficult to grow than other shrubs. Prairie gardeners have long known that such standards as 'Thérèse Bugnet', 'Blanc Double de Coubert', and the Altai rose (*Rosa pimpinellifolia* var. *altaica*) produce blossoms as fragrant and as exquisite as those of their tender relatives.

Over the past decades, Canadian rose breeders have produced many other beautiful shrub roses suited to northern prairie habitats. The Explorer and Parkland Series, especially, appeal to both novice and experienced gardeners alike. Not only are they dazzling, hardy, and easy to grow, but many are also fragrant, disease resistant, and feature long periods of continuous bloom rather than the single, short flushes of extravagant color common to other shrub roses.

Portrait

'Winnipeg Parks' is a complex hybrid in the Parkland Series that produces clusters of slightly fragrant, double, dark pink blossoms from early summer to frost. For sheer staying power, you can't beat this plant. It also has very attractive matte green leaves that are tinted red in cool weather, especially in fall.

Where to Grow

Tuck 'Winnipeg Parks' into a perennial or mixed border, or include it as part of a collection in a dedicated rose garden. You can also grow it as a showy hedge or feature it in a large summer container, as long as you heel it into the ground before winter.

How to Grow

For best flower production, plant 'Winnipeg Parks' in fertile, moist, well-drained soil, in a sheltered spot that receives 8 to 10 hours of direct sunlight; without enough light, growth will be spindly and flowers sparse. An annual top

Plant at a Glance

TYPE: deciduous shrub
HEIGHT: 76 cm (30 in.)
WIDTH: 76 cm (30 in.)
SOIL: fertile, moist, well drained
LIGHT: full sun
FLOWERING TIME: early summer to fall

PHOTO – PAGE 171

dressing of compost or well-rotted manure in early spring gives this rose all the nutrition it needs. If you use a commercial rose food, stop feeding in mid-August to allow the plant to harden off for winter.

Deadhead 'Winnipeg Parks' to encourage continuous bloom. However, stop deadheading toward the end of summer so that rosehips can form, signalling it's time for the plant to prepare for winter.

Prune this shrub when leaf buds begin to swell in the spring, removing winter tip kill, crossing branches, and old, woody canes.

The only winter protection that 'Winnipeg Parks' requires is organic mulch spread around its base to help moderate soil temperatures during harsh winters.

'Winnipeg Parks' foliage shows good resistance to powdery mildew and blackspot; however, be vigilant and remove and destroy infected leaves as soon as they appear. Provide good air circulation and bottom-water early in the day to help prevent these and similar diseases.

Perfect Partners
The dark pink blossoms of 'Winnipeg Parks' are enchanting juxtaposed with purplish blue-flowering plants such as delphinium, stiff beardtongue (*Penstemon strictus*), bellflower (*Campanula* spp.), sage (*Salvia* spp.), love-in-a-mist (*Nigella damascena*), forget-me-nots (*Myosotis* spp.), and alpine scabiosa.

Collectors' Choice
The following hybrids belong to the Parkland and Explorer Series of hardy shrub roses.

§ For a small garden, choose roses that reach no more than 90 cm (36 in.) tall: 'Charles Albanel' (fragrant, medium red), 'Frontenac' (fragrant, double, deep pink), 'George Vancouver' (abundant, double, medium red), 'Henry Hudson'

"'Winnipeg Parks' is a beautiful double, dark pink to red rose that overwinters well and has shiny foliage that is resistant to blackspot. I have found that this small shrub rose establishes easily in a sunny location and produces many flowers over the summer."

JOCK MATHIESON
OLDS, ALBERTA

(fragrant, double, white), 'John Franklin' (double, medium red), 'J. P. Connell' (very fragrant, double, pale yellow), 'Morden Amorette' (double, deep pink), 'Morden Blush' (fragrant, double, ivory with soft pink centers), 'Morden Cardinette' (double, cardinal red), 'Morden Fireglow' (double, bright scarlet), 'Simon Fraser' (profuse, semi-double, medium pink).

§ For a large garden, choose hardy shrub roses over 90 cm (36 in.) tall: 'Alexander McKenzie' (fragrant, double, medium red), 'Champlain' (double, dark red), 'Cuthbert Grant' (semi-double, crimson), 'David Thompson' (fragrant, double, deep fuchsia), 'Jens Munk' (fragrant, double, medium pink), 'Martin Frobisher' (fragrant, double, light pink), 'Morden Centennial' (fragrant, double, medium pink, in clusters), 'Morden Ruby' (double, pink speckled with red).

§ True climbing roses are not prairie hardy; however, the following tall hardy shrub roses may be tied to supports to give the effect of a climbing rose: 'Henry Kelsey' (fragrant, double, medium red), 'John Cabot' (fragrant, double, deep cherry-pink), 'John Davis' (fragrant, double, medium pink), 'William Baffin' (semi-double, deep pink, in large clusters).

Rudbeckia fulgida var. *sullivantii* 'Goldsturm'

(rude-*beck*-ee-ah *full*-gi-dah var. sull-i-*van*-tee-ee)

Rudbeckia, Coneflower

Bold and beautiful, golden rudbeckias are bright stars in the late-summer and autumn garden. Sun-loving rudbeckias are upright, clump-forming plants that bloom generously until hard frost, all the while attracting butterflies and other beneficial insects. Deer-proof and virtually pest and disease free, they are the perfect prairie plant. This genus of North American natives includes perennials, biennials, and annuals, all commonly called black-eyed Susans or coneflowers.

Carl Linnaeus, the father of modern botanical nomenclature, named the genus *Rudbeckia* after an illustrious pair of Swedish botanists. Olof Rudbeck lived from 1630 to 1702, and founded the Uppsala Botanic Garden. His son, Olof Rudbeck the younger, lived from 1660 to 1740, and was a professor at Uppsala University and a patron of Linnaeus. Father and son were responsible for pro-

ducing a volume of all the then-known plants, complete with thousands of woodcuts. Unfortunately, it was destroyed in a disastrous fire that burned much of Uppsala in 1702.

Rudbeckia fulgida, the orange coneflower, is a well-known and long-lived perennial species. The hardiest and most versatile rudbeckia for prairie conditions, it aptly derives its species name from the Latin word for "shining."

Portrait

Rudbeckia fulgida var. *sullivantii* 'Goldsturm' is a sturdy, compact perennial with rough, dark green, oval- to lance-shaped leaves. The branching, stiff stems bear 8-cm (3-in.), daisylike flowers with dark brown centers composed of disk florets, and golden yellow ray petals. 'Goldsturm' is a superb and long-lasting cut flower, and the seed heads may be dried for use in flower arrangements.

Although 'Goldsturm' was developed in Germany in the late 1930s, it has only become popular in North America since the 1980s. In 1999 it was named the Perennial Plant of the Year by the Perennial Plant Association.

Other members of this species are *Rudbeckia fulgida* var. *speciosa* (76 cm, 30 in.), and 'Pot of Gold' and 'Viette's Little Suzy' (40 cm, 16 in.), which look like dwarf 'Goldsturm'.

Where to Grow

Mass-plant 'Goldsturm' for a stunning

Plant at a Glance

TYPE: perennial
HEIGHT: 60 cm (24 in.)
WIDTH: 60 cm (24 in.)
SOIL: average to fertile, well drained
LIGHT: full to part sun
FLOWERING TIME: mid-summer to fall

PHOTO – PAGE 125

effect, or integrate small groups into perennial or mixed borders. It is also an ideal candidate for a cutting garden, or a natural prairie garden.

How to Grow

'Goldsturm' prefers a warm, sunny, location and well-drained soil high in organic matter. It is moderately drought tolerant once established, but also thrives in moist soil.

Deadhead to tidy the plant and to prevent self-seeding, unless you wish to allow some of the seed heads to remain to beautify the winter garden. Divide clumps every three or four years in the spring. Unlike many cultivars, 'Goldsturm' can be grown from seed, although the resultant plants may be more variable than those propagated by division.

Perfect Partners

Plant 'Goldsturm' with purple coneflower (*Echinacea purpurea*) and ornamental grasses such as *Molinia caerulea* 'Moorhexe' to achieve the look of a prairie meadow. Suitable border companions include *Sedum* 'Autumn Joy', Russian sage (*Perovskia atriplicifolia*), sea holly (*Eryngium* spp.), asters, yarrow (*Achillea* spp.), hardy garden mums, 'Starfire' red phlox, and *Verbena bonariensis*.

Collectors' Choice

When purchasing rudbeckias, check labels carefully so that you know whether you are buying a perennial species or one that must be grown as an annual on the prairies.

- *Rudbeckia hirta*, gloriosa daisy, is a biennial or short-lived perennial commonly grown as an annual. The species has orange-yellow ray petals around a dark brown center. Cultivars may be double or single, with golden or yellow flowers, some marked with mahogany or

bronze streaks. Some of the best are: 'Indian Summer' (90 cm, 36 in.), huge, single and semi-double, golden yellow blooms with black centers; 'Goldilocks' (60 cm, 24 in.), double, golden yellow flowers; 'Toto' and 'Becky', dwarf, single-flowered cultivars (25 cm, 10 in.).

- *Rudbeckia laciniata* (1.8 m, 6 ft.), ragged or green-headed coneflower, is a perennial species with deeply cut or lobed leaves, and yellow ray petals drooping from a green center. 'Golden Glow' is a king-sized rudbeckia with showy double yellow flowers; it may require staking. 'Autumn Sun', also known as 'Herbstsonne' (1.5 m, 5 ft.) has reflexed, wide, yellow ray petals. 'Golddrop', also called 'Goldquelle' (90 cm, 36 in.) is compact, with double, yellow blooms.

There are many perennial yellow daisies suited to prairie gardens. Inula has a more delicate flower than most members of this assertive group.

- *Inula ensifolia* (30 cm, 12 in.), swordleaf inula, has narrow, yellow ray petals, a golden disk, and small, lance-shaped leaves. *I. hookeri* (76 cm, 30 in.) has a fringe of fine, yellow ray petals, a golden disk, and coarser leaves. Inula prefers moist, well-drained soil, and thrives in sun or light shade.

Salix silicola 'Polar Bear'

(*say*-licks sill-ee-*ko*-lah)

Willow

Although willow trees do not suit the growing conditions that prevail in the average prairie garden—they crave big space and big water—the opposite is true for shrub willows. They tolerate a much wider range of soil and moisture conditions than their stately cousins, and their fluffy catkins, handsome foliage, and brightly colored bark make them welcome additions to any mixed or shrub border.

Willows have long been the source of the catkins or "palms" collected by children to decorate churches on Palm Sunday. Their bark was also used for centuries by Egyptians, Greeks, and even North American Natives to cure fevers, headaches, and toothaches. Salicin, the active ingredient in willow bark that brought relief to the ancients, served as inspiration for a large German pharmaceutical company to formulate a synthetic equivalent. The result, of course, was Aspirin (acetylsalicylic acid)—the most widely used synthetic drug ever created.

Portrait
'Polar Bear' shrub willow, a fast-growing, non-spreading, Canadian introduction, does its namesake proud; from tip to toe, it has a furry look and feel to it. It is a striking, multi-stemmed shrub consisting of hairy, slender, flexible branches festooned with silvery white, linear foliage that is also soft and hairy. Before the leaves appear, the entire shrub is covered in large, fuzzy catkins that mimic the equally fuzzy stems.

Where to Grow
Plant 'Polar Bear' as a tall accent shrub at the back of mixed or shrub borders. It also looks natural and elegant at the edge of a pond, or in any low-lying wet area where not much else will grow.

How to Grow
'Polar Bear' prefers fertile, moist, well-drained soil, although it will tolerate a wide range of soil conditions and short periods of drought, once established. It enjoys basking in full sun to light shade. As for all trees and shrubs, Chinook zone gardeners should ensure that 'Polar Bear' is especially well watered until freeze-up. A winter mulch around the shrub is also helpful.

For this and other shrub willows, regular removal of dead, diseased, or damaged branches should take place in late winter

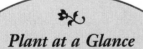

Plant at a Glance

TYPE: deciduous shrub
HEIGHT: 3 m (10 ft.)
WIDTH: 1.5 m (5 ft.)
SOIL: fertile, moist, well drained
LIGHT: full sun to light shade

PHOTO – PAGE 172

or early spring when shrubs are still dormant. Shrub willows also benefit from a hard rejuvenation pruning every three or four years to maintain vibrant branch colors.

Propagate 'Polar Bear' by softwood cuttings in late spring or by hardwood cuttings in winter.

Perfect Partners

In mixed borders, 'Polar Bear' makes a silvery background for perennials that bloom in vivid colors such as dark blue delphiniums, purple bellflowers (*Campanula* spp.), pink, orange, and yellow lilies, or blue Siberian iris.

In shrub borders, group it with such colorful favorites as pink-flowering shrub roses (*Rosa* spp.), purpleleaf sand cherry (*Prunus* x *cistena*), golden elder (*Sambucus* spp.), ninebark (*Physocarpus* spp.), and pink-flowering spireas.

Collectors' Choice

Several shrub willows perform well in urban gardens; they all benefit from rejuvenation pruning to encourage the growth of colorful new shoots. Willows are either male or female; male plants usually produce the showiest catkins.

- *Salix brachycarpa* 'Blue Fox' (1 m, 3.3 ft.) is a lovely tidy, little shrub with branches covered in reddish brown bark and linear, silvery blue foliage. It provides contrast in borders and requires very little pruning.
- *Salix caprea* 'Pendula' (1.8 m, 6 ft.), weeping pussy willow, is almost always grown as a grafted standard. Its long, flexible branches weep down to and trail along the ground. Bare branches are first covered in showy catkins; these are followed by elliptical, toothed leaves that are dark green above and gray-green beneath. Although this shrub is hardy on the prairies, its

"'Polar Bear' willow lights up a dark corner with its warm, fuzzy, silver contrasting foliage. It is undemanding, pest free, fully hardy, and a particular joy in the early spring when most other plants are still dormant."

BIRGITTA MICK
SASKATOON, SASKATCHEWAN

flower buds sometimes succumb to intense cold and hard frosts. In years when this happens, catkins do not develop.

- *Salix exigua* (4 m, 13 ft.), coyote willow, closely resembles bamboo when used in moist to wet locations. The feathery, lance-shaped foliage is silver-gray, lending a graceful air to boggy areas.
- *Salix* 'Flame' (5 m, 16 ft.), flame willow, is a compact shrub that displays golden yellow fall foliage and brilliant orange-red bark in winter. This cultivar does not produce catkins.
- *Salix integra* 'Alba Maculata' (1.5 m, 5 ft.), Hakura Nishiki Japanese willow, is sometimes called white spotted willow. Its wine-red branches and striking foliage, variegated creamy white and green, make a dramatic combination. Although this willow may not be hardy everywhere on the prairies, it is definitely worth a try.
- *Salix purpurea* 'Nana' (1.2 m, 4 ft.), dwarf arctic willow, has straight, non-branching, purplish red stems that produce long, slender catkins in mid-spring, followed by linear, blue-green foliage. Its leaf form and color create a delightful contrast in shrub collections; it also is perfect for a tidy, sheared hedge. 'Nana' dies back to the snow-line.

Sambucus racemosa

(sam-*boo*-kus rah-kay-*moh*-sah)

European red elder

Elders, with their attractive foliage, delicately scented blossoms, and colorful, juicy fruit, are a must for prairie gardens. Whether you grow them strictly for their ornamental value or for their tasty fruit, which makes excellent wine, jams, and jellies, elders are also an excellent source of food and shelter for songbirds. Butterflies, too, rely on their sweet nectar for survival.

In cultivation for centuries, elders have inspired a rich, though often contradictory, folklore. Some believed that burning or cutting elder wood inspired sorcery and witchcraft. Others believed elder wood could be harvested without dire consequences as long as permission was requested and granted from the tree spirits dwelling within. Still others planted elders by the front door to ward off evil spirits and lightning.

However, two things are certain: elders planted by outhouses kept the flies away,

thanks to unique repellent qualities, and elderberries, then as now, make a mighty fine liqueur—the Italian sambuca.

Portrait

The European red elder is an erect, deciduous shrub with slightly arching branches characterized by a rusty-colored pith at the core. Young foliage has a reddish purple tinge that changes to dull green on top and slightly hairy, blue-gray underneath. The leaves are divided into five or seven leaflets and have an unpleasant aroma when rubbed. Legend has it they only acquired this odor after Judas Iscariot hanged himself from an elder tree.

The small, pleasantly scented, pale yellow flowers are arranged in large, conical clusters and appear in late spring. They mature into juicy, pea-sized, bright red elderberries that are edible once cooked or heated. The stone in the fruit, and some other plant parts, are slightly poisonous.

'Redman' is a heavily fruiting selection of the species. Three golden-leaved cultivars are also available: 'Sutherland Golden' is a medium-sized shrub with finely dissected, golden leaves; 'Goldenlocks' is a dwarf, ball-shaped version of 'Sutherland Golden'; and 'Plumosa Aurea' has deeply incised, dull golden foliage.

Where to Grow

Use European red elder as a specimen plant at the back of shrub or mixed borders if it is to be grown to full size or pruned into the shape of a small tree.

Plant at a Glance

TYPE: deciduous shrub
HEIGHT: 4 m (13 ft.)
WIDTH: 3 m (10 ft.)
SOIL: fertile, moist, well drained
LIGHT: full sun to light shade
FLOWERING TIME: late spring

PHOTO – PAGE 172

Move the shrub forward in borders if you plan to keep it pruned to a modest size. It also creates a woodland effect when planted under other trees.

How to Grow

European red elder will grow in almost any soil type but prefers a fertile, moist, well-drained location, in full sun; once established, it is fairly drought tolerant. It tolerates light shade but produces fewer flowers. The golden-leaved varieties need full sun to maintain their intense color, yet will burn if the sun gets too hot.

European red elder is a vigorous grower; to maintain a compact, bushy shrub profile, prune it in early spring before leaves appear. All elders will tolerate severe pruning right back to the ground for rejuvenation or to stimulate growth after winterkill. They are also good subjects for pruning into the shape of a small tree.

Propagate this elder by softwood cuttings in the summer or by hardwood cuttings in the winter. It is also easy to grow from the stone produced by the fruit.

Perfect Partners

Plant European red elder next to woody plants of contrasting color, such as golden ninebark (*Physocarpus opulifolius*), golden variegated dogwood (*Cornus alba* 'Gouchaultii'), or golden-leaved elder cultivars (*Sambucus* spp.). The golden-leaved elders themselves make a lovely contrast with dark green evergreens such as cedar (*Thuja* spp.), junipers (*Juniperus* spp.), and globe spruce (*Picea pungens* f. *glauca* 'Globosa').

Collectors' Choice

Two other species of elder are available to home gardeners.

§ *Sambucus canadensis* (2 m, 6.5 ft.),

"I love the bushy, rounded shape of elder combined with its attractive golden foliage color. In addition, the winter birds love its bright red berries."

LORRAINE BOYLE
SWIFT CURRENT, SASKATCHEWAN

American elder, is a fast-growing, native North American shrub, well suited to an informal or wild garden. Its leaves are each composed of nine or more light green, toothed leaflets; pale white flowers are borne in flattened clusters in early summer and mature into dark purple berries. 'Aurea' is golden-leaved and produces red berries.

§ *Sambucus nigra* (7 m, 23 ft.), black elder, is an upright shrub with leaves composed of five toothed, medium green leaflets. White flowers are musk scented and borne in flattened clusters in early summer. Dark purple fruit suspended on beet red fruit stalks follows in late summer. 'Aurea' has golden foliage; a recent introduction, 'Guincho Purple', has dark purple leaves and pink-tinged flowers with purple stalks. Although both of these elders die back to the ground in prairie winters, they will regrow each year to form compact, colorful shrubs, but will never attain their full and considerable height.

Saxifraga x *urbium* 'Aureopunctata'
(sacks-*iff*-ra-gah x *er*-bee-um)

Saxifrage, Golden London pride

Most of the amazing little saxifrages are native to mountainous regions of the Northern Hemisphere, which explains why every spring they indulge in lavish floral displays that completely overshadow their lovely but lowly, ground-hugging foliage. Alpine plants give a big color bang for the proverbial buck; it ensures their survival during a short growing season in a relatively hostile native habitat. Luckily saxifrage species insist on giving the same sensational performance every spring, whether they are growing in the wild or being cultivated on easy street by attentive gardeners.

The genus name *Saxifraga* derives from two Latin words: *saxum*, meaning "rock," and *frangere*, meaning "to break." Thus, saxifrages are described as "rock breakers," a name that likely evolved because of their natural affinity to rocky places. Their rock-breaking reputation might also stem from a medieval belief that an infusion of saxifrage parts could dissolve kidney, gall, and bladder stones. As interesting as it may be, there is no medical proof for this theory.

Portrait
Saxifraga x *urbium* 'Aureopunctata' is a leafy saxifrage that spreads to form a carpet of large, deep green rosettes splashed with irregular patches of brightest yellow. Individual leaves are fleshy, spoon-shaped, and slightly serrated. In early summer, abundant upright, branching stems boast masses of loosely clustered, tiny, star-shaped, white flowers that are flushed with pale pink and held high above the foliage.

'Miss Chambers', also known as 'Chambers Pink Pride', produces sprays of soft pink, star-shaped flowers.

Where to Grow
Because 'Aureopunctata' and other saxifrages are spectacular in bloom, give them a prominent spot in the garden. They are logical inhabitants for rock gardens, but they also go well at the front of perennial and mixed borders, as an edging along pathways, and as a groundcover in lightly shaded areas.

How to Grow
Plant 'Aureopunctata' in fertile, moist, well-drained soil, in light shade or a sunny spot favored with afternoon shade. Top dress with a thin layer of compost early in the season; deadhead after blossoms fade

Plant at a Glance

TYPE: perennial
HEIGHT: 30 cm (12 in.)
WIDTH: 30 cm (12 in.)
SOIL: fertile, moist, well drained
LIGHT: light shade to part sun
FLOWERING TIME: early summer

PHOTO – PAGE 172

to showcase its exquisite foliage.

The succulent rosettes of 'Aureopunc-tata' are evergreen and must be mulched during winter to protect them from wind-burn, especially in areas of low or no snow cover. Use a generous layer of shredded leaves or a heap of evergreen branches as insulation; this will also protect against frost heaving.

'Aureopunctata' is best propagated after flowering, from early summer on, by detaching rosettes from the parent plant and rooting them as cuttings before replanting them.

Perfect Partners

Plant 'Aureopunctata' with other low-growing groundcovers such as rock jasmine (*Androsace* spp.), pussytoes (*Antennaria* spp.), creeping veronica, and creeping Jacob's ladder (*Polemonium reptans*) to create a tapestry of colors and textures on the garden floor. It also pairs well with spring-blooming foamflower (*Tiarella* spp.), bleeding heart (*Dicentra* spp.), yellow corydalis, and astilbe, as well as making a striking combination with roses.

Collectors' Choice

Of the many saxifrage species and hybrids in cultivation, only some are suitable for growing in the average prairie garden; others require slightly more specialized growing conditions. Most popular among gardeners are the mossy, encrusted, and leafy saxifrages. Those listed here require the same care as 'Aureopunctata'.

- *Saxifraga* x *arendsii* (20 cm, 8 in.), mossy saxifrage, forms spongy hummocks of bright green, delicate, deeply divided foliage. In late spring, masses of short, bare stems sport upward-facing, cup-shaped blossoms in shades of deep red through pink to white. 'Cloth of Gold' forms a carpet of chartreuse

"*Saxifrages are perfect little mat- or cushion-forming plants that do well in rock gardens or the front edge of a well-draining border. Flowers are pretty and a sure sign that the growing season has begun in earnest. Most are easily grown.*"

MICHAEL HICKMAN
EDMONTON, ALBERTA

with white flowers; 'Bob Hawkins' has variegated foliage (green and white) with white flowers in spring; 'Apple Blossom' has pale pink flower buds that open to white.

- *Saxifraga cotyledon* (60 cm, 24 in.), pyramidal or Jungfrau saxifrage, forms rosettes of pale green, lance-shaped leaves with lime-encrusted teeth. In early summer, pyramid-shaped panicles of white, cup-shaped flowers, veined in red, are held high above the foliage. The very popular 'Southside Seedling' has white cup-shaped flowers, heavily spotted in red.

- *Saxifraga* x *geum* (20 cm, 8 in.), kidneyleaf saxifrage, is a leafy saxifrage that forms broad rosettes of leathery, spoon-shaped leaves, topped in mid-summer with sprays of tiny, white flowers, spotted in red or yellow, on slender stems.

- *Saxifraga paniculata* (15 cm, 6 in.), encrusted saxifrage, forms gray-green rosettes of toothed, spoon-shaped leaves that are rimmed with an interesting deposit of pale white lime. The rosettes form a cushion that is topped with tall, branching stems smothered in creamy white, cup-shaped flowers. Once a rosette has bloomed, it dies, but offshoot rosettes are always on standby, spreading easily to fill the gaps.

Scabiosa columbaria 'Butterfly Blue'

(scab-ee-*oh*-sah call-um-*bear*-ee-ah)

Scabiosa, Small scabious

It is interesting to contemplate why a flower as lovely as the old-fashioned scabiosa has been tagged with such an unlovely botanical designation. Its name derives from the Latin *scabies*, meaning "scruff" or "itch," and scabiosa's hairy leaves were indeed used to relieve and cure scab-forming itch and mange in days gone by. But why focus on such a utilitarian aspect of its heritage, when there is much else about the pretty scabiosa to attract attention? Its large, flat, saucer-shaped flowers with their fascinating pincushion-like centers come in a charming array of gentle pastel colors, making scabiosa the perfect addition to soft romantic groupings in flower borders. When planted in small drifts, it also serves as a delightful transition between neighbors of stronger, sometimes incompatible colors.

Scabiosa is a magnet for ever-helpful bees and butterflies, gardeners' best friends. Sadly, bee and butterfly populations have been declining steadily over the years due to environmental stress and loss of habitat, so gardeners should be making every effort to include plants like scabiosa in their perennial borders to help reverse this trend.

Portrait

'Butterfly Blue' is an attractive cultivar of *Scabiosa columbaria* and has been named the Perennial Plant of the Year for the year 2000. It forms a compact mound of large, dense, finely hairy basal foliage. The gray-green leaves thin out, become more deeply divided, and diminish in size toward the tops of open, upright, wiry stems. Cool lavender-blue, honey-scented flowers are borne singly and are in constant supply all summer long. The relatively flat blooms consist of multiple florets. Large, jagged, overlapping ray florets form an elegant ruffled collar around a central mound of small, densely packed disk florets. Dark stamens protrude from the central mound like pins from a pincushion, hence, its common name of pincushion flower.

'Pink Mist' is another fine *Scabiosa columbaria* cultivar. It is similar to 'Butterfly Blue' but sports delicate lavender-pink flower heads over long periods in the summer. Both cultivars make wonderful cut flowers.

Where to Grow

Plant 'Butterfly Blue' in a cottage garden or a cutting garden, or in the front to middle range of perennial and mixed borders.

Plant at a Glance

TYPE: perennial
HEIGHT: 45 cm (18 in.)
WIDTH: 30 cm (12 in.)
SOIL: average to fertile, moist, very well drained
LIGHT: full sun to light shade
FLOWERING TIME: early summer to fall

PHOTO – PAGE 172

How to Grow

'Butterfly Blue', like all scabiosas, prefers a sunny location and average to fertile, moist soil. Perfect drainage is also critical; this can be achieved by using raised beds (mounded dirt or specially constructed) and then adding generous amounts of sand or grit to the soil in the planting hole. Putting humus-rich compost in the planting hole provides nourishment and stores essential moisture to be used by the plant as needed. An organic mulch around the plant also helps conserve moisture.

Deadhead 'Butterfly Blue' on a regular basis to promote abundant flowering and to prevent self-seeding.

Flower production diminishes as plants mature but can be stimulated again by dividing and replanting established clumps in the spring. This is also the best way to propagate this cultivar.

Perfect Partners

'Butterfly Blue' is lovely combined with yellow-blooming yarrow (*Achillea* spp.), sneezeweed (*Helenium autumnale*), false sunflower (*Heliopsis helianthoides*), black-eyed Susan (*Rudbeckia* spp.), and goldenrod (*Solidago* spp.). It also heightens the romantic appeal of pink-flowered hardy roses, purple coneflower (*Echinacea purpurea*), dianthus, veronica, and phlox.

Collectors' Choice

Other scabiosas suitable for mixed borders are similar in appearance and habit to *Scabiosa columbaria*.

- 🌢 *Scabiosa atropurpurea* (90 cm, 36 in.) is a lovely annual scabiosa that produces solitary, fragrant, dark purple to lilac flower heads above a clump of medium green basal foliage.
- 🌢 *Scabiosa caucasica* (60 cm, 24 in.), the most well-known garden scabiosa, has gray-green basal leaves and solitary, pale blue, lavender, or white flower

heads that are 8 cm (3 in.) across. Cultivars worth trying include: 'Bressingham White' (clear white), 'Clive Greaves' (lavender-blue with white centers), 'Fama' (compact with strong blue, silver-centered flowers), 'Floral Queen' (violet-blue), 'Miss Wilmott' (creamy white), and 'Moerheim Blue' (dark blue).

- 🌢 *Scabiosa graminifolia* (25 cm, 10 in.) forms low, evergreen clumps of silver-green, grassy foliage and single, lilac-violet, saucer-shaped flowers.
- 🌢 *Scabiosa lucida* (20 cm, 8 in.) is similar to *S. graminifolia* but shorter.

Two equally lovely plants with scabiouslike flowers are worthy garden additions. *Cephalaria gigantea* and *Knautia macedonica*, both classified as *Scabiosa* at one time, thrive in fertile, moist, very well-drained soil, in a sunny spot.

- 🌢 *Cephalaria gigantea* (2.5 m, 8 ft.), formerly *Scabiosa gigantea* or *S. tartarica*, grows into a large clump of towering, thick stems topped by 6-cm (2.5-in.), primrose yellow, saucer-shaped flowers.
- 🌢 *Knautia macedonica* (60 cm, 24 in.), formerly *Scabiosa rumelica*, has unusual deep burgundy flowers that add a unique touch to flower borders.

Scilla sibirica 'Spring Beauty'
(skee-lah sy-bee-ri-kah)

Siberian squill, Bluebells

At a time when few other plants have emerged from hibernation, the enchanting blue bells of *Scilla sibirica* lift the spirits of all prairie dwellers longing for spring. Gardeners who nostalgically yearn for English bluebells, which are not hardy on the prairies, should waste no time in adding these small treasures to their gardens.

The genus name *Scilla* is derived from the Greek *skilla*, the name for sea squill. At least five members of this genus, which like the English bluebell belong to the *Liliaceae* family, are known to have been in cultivation at the end of the sixteenth century, when the plants were used for medicinal purposes and for producing starch to stiffen Elizabethan collars.

Among the 80 members of the genus, *Scilla sibirica* is the most widely cultivated. Native to southern Russia, the Caucasus, and western Asia, they are among the hardiest and most desirable of spring bulbs, blooming reliably and spreading their patches of intense blue wider each year.

Portrait

'Spring Beauty' bursts forth each April with straplike, emerald green basal leaves above which rise spikes of loosely arrayed, deep blue, nodding bells. Individual flowers resemble dainty fairies' caps, with each of the six flared petals marked with a deeper blue stripe. You may also see 'Spring Beauty' sold as 'Atrocaerulea'. *Scilla sibirica* var. *taurica* is a lighter blue form.

Gardeners who love the cool purity of a white spring garden should try *Scilla sibirica* var. *alba*, perhaps in combination with white crocus, snowdrops, narcissus, hepatica, and rock cress (*Arabis* spp.).

Where to Grow

Plant 'Spring Beauty' in perennial beds and rock gardens, on banks, and beside pathways. It's a perfect, easy-to-grow little plant for naturalizing under deciduous trees and shrubs.

How to Grow

'Spring Beauty' prefers a sunny spot with average to fertile, well-drained soil. Plant the bulbs in early fall about 8 cm (3 in.) deep, and a similar distance apart. Like all spring-flowering bulbs, after blooming is finished the foliage should be left intact until it has died back. The small leaves of

Plant at a Glance

TYPE: hardy bulb
HEIGHT: 15 cm (6 in.)
WIDTH: 5 cm (6 in.)
SOIL: average to fertile, well drained
LIGHT: full to part sun
FLOWERING TIME: spring

PHOTO – PAGE 173

Siberian squill are much tidier and easier to disguise that those of larger bulbs.

'Spring Beauty' will increase by bulb offsets, often forming large clumps that may be dug up and divided if desired, although they will bloom cheerfully for years, left undisturbed.

Perfect Partners

Although generous drifts of 'Spring Beauty' are striking on their own, the deep blue, nodding bells are complemented beautifully by dwarf narcissus, snowdrops (*Galanthus* spp.), and glory-of-the-snow (*Chionodoxa luciliae*). In a rock garden, plant them with brightly colored Iceland poppies (*Papaver croceum*) and rock cress (*Arabis* spp.).

Collectors' Choice

Siberian squill is not the only prairie-hardy *Scilla* species.

- *Scilla bifolia* (20 cm, 8 in.) has starry turquoise blue, white, pink, or violet blue flowers.
- *Scilla mischtschenkoana* (syn. *Scilla tubergeniana*) (15 cm, 6 in.) produces small spikes of pale blue flowers, each striped with darker blue.

Many other equally lovely and undemanding spring-flowering bulbs are available.

- *Fritillaria pudica* (15 cm, 6 in.), the yellow fritillary, is native to the prairies and bears drooping, yellow or orange bells. Intolerant of excessive moisture, it is suited to a rock garden with well-drained soil. *F. pallidiflora* (30 cm, 12 in.), the Siberian fritillary, has soft yellow, bell-shaped flowers with red checkering inside. *F. meleagris* (30 cm, 12 in.) is also known as the snake's head fritillary, or checkered lily. Like the other fritillaries, it has pendant, bell-shaped flowers with characteristic checkering within. Although the species are usually purple or pink, there

are several cultivars: 'Alba' and 'Aphrodite' (white), 'Poseidon' (white with purple veining), 'Artemis' (purple-gray), 'Charon' (deep purple), and 'Saturnus' (red-purple). *F. meleagris* is native to English meadows and woodlands, and prefers fertile, moist, heavy soil. Mulching is advised if snow cover is inadequate.

- *Muscari armeniacum* (20 cm, 8 in.), commonly known as grape hyacinth, produces spikes of tubular, blue flowers with white mouths that resemble clusters of grapes. The leaves are basal and grassy. *M. botryoides* is similar and has white and pink forms. *M. latifolium* (25 cm, 10 in.), sometimes known as Oxford and Cambridge, has two-tone flower clusters—the bottom half is dark purple, the top half a paler shade. *M. comosum* 'Plumosum' (25 cm, 10 in.) is even more unusual, with purple, threadlike clusters of flowers.
- *Puschkinia scilloides* (15 cm, 6 in.), striped squill, has spikes of dainty, bell-shaped flowers of the palest blue with darker stripes. *P. s.* var. *libanotica* 'Alba' is a white variety.

"The little blue flowers of Siberian squill are so sweet and hopeful—they are the first blooms in my garden every spring!"

HELEN BUCHANAN
BATTLEFORD, SASKATCHEWAN

Sedum 'Autumn Joy'

(*see*-dum)

Showy sedum, Showy stonecrop

Versatile sedums have a host of endearing characteristics. Not only do they produce bright masses of blooms, but also succulent foliage that is attractive from spring to fall. They are low-maintenance, drought-tolerant perennials, untroubled by pests and diseases. Many are highly attractive to butterflies and bees, and some are even fragrant.

The generic name comes from the Latin *sedo*, "to sit," a reference to their manner of growth on rocks and walls. Low-growing types make ideal groundcovers and are suitable for rock gardens. Upright, clump-forming sedums are attractive border perennials.

Portrait

Sedum 'Autumn Joy', also known by its German name 'Herbstfreude', has fleshy, toothed leaves on sturdy stems topped with slightly rounded flower clusters. The developing flower heads add a pale green hue to the border before opening into tiny, pink, star-shaped blooms. Over the late summer and early fall, the flowers deepen to burgundy, and finally turn bronze. Fall flower arrangements will glow with the addition of a few bright stems of 'Autumn Joy'.

Where to Grow

Plant 'Autumn Joy' in groups or as a specimen plant in the middle of perennial borders.

How to Grow

Well behaved and easy to grow, 'Autumn Joy' tolerates all but excessively wet soil conditions. This congenial perennial performs best in full sun, and average to fertile, well-drained soil.

'Autumn Joy' does not require frequent watering and bears up well during hot, dry summers. Fertilizing is unnecessary; in fact, excessive nitrogen may cause stems to become floppy and weak.

Many gardeners leave the flower heads in place to add texture to the winter garden. Plants may be cut back to the ground in early spring.

Propagate by division or stem cuttings. Unless these plants become too large they do not require regular division and may be left undisturbed for many years.

Perfect Partners

'Autumn Joy' is a glorious addition to any collection of late-blooming perennials.

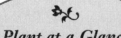

Plant at a Glance

TYPE: perennial
HEIGHT: 60 cm (24 in.)
WIDTH: 60 cm (24 in.)
SOIL: average to fertile, well drained
LIGHT: full sun
FLOWERING TIME: late summer to fall

PHOTO – PAGE 173

Plant it beside 'Audrey' or 'Professor Kippenberg' asters, hardy garden mums, rudbeckia, purple coneflower (*Echinacea purpurea*), Russian sage (*Perovskia atriplicifolia*), and ornamental grasses, particularly blue oat grass (*Helictotrichon sempervirens*). It is also brilliant next to gray- or silver-leaved plants, such as 'Valerie Finnis' artemisia.

Collectors' Choice

From perennial border to rockery, there is a low-maintenance sedum to fit any niche in the garden.

- ❧ *Sedum acre* (8 cm, 3 in.), also called goldmoss or golddust stonecrop, is a creeping sedum with tiny, evergreen leaves and yellow flowers in early summer. It can become invasive and is best kept out of rock gardens. 'Aureum' has bright yellow leaves.

- ❧ *Sedum* x 'Bertram Anderson' (20 cm, 8 in.) forms spreading clumps of dark burgundy leaves crowned with purple-red flowers in mid to late summer.

- ❧ *Sedum kamtschaticum* (15 cm, 6 in.) has dark green, toothed leaves and produces golden yellow flowers all summer. 'Variegatum' (25 cm, 10 in.) has attractive cream, green, and pink variegated leaves and orange-yellow flowers.

- ❧ *Sedum* x 'Mohrchen' (45 cm, 18 in.) has burgundy foliage and pink flowers in late summer.

- ❧ *Sedum sieboldii* (23 cm, 9 in.), also called October daphne, has pink-edged, blue-green leaves and pink flowers. It is one of the latest-blooming of the low-growing sedums. 'Mediovariegatum' (15 cm, 6 in.) has cream and blue-green variegated leaves.

- ❧ *Sedum spectabile* (50 cm, 20 in.), showy stonecrop, has blue-green foliage and 10-cm (4-in.) flower clusters in late summer. There are several outstanding cultivars including: 'Brilliant', which is similar to 'Autumn Joy' but with brighter mauve-pink flowers; 'Carmen', dark carmine pink; and 'Stardust', which has paler green foliage and white flowers.

- ❧ *Sedum spurium* (15 cm, 6 in.), or two row stonecrop, forms low mats of rounded leaves and produces abundant flowers in summer. 'Dragon's Blood' (10 cm, 4 in.) has reddish purple leaves and rose-red flowers. 'Ruby Mantle' (15 cm, 6 in.) has red foliage and cerise flowers.

- ❧ *Sedum* x 'Vera Jameson' (30 cm, 12 in.) is a popular low-growing sedum with red-purple foliage and pink flowers in late summer.

Another popular sun-loving succulent for the prairie garden offers delightful foliage shape and color, which is particularly appealing to very young gardeners.

- ❧ *Sempervivum* hybrids (up to 8 cm, 3 in.), also called hen and chicks or houseleeks, are hardy little plants that grow in evergreen rosettes surrounded by smaller rosettes, the "chicks." They are available with pointed or rounded leaves and in many shades of green, red, and purple. Cobweb varieties (*S. arachnoideum*) have silvery hairs. Mature plants die after producing flower stalks topped with star-shaped flowers, although the "chicks" live on.

> *"When everything else is frozen in the fall, 'Autumn Joy' sedum and Morden mums are at their best. Their colors blend with the autumn leaves, keeping the border aglow for a few more weeks."*
>
> CAROL CLEGG
> LAC DU BONNET, MANITOBA

Shepherdia argentea

(shep-*ur*-dee-ah are-*jen*-tee-ah)

Silver buffaloberry

Some prairie gardens are lush little microclimates where skilled and single-minded gardeners miraculously coax into bloom plants that really have no business at all growing here. If this describes your garden, don't even think of planting a silver buffaloberry (*Shepherdia argentea*). On the other hand, if you have a large, windswept lot, or a sun-scorched acreage or farm, this rugged native shrub will settle in happily.

The small *Shepherdia* genus consists of three species of North American shrubs. It was named for John Shepherd (1764–1836), curator of the Liverpool Botanic Gardens. The species name *argentea*, means "silvery." Buffaloberry fruit was mixed with bison meat by the Native peoples of the North American plains, thus, the common name.

Plant at a Glance

TYPE: deciduous shrub
HEIGHT: 3 m (10 ft.)
WIDTH: 2 m (6.5 ft.)
SOIL: poor to average, well drained
LIGHT: full sun
FLOWERING TIME: spring

PHOTO – PAGE 173

Portrait

Native from Alberta to Manitoba and down to Nevada, silver buffaloberry is a large, deciduous shrub notable for its narrow, silver-gray foliage and stems tipped with 2.5- to 5-cm (1- to 2-in.) thorns. It has an irregular growth habit and spreads by suckers to form substantial thickets. This shrub produces small, inconspicuous, yellow flowers in the spring and is dioecious—male and female flowers are produced on separate plants. If pollinated by a male plant, a female plant will bear clusters of sour, but edible, red or yellow fruit in mid-summer. The red fruit, in particular, stands in brilliant contrast to the silvery leaves. 'Goldeye' is a yellow-fruited cultivar.

Like legumes, silver buffaloberry fixes atmospheric nitrogen, that is, it converts the nitrogen in the air into a form useable by the plant, thus enriching the surrounding soil.

Where to Grow

Silver buffaloberry is an ideal shelterbelt or barrier shrub, and may be sheared to form a hedge. It provides cover and food for birds in informal plantings. Because of its size and tendency to sucker, it is not recommended for small gardens, although this shrub may be pruned into an interesting tree form that will fit into most urban properties. Alternatively, plant it in a restricted space, for example, between concrete pathways and a driveway, house, or garage. Used as a background, this shrub will add depth to any landscape.

How to Grow

Silver buffaloberry is a low-maintenance shrub that thrives on neglect, scorning such niceties as fertilizer, rich soil, and ample water. Plant it in full sun, in poor to average, well-drained soil. It is tolerant of both alkaline and saline soil, and requires no supplemental water.

Pruning is not usually necessary, but should you wish to trim the shrub, it is best done in late winter or early spring.

Perfect Partners

Silver buffaloberry contrasts beautifully with the dark green to blue-green foliage of Colorado spruce (*Picea pungens*) and Black Hills spruce (*P. glauca* 'Densata'). The flaming fall colors of cotoneaster and saskatoon (*Amelanchier alnifolia*) are also a rich foil to the silver leaves.

Collectors' Choice

A smaller native *Shepherdia* species is more suitable for urban gardens.

- *Shepherdia canadensis* (2 m, 6.5 ft.), russet buffaloberry, has gray-green foliage with brown undersides and yellow flowers, and bears red to orange fruit. It grows in full sun to light shade, but is more compact in habit if planted in a sunny location.

Several other tough, silver-leaved shrubs are tailor-made for large prairie gardens. They are all tolerant of drought, wind, and alkaline and saline soils, preferring poor to average soils and a sunny location. Like buffaloberry, all are nitrogen fixers.

- *Elaeagnus commutata* (2.5 m, 8 ft.), wolf willow or silverberry, is a native prairie plant with silvery white foliage and branches. This upright shrub produces fragrant silver and yellow flowers and small, dry, silver fruit. Because of its suckering, thicket-forming nature, it is best used in natural plantings. If purchased grafted onto Russian olive

rootstock, it will not sucker and may be used in borders.

- *Halimodendron halodendron* (2 m, 6.5 ft.) is commonly called salt tree or Siberian salt tree. A member of the legume family, it has woolly, compound leaves and pretty purplish pink blossoms resembling pea flowers. The salt tree is sometimes sold grafted onto caragana rootstock to reduce suckering. It may be pruned into an attractive single-stemmed, small tree.

- *Hippophae rhamnoides* (4 m, 13 ft.), sea buckthorn or Russian sand-thorn, is a Eurasian native with narrow leaves and sharp thorns. Like the silver buffaloberry, sea buckthorn is dioecious, both male and female plants producing unremarkable small, yellow flowers in spring. If pollinated by the male plants, the females produce large clusters of showy orange fruit that will persist on the shrubs all winter, if not consumed by birds. Sea buckthorn, which has a tendency to sucker profusely, may be grown as a dense shrub or pruned into a tree shape. Cultivars are 'Frugana', 'Hergo', and 'Leikora'.

Sorbus decora 'Grootendorst'

(*sore*-bus day-*cor*-ah)

Showy mountain ash,
Elder-leaf mountain ash

The best garden trees earn their keep during all four seasons of the year. This is certainly true of the mountain ash, which gives the gardener full value with spring blossoms, attractive foliage with fiery fall color, and brightly colored fruit that is retained on the tree until hordes of hungry waxwings descend to pick it clean.

The genus *Sorbus* includes 23 species of mountain ash trees. Most are medium-sized trees distinguished from other members of the genus by leaves that are divided into smaller leaflets. These leaves are termed "pinnate," for their resemblance to the shape of a feather. The conspicuous clusters of fruit are usually orange or red, but in some species they may be pink, yellow, or white. The berries are edible, though not necessarily appetizing.

Like many members of the *Rosaceae* family, mountain ash trees are susceptible to fireblight, a bacterial disease that pro-duces cankers and twigs that appear to have been scorched by fire. Proper sterilization of pruning shears, destruction of infected material, and prudent maintenance of the overall health of trees are all important steps in keeping the disease at bay. But perhaps most important is choosing a fireblight resistant species or cultivar, such as *Sorbus decora* 'Grootendorst'.

Portrait

Sorbus decora 'Grootendorst', the showy or elder-leaf mountain ash, is the hardiest and most fireblight resistant selection for the prairies. By a happy coincidence it is also the most beautiful; indeed, the botanical name may be translated as "showy" or "comely," which also inspires the common name. This is a dense, slow-growing tree with splendid dark green foliage, each compound leaf composed of 11 to 17 leaflets. The flat clusters of white flowers, called corymbs, are up to 11 cm (4.5 in.) across and bloom longer than those of other commonly grown mountain ash species. In addition, the berries are larger and redder than those of other species. In autumn, it is aflame with red and orange foliage.

Where to Grow

'Grootendorst' is a suitable tree for all but very small urban gardens. Use it where light shade is desired, or as a specimen tree that provides year-round interest.

Plant at a Glance

TYPE: deciduous tree
HEIGHT: 8 m (26 ft.)
WIDTH: 5 m (16 ft.)
SOIL: average to fertile, well drained
LIGHT: full to part sun
FLOWERING TIME: spring

PHOTO – PAGE 173

How to Grow

Plant 'Grootendorst' in average to fertile, well-drained soil, in full to part sun. Avoid wet or low-lying locations. Mulch around the tree to conserve moisture, and water well during dry spells.

Prune young trees lightly to shape once they have fully leafed out and finished blooming. They may also be pruned in late winter or early spring while they are still dormant, but some flowers may be sacrificed. Mature trees require very little pruning, except to remove dead or damaged material.

If a mountain ash tree is planted in an extremely sunny location, the smooth bark may suffer sunscald, a winter injury occurring due to the reflection of sun off the snow. This may be avoided either by locating the tree where the trunk is partly shaded during the warmest parts of the day, or by using tree wraps on the trunk during the winter.

Perfect Partners

Plant 'Grootendorst' against a backdrop of evergreens to show off its blazing fall color and the bold red of its berries.

Collectors' Choice

Other commonly available mountain ash species have variable forms that may appeal to prairie gardeners.

- *Sorbus americana* (8 m, 26 ft.), American mountain ash, is the second best choice for hardiness and disease resistance. This tree may be oval crowned, with a single trunk, or may grow in a more spreading form with several stems. American mountain ash bears ivory flowers and scarlet berries, and welcomes autumn with a blaze of red and orange foliage.
- *Sorbus aucuparia* (8 m, 26 ft.) is commonly called European mountain ash or the rowan tree. A single-trunked or

"I like mountain ash because its colorful bark looks great against the snow in winter, it flowers in late spring, and it has red berries for color and the birds. Also, it's not too large for city lots."

NIA MASSEY
SELKIRK, MANITOBA

multi-stemmed tree, it has been grown in North America since the eighteenth century and is readily available across the prairies. This species has an oval to round crown and dark green leaves with gray undersides that change to a pleasing red, orange, or even yellow in fall. It bears creamy white flowers, succeeded by small orange berries. Slightly less hardy than *Sorbus decora* or *Sorbus americana*, it is also more prone to fireblight and sunscald. Nonetheless, there are some very attractive forms of this species. 'Rossica' (8 m, 25 ft.), the Russian mountain ash, has an upright dense form, dark green leaves with toothed edges, and orange-red berries. 'Fastigiata' (6 m, 20 ft.), is a narrow columnar tree with scarlet fruit that spreads only 2 m (6 ft.)—an ideal selection for small gardens.

Spiraea japonica 'Little Princess'
(spy-*ree*-ah ja-*pon*-ih-kah)

Japanese spirea

The beauty and versatility of shrubby spireas is apparent to all who grow them. It's easy to be impressed by the delicate, rosy pink flowers and amazingly colorful foliage of summer-blooming spireas. Happily, spring-blooming varieties are equally appealing, with their flowers of purest white arranged in clusters along the length of slender, arching branches. It doesn't take much to imagine transforming such flower-laden boughs into perfect garlands with no more than a quick snip, twist, tie, and voilà! This image didn't escape the botanist who gave spirea its generic name: *Spiraea* derives from the Greek *speiraira*, which refers to plants used for garlands.

Portrait
Spiraea japonica 'Little Princess' is a compact, mounded, deciduous shrub with jagged, lance-shaped, dark green leaves that are a pale gray-green underneath.

The attractive foliage turns deep red in fall. Tiny, bowl-shaped, rosy pink and white flowers are borne at the ends of branches in early summer, forming flat-topped clusters in which the outer flowers open first.

'Shirobana', also known as 'Shiburi', is a Japanese spirea with a unique flowering habit—it produces flowers in shades of deep red, rose, and white on the same plant and sometimes even within the same flower cluster. Its foliage is also multi-colored in shades of green. Plant it in a sheltered area.

'Golden Princess' produces foliage that starts out bronze-red, changes to bright yellow, and ends up bright red in fall. Bright pink flowers appear in early summer. 'Mertyann' or Dakota Goldflame™ spirea (40 cm, 16 in.) is a dwarf cultivar that retains its yellow leaf color all summer.

Where to Grow
'Little Princess' is a perfect addition to the front of shrub and mixed borders. It also makes a low but attractive hedge or pathway edging.

How to Grow
Plant 'Little Princess' in fertile, moist, well-drained soil, in full sun to light shade. Deadhead flower clusters to help prolong bloom time.

Since this shrub flowers in mid-summer on the current year's growth, prune it back in early spring just as the buds begin to swell.

All spireas, including 'Little Princess', can be propagated by softwood cuttings in summer.

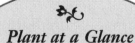

Plant at a Glance

TYPE: deciduous shrub
HEIGHT: 60 cm (24 in.)
WIDTH: 90 cm (36 in.)
SOIL: fertile, moist, well drained
LIGHT: full sun to light shade
FLOWERING TIME: summer

PHOTO – PAGE 174

Perfect Partners

Plant 'Little Princess' as a specimen shrub toward the front of mixed borders, surrounded with contrasting, low-growing perennials such as dianthus, bellflowers (*Campanula* spp.), Iceland poppies (*Papaver croceum*), and coreopsis. In a shrub border, plant 'Little Princess' with shrubs of contrasting foliage such as golden ninebark (*Physocarpus opulifolius*), purpleleaf sand cherry (*Prunus* x *cistena*), or the golden-leaved spireas.

Collectors' Choice

Spring-blooming spireas have tiny, white blossoms produced in showy clusters along the entire length of arching branches. They should be pruned after flowering has stopped.

- *Spiraea* x *arguta* (1.8 m, 6 ft.), garland spirea, produces flat clusters of small, white flowers and bright green, lance-shaped, sharply toothed leaves. 'Compacta' is a condensed version that grows to 1.2 m (4 ft.).
- *Spiraea* x 'Snowhite' (1.2 m, 4 ft.) is similar to bridalwreath spirea but much hardier. It produces tiny, white flowers with prominent stamens.
- *Spiraea trilobata* (90 cm, 36 in.), three-lobed spirea, is a compact shrub that produces distinctive dark green, three-lobed foliage and flat clusters of tiny, pure white flowers. 'Fairy Queen' is a choice cultivar.
- *Spiraea* x *vanhouttii* (2.5 m, 8 ft.), bridalwreath spirea, is a tall, upright shrub that produces spreading branches veiled in clusters of white flowers.

Summer-blooming spireas have tiny, pink blossoms produced in flat-topped clusters at the tips of branches. The bumald hybrids generally bloom before the Japanese spireas. Prune these hybrids in early spring.

- *Spiraea* x *bumalda* 'Anthony Waterer'

(90 cm, 36 in.) forms a compact, upright, long-blooming shrub with coarsely toothed foliage that emerges red but eventually turns green. Tiny, crimson-pink flowers are produced in flat clusters in mid-summer. *S.* x *bumalda* 'Dart's Red' (90 cm, 36 in.) is an improved version of 'Anthony Waterer'. It forms a tight mound of mostly red, multi-colored foliage topped by dark red flowers that fade to pink.

- *Spiraea* x *bumalda* 'Flaming Mound' (60 cm, 24 in.) forms a tight, compact shrub with flaming red foliage that gradually turns yellow. The flower buds are brilliant red; the flowers themselves change from pink to red.
- *Spiraea* x *bumalda* 'Froebelii' (1.2 m, 4 ft.) is a vigorous shrub with foliage that emerges bronze-red and flat clusters of deep pink flowers.
- *Spiraea* x *bumalda* 'Goldflame' (90 cm, 36 in.) has colorful foliage that is bronzy gold in the spring, soft gold in the summer, and red in the fall. Light pink flowers bloom all summer.
- *Spiraea* x *bumalda* 'Goldmound' (60 cm, 24 in.) is a dwarf, ball-shaped shrub that produces golden foliage all season long. Light pink flowers appear in early summer.

> *"The jade green foliage of 'Little Princess' is a perfect background to its medium pink flowers. Blooming from the end of June until late summer, it is a very attractive small shrub for a mixed border, along a walk, or in a planter."*
>
> HUGH SKINNER
> ROBLIN, MANITOBA

Syringa meyeri 'Palibin'
(sih-*ring*-gah *may*-a-ree)

Dwarf Korean lilac, Meyer lilac

Across the prairies the wind whistles through decaying homesteads, where lilacs still stand sentinel, lovely and silent reminders of those who have passed through this land. Lilacs were considered lucky in Europe, and no doubt many plants arrived with early pioneers. The Canadian government gave free lilacs to prairie settlers, a promise of beauty in a challenging environment. Although not native to North America, lilacs have long been one of the most beloved shrubs throughout the continent, and there are 300-year-old plants growing in New Hampshire and Michigan.

Portrait
Syringa meyeri 'Palibin' (syn. *S. palibiniana*, *S. velutina*), dwarf Korean lilac, is a compact, rounded shrub that will fit into any garden. The small, oval, dark green leaves have wavy edges and turn red in autumn.

Plant at a Glance

TYPE: deciduous shrub
HEIGHT: 1.5 m (5 ft.)
WIDTH: 1.5 m (5 ft.)
SOIL: fertile, well drained
LIGHT: full to part sun
FLOWERING TIME: spring to
early summer

PHOTO – PAGE 174

In late spring or early summer, 'Palibin' is clothed with delicate 10-cm (4-in.) panicles of fragrant, lilac-pink blossoms that open from dark reddish purple flower buds. Unlike common lilacs, which may take several years to bloom profusely, this lilac rewards the gardener with a fine floral display within a year or two. It often reblooms lightly in late summer if the first flowers are deadheaded immediately after flowering.

This practically perfect little shrub is non-suckering and mildew resistant.

Where to Grow
'Palibin' is easy to slip into a shrub border or a rock garden. Its dense, compact form makes it a natural for mass-planting or for an informal hedge.

How to Grow
'Palibin' performs well in full to part sun, in a sheltered location. It should be lightly shaded from the blazing afternoon sun that decreases the longevity of its blooms. Provide well-drained soil amended with aged manure or compost; additional organic mulch around the plant will aid in retaining moisture. This cultivar tolerates dry spells, but is at its best given adequate water.

Unlike large, suckering lilacs, 'Palibin' requires very little pruning. Dead or damaged branches may be removed at any time, but other pruning, including the removal of spent flower heads, should be done immediately after flowering to avoid removing next year's flower buds. It may be propagated by cuttings.

Perfect Partners

Plant 'Palibin' in a shrub bed with 'Pink Beauty', 'Abbotswood', or 'Coronation Triumph' potentilla. Other excellent companions include the small to medium-sized hardy shrub roses 'Winnipeg Parks', 'Henry Hudson', and 'Morden Blush'.

Collectors' Choice

There are many superb hardy lilacs available to prairie gardeners. If you have the space for several, choose species and hybrids that bloom at different times and you will be rewarded with their elegant flower forms and evocative perfume all spring long.

- 🌿 *Syringa* x *hyacinthiflora* (3 m, 10 ft.), also called American hybrids or Skinner lilacs, are early-blooming lilacs that sucker less than common lilacs, and are noted for their profusion of scented blooms. Cultivars include 'Annabel' (double, pink), 'Assessippi' (single, lavender), 'Pocahontas' (single, deep violet), 'Gertrude Leslie' (double, white), 'Maiden's Blush' (single, light pink), and 'Mount Baker' (single, white).

- 🌿 *Syringa oblata* var. *dilatata* (5 m, 15 ft.) is a vigorous shrub with heart-shaped leaves that are bronze when young, then change to glossy green. Producing fragrant, lavender blue flowers, this variety is notable for its fine red-purple fall color.

- 🌿 *Syringa* x *prestoniae* (4 m, 13 ft.), Preston hybrids, are vigorous, non-suckering shrubs that bloom later than common lilacs, producing large flower clusters with a musky fragrance. Cultivars include 'Donald Wyman' (single, deep red-pink), 'James MacFarlane' (single, deep pink), 'Miss Canada' (single, bright rose-pink), 'Royalty' (single, violet-purple), and the smaller cultivar 'Minuet' (single, light purple).

"I rate this shrub very highly for its dense, semi-compact, and non-suckering growth habit, which makes it a versatile shrub to use in many situations. When planted in well-drained soil, it often takes on a purple autumn coloration not common in lilacs."

DALE HERMAN
FARGO, NORTH DAKOTA

- 🌿 *Syringa pubescens* subsp. *patula* 'Miss Kim' (1.8 m, 6 ft.), Korean or Manchurian lilac, is a compact, non-suckering variety with red-purple fall foliage. It bears small, fragrant, lavender flowers and blooms later than the common lilac.

- 🌿 *Syringa vulgaris* (5 m, 16 ft.), the common lilac, has been in cultivation for over 500 years. It produces fragrant, blue flowers in mid-spring. Although its suckering habit and large size make it a good windbreak, it can be a bit overwhelming for a small garden. The common lilac is a parent to many fabulous lilacs, generally called French hybrids, since many early named cultivars were bred in France by Victor Lemoine and son. Most nurseries carry only a handful of varieties, but it is worth shopping around for these fine lilacs: 'Beauty of Moscow' (double, white from pink buds), 'Charles Joly' (double, deep red-purple), 'Nadezhda' (double, blue), the dwarf cultivar 'Prairie Petite' (dwarf single, pink), 'President Grévy' (double, lilac blue), 'President Lincoln' (single, blue), 'Primrose' (creamy white to pale yellow), 'Sensation' (single, purple edged with white), and 'Wedgwood' (single, blue from pink buds).

Syringa reticulata
(sih-*ring*-gah reh-tih-kew-*lah*-tah)

Japanese tree lilac, Giant tree lilac

Lilacs are unquestionably one of the most beautiful and dependable flowering shrubs on the prairies, a source of abundant fragrant blooms in late spring and early summer. However, gardeners are much less familiar with the Japanese tree lilac, a frequently overlooked member of the genus that not only extends the lilac flowering season, but also does double duty as a small tree with year-round appeal.

Although the Japanese tree lilac was introduced into cultivation in North America in 1876, it is only recently that gardeners looking for smaller ornamental trees have come to appreciate its admirable qualities. Beautiful, drought tolerant, and long-lived, it deserves to be more widely used in prairie gardens.

Portrait

The Japanese tree lilac is a showy small tree with an upright, rounded crown and shiny, smooth, red-brown bark, much like that of a cherry tree. Bright green in spring, the pointed, oval leaves are 8 to 20 cm (3 to 8 in.) long. In early summer, just after the blossoms of other lilacs have faded, the Japanese tree lilac bursts forth with spectacular large clusters of fragrant, cream-colored flowers.

Cultivars tend to be more upright and compact than the species and include 'Ivory Silk', 'Summer Snow', and 'Regent'. The variety *Syringa reticulata* var. *amurensis* is recommended for the most northerly regions of the prairies.

Where to Grow

The Japanese tree lilac is an ideal feature tree to tuck into a small garden. It is also a superb addition to an informal shrub border.

How to Grow

The Japanese tree lilac is at its best when grown in full to part sun, in well-drained soil. Before planting, liberally amend the soil with compost or well-aged manure. Although it is wise to mulch around newly planted trees to conserve moisture, Japanese tree lilacs are drought tolerant once established.

As with other lilacs, spent flower heads may be pruned off immediately after flowering; however, this may prove impractical as the tree reaches its mature size and the

Plant at a Glance

TYPE: deciduous tree
HEIGHT: 6 m (20 ft.)
WIDTH: 4.5 m (15 ft.)
SOIL: fertile, well drained
LIGHT: full to part sun
FLOWERING TIME: early to mid-summer

PHOTO – PAGE 174

dried seed pods do not detract from its beauty.

Perfect Partners

Plant the Japanese tree lilac behind spring-blooming, double-flowering plum (*Prunus triloba* 'Multiplex'), and purpleleaf sand cherry (*Prunus* x *cistena*). Dwarf Korean lilac (*Syringa meyeri* 'Palibin') is also a pretty companion for this larger cousin, as are hardy shrub roses. Choose low-growing or dwarf evergreens such as spreading junipers (*Juniperus horizontalis*) or globe spruce (*Picea pungens* f. *glauca* 'Globosa') to complement the shiny bark in winter.

Collectors' Choice

Like the Japanese tree lilac, several other small flowering trees are notable for eye-catching bark texture and color, tremendous assets to the winter garden.

- *Maackia amurensis* (5 m, 16 ft.), Amur maackia, is a rarely grown small tree with an upright, open canopy. An attractive addition to any landscape, this tree has golden bark and pinnate, compound leaves, and bears clusters of creamy white flowers in early to mid-summer. A member of the pea family, Amur maackia is a nitrogen-fixing plant that produces pea-like seed pods. Plant it in a sunny location.

- *Prunus maackii* (12 m, 40 ft.), Amur cherry, is a tall, fast-growing, spreading tree that produces abundant off-white flowers in spring on the previous year's growth, followed by small, black, astringent cherries. Its exfoliating, shiny gold or bronze bark gives it a charming appearance all year long.

- *Prunus pensylvanica* (5 m, 16 ft.), pin cherry, is perfect for small, urban spaces. It has attractive maroon-brown bark, bears white flowers in spring, and produces tiny, red cherries that attract birds. 'Jumping Pound' has a compact,

"I don't think you could find a better lilac for the prairies than the Japanese tree lilac. It is beautiful, very hardy and vigorous, and never fails to bloom. The fragrant flowers are wonderful in a bouquet."

MARVIN JOSLIN
SPRUCE GROVE, ALBERTA

weeping habit; 'Miss Liss' grows larger fruit than the species; and 'Stockton' produces masses of double, white flowers.

The Morden hawthorn (*Crataegus* x *mordenensis*) is another attractive flowering tree that is suitable for small gardens. Morden hawthorn trees have an upright, oval shape and glossy, toothed leaves; they bear only a few thorns. The crimson fruit resembles small crabapples, but is sparsely produced. Plant these trees in well-drained soil, in sun to part sun.

Hawthorn trees are hardy to Zone 3 and thus suited to many areas of the prairies; however, their hardiness may be questionable in Zone 2. There are two cultivars now commonly available, but watch for more in the future.

- 'Snowbird' (5 m, 16 ft.), the hardiest cultivar, produces fragrant, double, white flowers in the spring.

- 'Toba' (5 m, 16 ft.) has lovely fragrant flowers that are white in bud but turn pink as they open. It is a slightly wider tree than 'Snowbird'.

Thalictrum delavayi 'Hewitt's Double'

(tha-*lick*-trum de-la-*vay*-ee)

Yunnan meadow rue

For most of us, color in the garden is synonymous with the myriad tints and hues of the painter's palette that saturate the petals of favorite flowers. It therefore comes as a surprise to many that the utterly delightful misty haze of meadow rue's purple, pink, and white blossoms is achieved with nary a petal in sight. That's right—meadow rue flowers don't have petals. Instead, they have colorful stamens and modified leaves called bracts, which together determine the ultimate appearance of flower clusters. In some species the bracts are small and bosses of filamentous stamens predominate, giving their flower heads a lacey, almost fibrous aspect. In other species the bracts are large compared to the stamens, resulting in masses of nodding, bell-shaped flowers.

Regardless of the flower shape, meadow rue is an outstanding addition to lightly shaded borders or woodland gardens, where its soft flower clusters evoke heady romance or help more vibrant neighbors reach a compromise between clashing colors.

Portrait

The compact Yunnan meadow rue *Thalictrum delavayi* "Hewitt's Double' (previously known as *T. dipterocarpum* 'Hewitt's Double') is unique among meadow rues. Like other meadow rues, 'Hewitt's Double' produces large, foamy sprays of nodding, petal-less flowers. Unlike other meadow rues, its once-prominent stamens have evolved into a second row of purple, petal-like structures, which define the double character of its flowers. This cultivar is one of the last meadow rues to bloom, putting on a show of soft violet-purple from mid-summer on. Its double flowers last much longer than the singles of other Yunnan meadow rue.

'Hewitt's Double' has refined, blue-green, fernlike foliage; the 30-cm (12-in.) leaves are divided into dainty, three-lobed, scalloped leaflets.

Where to Grow

Grow 'Hewitt's Double' on pond or stream margins, naturalized in a wildflower garden, or in the middle or background of mixed or perennial borders.

How to Grow

'Hewitt's Double' prefers a spot sheltered from the wind, in light dappled shade or in full sun with afternoon shade. It is a long-lived perennial that expands slowly in average to fertile, moist, well-drained soil.

Plant at a Glance

TYPE: perennial
HEIGHT: 90 cm (36 in.)
WIDTH: 1.8 m (6 ft.)
SOIL: average to fertile, moist, well drained
LIGHT: light shade to full sun
FLOWERING TIME: mid-summer to fall

PHOTO – PAGE 174

An annual top dressing of organic-rich compost is the only nourishment this plant needs; overfertilizing encourages the development of weak stems that may subsequently require staking. It does not like to dry out, so keep an eye on moisture levels, especially in hot, windy weather.

All meadow rue is slow to break dormancy in the spring. To prevent unintentional damage, mark its location clearly and take care when digging in its vicinity.

Mature, fading clumps of 'Hewitt's Double' can be refreshed by dividing them in early spring. New divisions will languish and sulk for a while before getting on with the business of growing again and may need two to three years to fill out. This cultivar may also be propagated by division or cuttings.

Perfect Partners

The airy flowers of 'Hewitt's Double' contrast beautifully with bold-flowered plants such as lilies (*Lilium* spp.), daylilies (*Hemerocallis* spp.), phlox, peach-leaved bellflowers (*Campanula persicifolia*), and black-eyed Susan (*Rudbeckia* spp.). They also are in accord with the frothy flowers of meadowsweet (*Filipendula* spp.) and bugbane (*Cimicifuga* spp.).

Collectors' Choice

Several meadow rue species that require similar growing conditions to 'Hewitt's Double' come in a range of sizes and bloom times.

- *Thalictrum alpinum* (30 cm, 12 in.) has much-divided, fernlike leaves and yellow flowers, and is suitable for lightly shaded rock gardens.
- *Thalictrum aquilegifolium* (90 cm, 36 in.), columbine meadow rue, blooms in spring, producing gray-green columbinelike foliage and clustered, lilac-purple, white, or rose stamens cupped in greenish white sepals.

Clusters of dangling, flat seeds follow. Well-known cultivars include 'Album' (white stamens), 'Thundercloud' (dark purple stamens, steely blue foliage), 'White Cloud' (yellow-tipped white stamens), and 'Atropurpureum' (violet stamens).

- *Thalictrum minus* (45 cm, 18 in.) has unremarkable greenish flowers in June, but its foliage is wonderful, resembling that of maidenhair ferns.
- *Thalictrum rochebrunianum* (1.8 m, 6 ft.), lavender mist, has purple-blue stems, finely divided, fernlike foliage, and masses of lavender blossoms with bright yellow stamens.

Meadowsweet (*Filipendula* spp.) produces airy flower heads similar in appearance to meadow rue and requires the same care as it does.

- *Filipendula rubra* (1.8 m, 6 ft.), queen-of-the-prairie, is a stately plant with 20-cm (8-in.), feathery clusters of pink or rose flowers.
- *Filipendula ulmaria* (90 cm, 36 in.), queen-of-the-meadow, has bold foliage and 15-cm (6-in.) plumes of tiny, fluffy, creamy white flowers.
- *Filipendula vulgaris* (60 cm, 24 in.), dropwort, has fernlike basal foliage and weak stems supporting flat clusters of creamy white flowers.

Thuja occidentalis 'Brandon'
(*thew*-ya awk-si-dent-*al*-liss)

Eastern or northern white cedar, Arborvitae

Eastern white cedar, the famed arborvitae or "tree of life," was so named by the French King Henry II in 1558 when he learned that explorer Jacques Cartier and his crew had been cured of scurvy in North America by drinking cedar tea, a brew rich in vitamin C. Subsequent to this discovery, cedars were often planted in cemeteries to commemorate longevity and the afterlife. Cedars themselves are long-lived, easily reaching an age of 300 years or more. The oldest known eastern white cedar in Ontario is more than 1,000 years old!

Even though eastern white cedars are bog-loving trees, there is something about their soft fragrant foliage and shaggy, aromatic bark that appeals to prairie gardeners who, ironically, love growing them in their drought-prone climate.

Plant at a Glance

TYPE: evergreen tree
HEIGHT: 4 m (13 ft.)
WIDTH: 1.5 m (5 ft.)
SOIL: average to fertile, moist, well drained
LIGHT: full sun to light shade

PHOTO - PAGE 175

Portrait
'Brandon' is one of the best cold-hardy, pyramidal cedars for the prairies. Developed in the early 1940s at the Patmore Nursery in Brandon, Manitoba, it is a relatively fast-growing, columnar evergreen with fan-shaped sprays of flat, scale-like, diamond-shaped leaves. The foliage is soft, very fragrant, and dotted with small, raisin-sized cones that turn a medium brown toward the end of summer. Contact with the foliage may aggravate skin allergies in some people. All cedar bark is a fibrous, reddish brown, and very aromatic. Insignificant male and female flowers are borne on separate branches of the same tree.

Where to Grow
This cedar makes an excellent accent tree in formal or semi-formal, mixed and shrub borders. A row of sheared 'Brandon' cedars also makes an attractive hedge.

How to Grow
'Brandon' cedar will tolerate almost any soil, as long as it is well drained. However, care must be taken to situate it in a sheltered spot—ideally, one that is sunny in summer and shaded in winter. All cedars are susceptible to desiccation during winter months, so direct exposure to sun and wind should be avoided as much as possible. If this can't be arranged naturally, then construct a small shelter from wooden supports and burlap, making sure to leave enough room for good air circulation.

Cedars are moisture-loving trees, so supplementary watering and a good water-conserving mulch are a must on the prairies, especially in the weeks leading up to winter dormancy. After a cold, dry winter, foliage tips may turn brown, but these are usually sluffed during summer and replaced by healthy new growth.

Repeated shearing of cedars results in a dense outer shell of greenery and bare branches toward the center of the tree; holes that penetrate the shell due to injury can be unsightly and difficult to repair.

Propagate 'Brandon' cedar by layering or by hardwood cuttings in winter.

Perfect Partners

An accent 'Brandon' cedar planted toward the back of a shrub or mixed border looks wonderful surrounded with deciduous shrubs such as Siberian coral dogwood (*Cornus alba* 'Sibirica'), white-flowering spirea (*Spiraea trilobata*, *S.* x *vanhouttii*), or hardy shrub roses ('Henry Hudson', 'J. P. Connell', 'David Thompson').

Collectors' Choice

The following tall, columnar or pyramidal cedars are readily available to prairie gardeners:

- 'Degroot's Spire' (2 m, 6.5 ft.) is slow growing, fine-textured, upright, and spire-shaped—perfect for a small spot.
- 'Emerald Green' (4.5 m, 15 ft.) is narrow, pyramidal, and bright green; it shows excellent heat tolerance and does not discolor in winter.
- 'Nigra' (4.5 m, 15 ft.), dark green cedar, forms a broad pyramid of dark green foliage; one of the finest cedars for hedging, it also maintains its color in winter.
- 'Techny' (also sold as 'Mission') (4 m, 13 ft.), one of the hardiest cedars for the Chinook zone, forms a broad,

> **"'Brandon' cedar is a hardy, narrow, pyramidal cedar with attractive dark green foliage. It may be grown as a hedge when planted one meter apart and properly clipped."**
>
> MAURICE CLARKE
> MARWAYNE, ALBERTA

columnar tree, perfect for hedging; it maintains its color in winter.

- 'Wareana' (3 m, 10 ft.), Siberian cedar, is the hardiest of the cedars; it forms a broad, pyramidal tree with dense, dark green foliage; it is tolerant of hot, dry conditions and does not brown in winter.
- 'Woodwardii' (1.5 m, 5 ft.), globe cedar, forms a large, globular tree dense with rich green foliage that stays green in winter; it is good for hedges and topiary.

Some short, globe cedars are also readily available.

- 'Danica' (30 cm, 12 in.) is one of the best globe cedars; it produces dense, bright green foliage in almost vertical sprays.
- 'Hetz Midget' (45 cm, 18 in.) is a slow-growing, spherical, dwarf cedar.
- 'Little Gem' (60 cm, 24 in.) is a dwarf, moderately spherical, dark green cedar.
- 'Little Giant' (45 cm, 18 in.) forms an upright, medium green oval that requires no pruning to maintain its habit; it does not discolor in winter.

Thymus serpyllum

(*ty*-mus sir-*pil*-lum)

Mother-of-thyme,
Mountain thyme

Renowned for its captivating fragrance, tiny, delicate flowers, persistent green foliage, and pleasing mat-forming growth habit, thyme is a desirable groundcover for gardeners everywhere. Its long and fascinating history as a culinary and medicinal herb adds to its appeal in the garden.

There are two main groups of thyme—common thyme and creeping thyme, the latter coming with a list of common names, such as mother-of-thyme, mountain thyme, wild thyme, hillwort, and shepherd's thyme. The taxonomy of this genus has been revised and various forms may be listed under several botanical names, including *Thymus praecox* subsp. *arcticus*.

Both groups are from the Mediterranean area, where they inhabit dry, rocky soil. These low, aromatic creepers belong to the mint family, with common thyme having a somewhat shrubbier aspect than creeping thyme.

All thymes may be used for cooking, although some are more flavorful than others. Mother-of-thyme (*Thymus serpyllum*) is an excellent choice for prairie gardeners, serving double duty as a decorative and hardy perennial groundcover and as a useful culinary herb.

Portrait

Mother-of-thyme has small, semi-evergreen, fragrant, almost oval leaves that come to a point and grow from 0.5 to 2 cm (0.25 to 0.75 in.). The diminutive flowers are two-lipped and tubular, growing in short spikes and dense clusters that smother the plants in blankets of mauve. Blooms persist from early June throughout most of the summer and are much favored by the industrious honeybee.

Other forms of *Thymus serpyllum* vary in bloom color: *album* (white), *coccineus* (bright red), and *roseus* (pink). 'Aureus' is a golden creeping thyme.

Where to Grow

Mother-of-thyme is an ideal plant for edging flowerbeds, and for underplanting taller inhabitants of a border. It is also useful in a terraced garden, providing a tapestry of color that cascades over walls. Plant it in crevices between stepping stones and pavers, where it will quickly develop into a continuous ribbon of green crowned with a profusion of lilac, pink, or white blossoms. If no garden space is available, it will grow happily in summer containers.

Plant at a Glance

TYPE: perennial groundcover
HEIGHT: 10 cm (4 in.)
WIDTH: 30 cm (12 in.)
SOIL: poor to average, well drained
LIGHT: full to part sun
FLOWERING TIME: early to late summer

PHOTO – PAGE 175

How to Grow

Plant mother-of-thyme in full sun to encourage optimum flowering. It revels in relatively poor but well-drained soil; good drainage is essential for this low, ground-hugging creeper which will occasionally succumb to fungus and other stem and root diseases. Like all thymes, mother-of-thyme expands slowly by means of delicate runners and can be tricky to transplant. Move plants no later than mid-summer, to enable them to re-establish their roots before the first hard freeze. Even established plants can be damaged by frost heaving from time to time. This plant benefits from winter protection in areas where snow cover is unreliable.

Eventually, clumps of thyme will die out at the center. When this occurs, divide them, then replant the outer living portions and discard the dead, woody, inner portion. Thyme can also be propagated from cuttings or grown from seed.

Perfect Partners

Plant a fragrant blooming carpet of mother-of-thyme around hardy roses and old-fashioned perennials such as phlox, daylilies, peach-leaved bellflower (*Campanula persicifolia*), or 'Munstead' lavender (*Lavandula angustifolia*). In a rock garden, thyme pairs well with white maiden pinks (*Dianthus deltoides*), sedum, and creeping veronica.

Collectors' Choice

Many species and cultivars of thyme are available; at least one variety can be found to suit every gardener's tastes and needs.

- *Thymus* 'Doone Valley' (10 cm, 4 in.), Doone Valley lemon thyme, is a gold-splashed thyme that seems to perform best if not allowed to bloom. *T. x citriodorus* 'Gold Edge', golden lemon thyme, has shiny green leaves edged in gold.

> *"I love the way mother-of-thyme covers the ground with its soft, open, airy foliage. The purple flowers are also very pleasing, and it releases a wonderful scent when you brush by it or water it. It's a great addition to a rock garden."*
>
> DEBBIE PETRINI
> GREAT FALLS, MONTANA

- *Thymus pseudolanuginosus* (5 cm, 2 in.), woolly thyme, spreads to form a soft carpet of tiny, woolly, gray leaves topped with pale pink flowers. It thrives in especially well-drained soil.
- *Thymus vulgaris* (15 cm, 6 in.), English thyme, is the hardiest shrubby, upright thyme and is highly valued for cooking. *T. vulgaris* 'Argenteus' is a silver-leaved cultivar.

Herbs thrive in the prairie sunshine. If you love cooking with fresh herbs, try these culinary classics.

- *Allium schoenoprasum* (38 cm, 15 in.), chives, is a hardy herb garden staple with purple flowers that share the onion flavor of the grassy leaves. 'Profusion'™ is a sterile cultivar with prolific flower production.
- *Origanum vulgare* subsp. *hirtum* (20 cm, 8 in.), Greek oregano, is indispensable in Mediterranean cooking; *O. vulgare* 'Aureum', golden oregano, is a creeping variety suited to rockeries or the front of a perennial border.
- *Salvia officinalis* (60 cm, 24 in.), common sage, is generally hardy across the prairies. Varieties with decorative foliage need winter mulch, and may need to be grown as annuals; try 'Tricolor' (green, cream, and purple), 'Purpurea' (purple), and 'Aurea' (green and gold).

Tilia x *flavescens* 'Dropmore'
(*till*-ee-ya x flav-*ess*-kens)

Linden, Basswood

The genus *Tilia* consists of approximately 45 species of deciduous trees native to northern temperate zones. Commonly known as linden, basswood, and lime trees, the latter name is the result of linguistic confusion between similar words since *Tilia* species bear no relation to the citrus lime trees. The botanical name *Tilia* is the Latin word for lime or linden tree and may be related to the Greek *tillein*, meaning "to pluck, to extract fibers from," referring to the fibrous inner bark of the linden. The Swedish word for linden is *linn*, which was the birth name of the originator of modern botanical nomenclature, Carl Linnaeus.

Lindens are graceful shade trees, many with heart-shaped leaves and creamy white to yellow flower clusters that are delightfully fragrant and so attractive to bees that another common name for linden is "bee tree." The fruit are small nutlets encased in papery bracts similar to maple tree samaras.

In many European countries, tea is brewed from linden flowers as a digestive tonic with soothing properties. The blossoms are also used cosmetically to cleanse and soften the skin.

Portrait
Tilia x *flavescens* 'Dropmore' was introduced in 1955 by Manitoba's Dropmore nursery; it is a hybrid of *T. cordata*, the little-leaf linden, and *T. americana*, the American linden. 'Dropmore' is faster growing and hardier than the little-leaf linden and tolerates drier soil. It is also immune to the linden mite, an insect that causes disfiguring galls to form on linden leaves.

'Dropmore' has a pyramidal form and a dense canopy of large, dark green leaves that are heart-shaped and pointed with serrated edges. The scented, yellow flowers appear in mid-summer.

Where to Grow
Use 'Dropmore' as a shade tree in large lots, rural settings, or parks.

How to Grow
'Dropmore' prefers a sunny location, and fertile, moist, well-drained soil, although it will tolerate part sun and a range of soil types. Mulch with organic material around the tree to conserve moisture.

Prune young trees lightly to achieve the desired shape. Mature trees require lit-

Plant at a Glance

TYPE: deciduous tree
HEIGHT: 15 m (50 ft.)
WIDTH: 12 m (40 ft.)
SOIL: fertile, moist, well drained
LIGHT: full to part sun
FLOWERING TIME: mid-summer

PHOTO – PAGE 175

tle pruning other than to remove dead or damaged branches. This should be done in late winter when the trees are still dormant.

Perfect Partners
'Dropmore' is an impressive shade tree standing on its own. Evergreen trees and shrubs planted nearby will accentuate its bright yellow fall foliage.

Collectors' Choice
Several other lindens have proven hardy or moderately hardy on the prairies, but all require regular watering and well-drained soil. These lindens may be less reliable in the Chinook zone than in other areas because of winter dryness and minimal snow cover.

- *Tilia americana* (18 m, 60 ft.), the American linden, is the hardiest North American linden, but its considerable spread of 15 m (50 ft.) limits its usefulness on small lots. It is a beautiful shade tree for parks or boulevards, with a broad, rounded crown of dense foliage when mature. This linden has large, dark green, toothed leaves and fragrant, yellow flowers, and it is native to parts of the eastern prairies. Another name for the tree is basswood, from "bast," the fiber from the inner bark of the linden that was used for rope, twine, and woven baskets and mats. Watch for new cultivars of this tree in the future.
- *Tilia cordata* (11 to 14 m, 35 to 45 ft.), little-leaf linden, grows in a neat, pyramidal form. It has fragrant, ivory flowers, heart-shaped, dark green leaves with lighter undersides, and yellow autumn color. This linden should be planted in a sheltered location; it may be slow to establish. Although this species is lovely indeed, several *T. cordata* cultivars developed in Manitoba

"The 'Dropmore' linden is a very hardy hybrid of the American and little leaf lindens, and is one of my favorites. It has a lovely shape with a strong, definite trunk and right-angle branching. This is an exceptional tree that we don't use enough."

NEIL HOLLAND
HARWOOD, NORTH
DAKOTA

specifically for the region are hardier and offer other appealing features. 'Golden Cascade' (14 m, 45 ft.) is named for its golden fall foliage color and cascading form. 'Ronald' (14 m, 45 ft.), also called Norlin™ linden, grows more rapidly than the species, and has good disease and sunscald resistance. 'Morden' (10 m, 33 ft.) has gray bark, an upright form similar to the species, fragrant, yellow flowers, and good fall color.

- *Tilia mongolica* (9 m, 30 ft.), Mongolian linden, is smaller than most lindens. It has a broad, pyramidal shape, toothed leaves that turn yellow in fall, and yellow flowers. 'Harvest Gold' (14 m, 45 ft.), an upright form developed in Manitoba, has many worthy attributes including thin, serrated leaves, golden buds, golden fall color, exfoliating bark, resistance to sunscald, and disease-free foliage. The crown spread of 7.5 m (25 ft.) is less than that of other hardy lindens, making it a suitable tree for large gardens.

Tradescantia x *andersoniana* 'Osprey'
(tra-des-*kant*-ee-ah x an-der-son-ee-*ah*-na)

Spiderwort, Widow's tears

For brush strokes of intense color among the cool greens of a light shade garden, be sure to plant small drifts of spiderwort. The luminous pink, blue, white, and purple flowers of this intriguing plant positively glow, and although individual blossoms are very short-lived, plants produce so many of them that they flourish from spring until late summer.

Named for John Tradescant, royal gardener to King Charles I of England and a plant collector of note, spiderwort's grassy foliage sets it apart from many other shade-loving plants and adds textural diversity to shaded borders. The strappy leaves, as angular and spindly as a spider's legs, were at one time used to heal spider bites, hence, its common name.

A fascinating peculiarity of spiderwort is its sensitivity to fluctuating levels of pollution. As atmospheric concentrations of pesticides, herbicides, auto exhaust, sulphur dioxide, and low-level radiation fluctuate, mutations occur that modify the color of spiderwort's stamens. These changes happen in as few as 10 to 15 days, making it an excellent indicator of harmful levels of pollution.

Portrait

'Osprey' spiderwort forms lax, grassy mounds smothered with a profusion of white blossoms touched with lavender purple, 4 cm (1.5 in.) across, that are especially brilliant in cool, moist weather. Each flower consists of a trio of gently scalloped, triangular petals encircling bright, yellow-colored stamens. Flower buds develop in tight clusters at the tips of succulent stems in late spring, and bloom in continuous succession from June to August. Like ephemeral daylilies, individual blossoms open in the morning only to fade in the afternoon, but these showy plants produce so many buds that their display of color is uninterrupted for weeks on end. The tufts of coarse, grassy spiderwort foliage start out a lovely fresh, purple-tinted blue-green, but may deteriorate about the time they finish flowering.

Spiderwort flowers have a curious habit that endears them to gardeners: instead of shriveling, drying, and dying as most flowers do, they turn to a runny liquid—thanks to a unique enzyme action—and just disappear. No deadheading!

Named spiderwort cultivars are among the best to use in cold climates. Excellent choices include 'Iris Pritchard' (white with

Plant at a Glance

TYPE: perennial
HEIGHT: 60 cm (24 in.)
WIDTH: 60 cm (24 in.)
SOIL: average to fertile, moist
LIGHT: full sun to light shade
FLOWERING TIME: early to late summer

PHOTO – PAGE 175

a violet blush), 'Isis' (Oxford blue), 'Purple Dome' (rich purple), 'Red Cloud' (rose red), 'Snowcap' (pure white), and 'Zwanenburg Blue' (royal blue).

Where to Grow

Spiderworts are charming massed in natural woodland areas, edging a stream or pond, or tucked into an informal cottage garden. You can also plant them in mixed borders much as you would hardy bulbs—in diagonal drifts mingled with plants that will disguise tired foliage in August.

How to Grow

Spiderwort grows in any reasonable soil but prefers a rich, woodsy, fertile environment. Moisture is the key to healthy plants. It flowers best in full sun, but unless it is kept cool and moist enough, its foliage will scorch to a dull brown, and may even go dormant. That is why in the prairies it is wise to plant it in light shade, where it still blooms beautifully, and to water it regularly. Applying organic mulch around the plant also helps retain moisture and keeps plants looking their finest. If, despite careful attention, your spiderwort gets that bedraggled look, cut it back to encourage fresh new growth and, with luck, you will experience a second flush of flowers during the occasional, unseasonably warm fall.

Divide spiderwort in spring or fall. Although it is an abundant self-sower, seedlings may not be the same color as the parent. You can prevent self-seeding by picking seed pods before they turn brown.

A generous winter mulch applied in late fall can help prevent damage that otherwise might result during extremely cold prairie winters with little or no snow cover.

"Spiderwort's interesting grassy foliage and need for a lightly shaded, moist spot make it perfect for pondside plantings. Although individual blossoms are short-lived, so many of them are produced that the plant seems to bloom continuously, all summer long."

ANGELA DU TOIT
BRAGG CREEK, ALBERTA

Perfect Partners

Spiderwort combines well with lady's mantle (*Alchemilla mollis*), astilbe, coral bells (*Heuchera* spp.), hostas, and ferns. Other good companions include columbine (*Aquilegia* spp.), leopard's bane (*Doronicum columnae*), cranesbill (*Geranium* spp.), and pulmonaria.

Collectors' Choice

Another plant that tends to dormancy in late summer but is a "must have" for the woodland or shade garden is the Virginia bluebell, or its native cousin, *Mertensia paniculata*.

- *Mertensia paniculata* (60 cm, 24 in.) forms a bushy plant with lance-shaped, hairy leaves, smothered with intensely blue, tubular flowers in early spring.
- *Mertensia virginica* (60 cm, 24 in.) has fragrant, sapphire blue flowers sporting small tubes that flare into scalloped, bell-shaped cups; they form clusters that arch over soft gray-blue-green leaves. Plant these spring bloomers for a carpet of blue amongst hostas, ferns, and bleeding hearts that will fill the gaps after the Virginia bluebells have departed for the summer.

Tulipa tarda
(*tew*-lip-ah *tar*-dah)

Tarda tulip

Tulips were first introduced to Europe in 1554 from Turkey, where they had been grown for centuries. The botanical name "tulip" is derived from *tulband*, the Turkish word for turban, due to the flower's resemblance to the headgear. By the seventeenth century, tulips became so popular that bulbs traded for vast sums of money during the famous Dutch "tulipomania" of 1634 to 1637. Many fortunes were lost when the market collapsed. Luckily, tulips continued to be cultivated and hybridized so widely that there are now thousands of known varieties available.

Today, for a very modest investment, any garden can bloom from April until June with the sumptuous shades and elegant shapes of tulips. Although large, showy cultivars remain popular, an increasing number of hardy and beautiful little species (wild) tulips are popping up every spring across the prairies.

Plant at a Glance

TYPE: hardy bulb
HEIGHT: 15 cm (6 in.)
WIDTH: 15 cm (6 in.)
SOIL: fertile, well drained
LIGHT: full sun
FLOWERING TIME: spring

PHOTO – PAGE 176

Portrait
A native of Turkestan, *Tulipa tarda* (formerly *T. dasystemon*) is an early-blooming species tulip with shiny, lance-shaped bright green leaves. Each flower stem bears clusters of three or more star-shaped golden yellow flowers tipped with white. A long-lived species, it will spread into patches by producing many little bulblets that mature into new plants.

Where to Grow
Tulipa tarda is suitable for rockeries, the front of borders, and around shrubs. This dwarf species is a good choice for mass-planting in exposed sites where larger tulips may be damaged by wind.

How to Grow
Plant *Tulipa tarda* in fertile, well-drained soil where it will receive at least five hours of sun per day. For the most striking effect, the small bulbs should be planted no more than 5 cm (2 in.) apart.

This and other species tulips may be left undisturbed for many years, although if clumps increase in size, bulbs and bulblets may be dug up and redistributed in early fall.

Perfect Partners
Plant *Tulipa tarda* in a rockery with other species tulips, including *T. acuminata*, *T. kaufmanniana* and its hybrids, and *T. kolpakowskiana*. Deep blue Siberian squill (*Scilla sibirica*) and dwarf narcissus are also charming companions.

Collectors' Choice

There are so many fine varieties of tulips that it would take a gardening lifetime to try them all. Make a point of adding a few new ones each fall, starting with the early-blooming species tulips.

- *Tulipa acuminata* (45 cm, 18 in.) is an unusual light red or yellow tulip with slender, spiky petals and linear, gray-green leaves.
- *Tulipa greigii* (30 cm, 12 in.) has orange-scarlet flowers; named varieties often feature attractive purple-striped foliage. Look for 'Red Riding Hood' (scarlet), 'Pinocchio' (yellow striped with red), and 'Cape Cod' (yellow striped with red).
- *Tulipa kauffmanniana* (25 cm, 10 in.) is aptly named the waterlily tulip for the open-bowl shape of the lovely creamy yellow and red blooms. This robust species has gray-green, slightly wavy leaves. Kaufmanniana hybrids frequently have purple-brown striped or mottled leaves. Outstanding named varieties include 'Stressa' (yellow), 'Shakespeare' (red with yellow base), and 'Heart's Delight' (red and yellow).
- *Tulipa kolpakowskiana* (15 cm, 6 in.) has narrow leaves and yellow, cup-shaped flowers.
- *Tulipa praestans* (30 cm, 12 in.) produces clusters of red flowers. Try 'Fusilier' (scarlet red), and 'Unicum' (scarlet red with cream and green variegated foliage).

Tulips are classified into 15 divisions based upon origin and bloom shape. For flower variety and a continuous blaze of color throughout the spring, choose a selection from early, mid-spring, and late spring blooming varieties.

- Double early tulips (early to mid-spring) are usually short-stemmed and fragrant: try 'Monte Carlo' (golden yellow), 'Peach Blossom' (light pink), and 'Electra' (magenta).
- Fosteriana tulips (early to mid-spring) are long-stemmed with large flowers: try 'Purissima', also called 'White Emperor' (white), 'Juan' (orange-red with golden-yellow base), and 'Red Emperor', also called 'Madame Lefeber' (glossy red).
- Triumph tulips (mid-spring) are tall with large, cup-shaped flowers: try 'Lustige Witwe', also called 'Merry Widow' (red edged with white), 'Dreaming Maid' (violet edged with white), and 'Golden Melody' (yellow).
- Darwin hybrid tulips (mid-spring) have large flowers on tall stems: try 'Apeldoorn' (red), 'Golden Parade' (yellow), and 'Elizabeth Arden' (salmon pink).
- Single late tulips (late spring) are a variable group with a large color range: try 'Union Jack' (red and white streaked), 'Queen of Night' (maroon black), and 'Blue Aimable' (lilac).
- Lily-flowered tulips (late spring) are tall with elegantly shaped, long-petalled blooms: try 'White Triumphator' (white), 'West Point' (yellow), and 'Mariette' (rose pink).

> *"Tulips are my harbinger of spring. By planting early, mid-season, and late-blooming varieties, my gardens have color long before any annuals begin blooming. Then I can still plant annuals when the tulips have disappeared."*
>
> MARGARET JOHNSTON
> CARMAN, MANITOBA

Verbascum chaixii 'Album'
(ver-*bass*-kum *shay*-zee-ee)

Nettle leaved mullein

It's hard to believe that the coarse, often ungainly, giant mullein (rhymes with sullen) seen naturalized by dry, dusty roadsides across North America has relatives elegant enough to grace the most formal of borders. Yet for many prairie gardeners, mullein has become a plant of choice for dry, sunny locations. Usually a biennial or short-lived perennial, this lovely plant can also be a long-lived perennial. Its slender spires of delicate flowers bloom profusely in shades of soft yellow, purple, pink, and white, ascending above remarkable soft, gray-green rosettes of foliage. Add to this its dramatic pose, carefree nature, and ability to withstand heat and drought, and the verdict is clear—mullein is an outstanding garden plant.

Portrait
The elegant *Verbascum chaixii* 'Album' is a study in charm. Green foliage is toothed and deeply veined, forming large clumps that slowly increase in size. Hairy stems sport smaller leaves and develop into sturdy flower spikes smothered in tight buds by early summer. Individual buds blossom into pure white, five-petalled, outward-facing, saucer-shaped flowers that open singly, but continuously, until summer's end. At each flower's center is a sparkling eye of wine-red or mauve stamens.

The species *Verbascum chaixii* sprouts lovely pale yellow blossoms with a reddish purple eye.

Where to Grow
Its tall, white spires make 'Album' an excellent accent plant for the back of dry, sunny borders, although it is equally suitable toward the front, where its showy foliage rosettes are attractive in their own right. The flower spikes are so narrow they do not obscure the plants behind them. This cultivar is also a natural for herb gardens and wildflower meadows.

How to Grow
'Album' is a heat- and drought-resistant plant that thrives in a warm, sunny spot, in poor to average, well-drained, sandy or gravelly soil. This makes it a star performer in xeriscape (water-wise) landscapes. It also does reasonably well in moist, fertile soil, but is more likely to perform as a perennial in drier locations. Soil that is too fertile and moist encourages this plant to lead a biennial or even annual existence; it also necessitates staking from time to time.

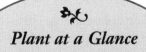

Plant at a Glance

TYPE: perennial
HEIGHT: 90 cm (36 in.)
WIDTH: 45 cm (18 in.)
SOIL: poor to average, well drained
LIGHT: full sun
FLOWERING TIME: mid to late summer

PHOTO – PAGE 176

Cut back flower stalks after blooming to tidy 'Album' and stimulate the formation of basal rosettes; alternatively, leave them in place for drama in the winter garden and a treat for feathered friends.

'Album' seldom needs dividing, although it can be propagated from root cuttings or by carefully separating and replanting secondary basal leaf rosettes. A generous self-sower, it does not necessarily grow true from seed. However, as for all mulleins, it hybridizes so enthusiastically that most seedlings develop into plants every bit as beautiful as the parents.

Disease or pests rarely bother 'Album', although in damp flower borders, cruising slugs sometimes pause for lunch. Be vigilant!

Perfect Partners
'Album' looks natural when paired with other heat-loving, drought-resistant plants such as potentilla, hen-and-chicks (*Sempervivum* spp.), stonecrop (*Sedum* spp.), globe thistle (*Echinops* spp.), and sea holly (*Eryngium* spp.). It also contrasts beautifully with blue-flowering Russian sage (*Perovskia atriplicifolia*).

Collectors' Choice
The following species of mullein are most likely to succeed as perennials if given the sunny, dry conditions they prefer.

- *Verbascum* x *hybridum* (to 90 cm, 36 in.) comprise a series of hybrids in a range of colors: 'Cotswold Beauty' (pink-purple, dark eye), 'Cotswold Queen' (buff-orange, purple eye), 'Gainsborough' (light yellow), 'Mont Blanc' (white), 'Pink Domino' (pink), and 'Helen Johnson' (coppery orange).
- *Verbascum nigrum* (90 cm, 36 in.), black mullein, produces basal rosettes of medium green, oblong leaves that are hairy underneath and 60-cm (24-in.)

"Verbascums, which come in every conceivable shade of cream, yellow, pink, and purple, are superb plants for novice or beginner gardeners. They are so hardy, so drought tolerant, and frost doesn't make them turn a hair."

ANNE VALE
BLACK DIAMOND, ALBERTA

spikes of yellow flowers with reddish brown centers.

- *Verbascum phoeniceum* (60 cm, 24 in.), purple mullein, is one of the showiest mulleins. It produces unbranched spikes of purple, pink, red, or white, delphiniumlike flowers in early summer above shiny, green, ground-hugging foliage. It is a common parent of mullein hybrids.

Two other tall biennial or short-lived perennial plants worth growing for their dramatic effect are foxglove and teasel.

- *Digitalis purpurea* (1.5 m, 5 ft.), common foxglove, forms dense rosettes of broad, lance-shaped leaves, stout, leafy stems, and tall, one-sided spikes of funnel-shaped flowers in purple, pink, white, or yellow; the flowers are often spotted inside. The yellow *D. grandiflora*, though less showy, is more reliably perennial on the prairies.
- *Dipsacus fullonum* (1.5 m, 5 ft.), fuller's teasel, is a prickly plant that forms rosettes of spiny, toothed, dark green leaves and tall, upright stems that culminate in large, oval, thistlelike pinkish purple or white flower heads.

Veronica x 'Sunny Border Blue'

(ver-*on*-ih-kah)

Veronica, Speedwell

The genus *Veronica* embraces a versatile collection of beautiful, trouble-free, long-lived perennials that are assets to any prairie garden. Chiefly renowned for their vivid blue flowers, hardy veronicas can display richly colored, bottle-brush spikes or creeping mats of brillant, tiny flowers.

The history of the name Veronica is as lovely as the flowers themselves. As a female name it may derive from the legend of St. Veronica, who was said to have wiped the sweat from Christ's brow with her veil as he carried the cross to his crucifixion. Another origin may be from the medieval Latin *veronicus*, meaning "of the city of Verona," that most romantic of Italian cities where Shakespeare sets his woeful tale of Romeo and Juliet. In addition, sometime during the Renaissance, Verona claimed to possess the veil of St. Veronica. It is unclear why this name became associated with the flower, although many flowers throughout history have been given a woman's name.

Speedwell, the common name, seems to refer to the ability of veronica to effect a quick cure for illness; however, it could also be associated with the meaning "farewell," referring to one species' habit of shedding its petals as soon as the flowers were gathered.

Portrait

The hybrid 'Sunny Border Blue' has showy, deep violet-blue flower spikes composed of many small individual blooms. Even more impressive, these flowers are produced all summer. Compact and sturdy in habit, it does not become floppy, and the glossy and crinkled-toothed leaves remain fresh-looking throughout the growing season. As with all veronicas, this popular hybrid may develop powdery mildew when stressed by drought.

Where to Grow

'Sunny Border Blue' is a superb plant for massing in sunny perennial beds or for planting in a cutting garden, as the intensely blue flower spikes are striking additions to floral arrangements. Its long bloom period also makes it an excellent candidate for summer container plantings, but plants should be moved out of the containers and into the garden for winter.

How to Grow

'Sunny Border Blue' thrives in full to part sun, although the more sun it receives, the

Plant at a Glance

TYPE: perennial
HEIGHT: 60 cm (24 in.)
WIDTH: 30 cm (12 in.)
SOIL: average to fertile, moist, well drained
LIGHT: full to part sun
FLOWERING TIME: early summer to fall

PHOTO – PAGE 176

better the bloom production. Plant it in average to fertile, moist, well-drained soil and top dress it with compost each year; no additional fertilizer is necessary. Like most veronicas, this one prefers consistent moisture. An organic mulch around the plant will help retain moisture during the hot summer months.

Propagate 'Sunny Border Blue' by taking stem cuttings or by division. Plants should be divided every three or four years in spring, shortly after new growth appears.

Perfect Partners
'Sunny Border Blue' is congenial company for a wide assortment of perennials. Among the best partners are daylilies (*Hemerocallis* spp.), coreopsis and other yellow, daisylike flowers, ornamental grasses, garden phlox, cranesbill (*Geranium* spp.), and yarrow (*Achillea* spp.).

Collectors' Choice
Other upright, spike-flowered veronicas to try in the border include these two.
- *Veronica austriaca*, Hungarian speedwell, blooms in early summer. 'Crater Lake Blue' (38 cm, 15 in.) boasts intensely blue flowers and, unlike most cultivars, will frequently come true from seed.
- *Veronica spicata*, spike speedwell, blooms from early to mid-summer. Outstanding cultivars are 'Blue Charm' (76 cm, 30 in.), the deep blue 'Goodness Grows' (38 cm, 15 in.), rose-pink 'Heidekind' (25 cm, 10 in.), rose-red 'Red Fox' (38 cm, 15 in.), and pure white 'Icicle' (60 cm, 24 in.). *V. s.* var. *incana*, formerly *V. incana* (30 cm, 12 in.) has silvery foliage and bright blue flower spikes.

Many veronicas have a mat-forming or creeping habit and are useful for the front of borders, as groundcovers, and in rockeries.

"I value veronicas for their subtle beauty, but this cultivar has a presence of its own. With its dense, blue flower spikes, shiny, crinkled foliage, and long bloom period, it is worthy of a place near the sitting area on my low deck."

SHARON LANIGAN
SASKATOON, SASKATCHEWAN

- *Veronica gentianoides* (40 cm, 16 in.), gentian veronica, has dark green leaves and produces light blue flowers in late spring. 'Variegata' sports green and white leaves.
- *Veronica pectinata* (10 cm, 4 in.), commonly known as comb speedwell, is an excellent rock garden plant with furry, gray-green leaves and deep blue flowers with a white eye. 'Rosea' is a pink cultivar.
- *Veronica prostrata* (10 cm, 4 in.), harebell speedwell, is another creeping veronica with tiny, gray-green leaves. The species has blue flowers and several cultivars are available, including 'Heavenly Blue', 'Alba' (white), and 'Mrs. Holt' (rose-pink).
- *Veronica spicata* subsp. *nana* 'Blue Carpet' (10 cm, 4 in.) is an outstanding compact plant with mat-forming foliage and deep blue flowers in July.
- *Veronica* x 'Waterperry Blue' (10 cm, 4 in.) has slowly creeping, red-tinted foliage; soft lavender blue flowers bloom from summer through to frost.

Viburnum trilobum
(vye-*burr*-num try-*loh*-bum)

American highbush cranberry

Highbush cranberries and their immediate relatives are thrice-blessed from the point of view of prairie gardeners. They are covered in charming hydrangealike clusters of white flowers in late spring and early summer; they produce colorful fruit (not to be confused with cranberries of Thanksgiving fame) that is attractive to birds and persists through freezing temperatures for visual interest in the winter garden; and their fall foliage is brilliant, varying from yellow, to crimson, to deep wine red, and even to purple. What's more, all cranberries can be grown as multi-stemmed shrubs or pruned into single-stemmed, small trees—perfect substitutes for full-sized trees when space is limited.

Portrait
The American highbush cranberry grows dark green, three-lobed, maplelike leaves;

these are tinged bronze when young and change to yellow, then red, in fall. It produces fragrant, lacy, flat-topped flower clusters in early summer, which are composed of small, fertile, tubular, white flowers in the middle, ringed by showy, flat, sterile ray florets. Blossoms transform into small, juicy, red fruit called drupes. Much appreciated by feathered friends, especially waxwings, the edible fruit also makes delicious jam.

'Alfredo' is attractive but less prolific than the species; 'Andrews' is a compact form with early-ripening fruit; 'Bailey's Compact' has rich red fall color; 'Garry's Pink' produces light shell-pink flower clusters; and 'Wentworth' is a heavy bloomer and prolific fruit producer.

Where to Grow
Place American highbush cranberry at the back of mixed or shrub borders, or at the sunny edge of a woodland garden. Because this and other cranberries often show "self-incompatibility," make sure several different clones of the same species are growing in relatively close proximity to ensure cross-fertilization and successful fruit production. This shrub also makes an excellent hedge.

How to Grow
American highbush cranberry is easy to grow. Plant it in fertile, moist, well-drained soil in full sun or light shade. For best fall color, allow it to dry out a bit by summer's end. Do not deadhead if you wish fruit to set.

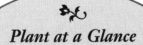

Plant at a Glance

TYPE: deciduous shrub
HEIGHT: 4 m (13 ft.)
WIDTH: 3 m (10 ft.)
SOIL: fertile, moist, well drained
LIGHT: full sun to light shade
FLOWERING TIME: late spring to early summer

PHOTO – PAGE 176

Because this shrub flowers on the previous or current year's growth, refrain from pruning for shape until after flowering is complete. Dead or damaged growth can be removed earlier.

All cranberries are susceptible to aphids so keep an eye out for them, and flush them with a long, strong spray of water as soon as they appear. A telltale sign is curled, puckered foliage.

Propagate by softwood cuttings in summer; sow seed in autumn.

Perfect Partners

Interplant American highbush cranberry with shrubs of contrasting leaf color such as purpleleaf sand cherry (*Prunus* x *cistena*), golden-leaved spireas, or golden variegated dogwood (*Cornus alba* 'Gouchaultii'). If pruned into the shape of a small tree, it can be underplanted with shade-loving, woodland dwellers such as foamflower (*Tiarella* spp.), primula, ferns, and hostas.

Collectors' Choice

Several other viburnums are good choices for prairie gardens; care for them as you would American highbush cranberry.

- *Viburnum dentatum* (3 m, 10 ft.), arrowwood, produces glossy, strongly toothed, green leaves that turn yellow, brilliant red, or reddish purple in the fall. Tiny, tubular, white flowers form flat clusters in early summer, followed by pea-sized, blue-black fruit. Although not as ornamental as other viburnums, arrowwood tolerates heavy, clay-rich, alkaline soils.
- *Viburnum lantana* (4 m, 13 ft.), wayfaring tree, is covered in wrinkled, fuzzy, gray-green foliage that is finely toothed and turns red-purple in the fall. Small, tubular, white flowers appear in loosely domed clusters in early summer; they develop into small, pea-sized, red fruit clusters that ripen to a dark blue-black.

"*Every year our highbush cranberry is loaded with beautiful white blossoms and later bears gorgeous red fruit, which the birds love to feast upon.*"

PATRICIA NOWELL
REGINA, SASKATCHEWAN

'Mohican' is a compact variety with dark green foliage and orange-red fruit.

- *Viburnum lentago* (4 m, 13 ft.), nannyberry, forms an upright shrub with oval, finely toothed, shiny green foliage that turns red and purple in the fall. Small, tubular, fragrant, white flowers are borne in flat-topped clusters in early summer and develop into blue-black fruit by August.
- *Viburnum opulus* (5 m, 16 ft.), European highbush cranberry or Guelder rose, sprouts three-lobed, maplelike, dark green leaves that turn wine red or crimson in the fall. In early summer it produces lacy, flattened flower heads composed of small, white, tubular, fertile flowers at the center ringed by large, white, flat, sterile ray florets; these are followed by fleshy, bright red fruit. 'Aureum' has yellow leaves and performs best in a shady spot. 'Compactum' flowers and fruits like the species but is smaller. 'Nanum' is a dwarf variety that rarely flowers or sets fruit, but is useful for hedging. 'Roseum', or 'Sterile' as it is sometimes called, produces large, sterile, snowball-shaped clusters of white flowers, but no fruit. 'Xanthocarpum' fruit is bright yellow.

Annuals

Botanical name	Common name	Full sun	Part sun	Light shade	Full shade	<30 cm (<12 in.)	30–60 cm (12–24 in.)	60–90 cm (24–36 in.)	>90 cm (>36 in.)	White	Yellow	Orange	Red	Pink	Purple	Blue	Spring	Early Summer	Mid-Summer	Late Summer	Fall	Fragrant	Great foliage	Poisonous	Birds	Butterflies	Bees	Page number
Antirrhinum majus Floral Showers Series	Snapdragon	•	•	•		•				•	•	•	•	•	•					•	•	•					•	26
Consolida ajacis 'Dwarf Hyacinth Flowered'	Larkspur	•	•				•			•				•		•		•						•				48
Eschscholzia californica 'Thai Silk Mixed'	California poppy	•				•						•	•					•			•				•			70
Gladiolus callianthus	Peacock orchid	•		•				•		•												•						88
Helianthus annuus 'Floristan'	Sunflower	•							•	•	•	•	•												•			90
Helichrysum petiolare	Licorice plant	•	•	•		•								•							•		•					92
Impatiens walleriana Super Elfin Series	Impatiens			•	•					•			•	•	•					•	•							106
Lathyrus odoratus 'Old Fashioned Mixed'	Sweet pea								•	•			•	•	•					•	•	•						116
Nicotiana sylvestris	Flowering tobacco	•		•					•	•										•	•	•		•				144
Pelargonium x hortorum	Zonal pelargonium	•	•				•	•		•		•	•	•	•			•		•	•	•				•		152
Petunia Wave Series	Petunia	•	•			•								•	•			•		•	•							156

Perennials

Botanical name	Common name	Full sun	Part sun	Light shade	Full shade	<30 cm (<12 in.)	30–60 cm (12–24 in.)	60–90 cm (24–36 in.)	>90 cm (>36 in.)	White	Yellow	Orange	Red	Pink	Purple	Blue	Spring	Early Summer	Mid-Summer	Late Summer	Fall	Fragrant	Great foliage	Poisonous	Birds	Butterflies	Bees	Page number
Achillea Galaxy Series	Yarrow	•						•		•	•		•	•						•	•		•			•		10
Aconitum 'Bressingham Spire'	Monkshood	•	•	•				•							•	•				•	•			•				12
Ajuga reptans 'Burgundy Glow'	Ajuga	•	•	•		•									•		•						•					16
Alchemilla mollis	Alchemilla	•	•	•			•				•							•					•					18
Allium aflatunense 'Purple Sensation'	Allium	•	•					•							•		•	•					•			•	•	20
Antennaria rosea	Pussytoes	•	•			•								•				•										24
Aquilegia canadensis	Columbine	•	•	•				•					•					•									•	28
Artemisia ludoviciana 'Valerie Finnis'	Artemisia	•					•											•					•					30
Aster novi-belgii 'Audrey'	Michaelmas daisy	•	•						•					•							•	•			•	•		32
Astilbe x arendsii 'Fanal'	Astilbe		•	•	•								•					•								•		34
Bergenia 'Sunningdale'	Bergenia	•	•	•			•							•			•						•					36
Campanula persicifolia 'Chettle Charm'	Peach-leaved bellflower	•	•					•		•								•										40
Chrysanthemum x rubellum 'Clara Curtis'	Hardy mum	•	•					•						•							•				•			44
Clematis viticella 'Purpurea Plena Elegans'	Italian clematis	•	•						•						•			•					•					46
Coreopsis verticillata 'Zagreb'	Coreopsis	•					•				•							•										50
Corydalis lutea	Yellow corydalis		•	•		•					•							•					•		•	•		54
Crocus chrysanthus 'Cream Beauty'	Snow crocus	•	•			•					•						•											56
Delphinium x elatum 'Magic Fountain Hybrids'	Delphinium	•					•			•				•	•	•		•						•	•			58

Perennials – *continued*

Botanical name	Common name	light				height				color							season of bloom					features			wildlife			Page number
		Full sun	Part sun	Light shade	Full shade	<30 cm (<12 in.)	30–60 cm (12–24 in.)	60–90 cm (24–36 in.)	>90 cm (>36 in.)	White	Yellow	Orange	Red	Pink	Purple	Blue	Spring	Early Summer	Mid-Summer	Late Summer	Fall	Fragrant	Great foliage	Poisonous	Birds	Butterflies	Bees	
Dianthus gratianopolitanus 'Tiny Rubies'	Cheddar pink	•	•			•								•				•					•		•	•		60
Dicentra x 'Luxuriant'	Fernleaf bleeding heart	•	•	•			•						•				•	•	•	•				•				62
Doronicum columnae 'Miss Mason'	Leopard's bane	•	•	•			•				•						•	•										64
Echinacea purpurea 'Magnus'	Purple coneflower	•	•					•						•					•	•	•				•	•	•	66
Echinops ritro 'Veitch's Blue'	Globe thistle	•	•					•								•			•	•	•							68
Gaillardia x *grandiflora* 'Goblin'	Gaillardia	•	•			•							•					•	•	•	•					•		82
Geranium x *magnificum*	Showy cranesbill	•	•	•			•								•		•	•					•					84
Geum triflorum	Three-flowered avens	•	•	•			•								•			•	•				•					86
Hemerocallis 'Catherine Woodbury'	Daylily	•	•	•				•						•					•	•					•			94
Heuchera x *brizoides* 'Brandon Pink'	Coral bells	•	•	•			•								•			•	•						•			96
Hosta sieboldiana 'Elegans'	Hosta		•	•	•			•		•					•					•			•					98
Humulus lupulus	Hops	•	•	•					•	•									•	•								100
Iberis sempervirens 'Snowflake'	Perennial candytuft	•	•			•				•							•								•			104
Iris pumila hybrids	Dwarf bearded iris	•	•			•				•								•										108
Iris sibirica 'Silver Edge'	Siberian iris	•	•					•								•		•							•			110
Liatris spicata 'Kobold'	Liatris	•	•				•							•	•				•	•					•			118
Ligularia dentata 'Othello'	Ligularia		•	•					•			•								•			•		•			120
Lilium x Orientpets	Lily	•	•						•			•	•	•				•	•	•					•	•	•	130
Lysimachia punctata	Lysimachia	•	•					•			•								•	•						•		132

Perennials – *continued*

Botanical name	Common name	Full sun	Part sun	Light shade	Full shade	<30 cm (<12 in.)	30–60 cm (12–24 in.)	60–90 cm (24–36 in.)	>90 cm (>36 in.)	White	Yellow	Orange	Red	Pink	Purple	Blue	Spring	Early Summer	Mid-Summer	Late Summer	Fall	Fragrant	Great foliage	Poisonous	Birds	Butterflies	Bees	Page number
Molinia caerulea 'Moorhexe'	Purple moor grass	•	•	•				•							•					•					•	•	•	136
Monarda didyma 'Gardenview Scarlet'	Monarda	•	•	•				•					•						•	•	•				•	•	•	138
Narcissus 'Minnow'	Miniature narcissus	•	•	•		•					•						•							•				140
Nepeta x faassenii 'Dropmore'	Catmint	•	•	•			•									•		•				•						142
Osmunda regalis	Royal fern			•	•				•														•					146
Paeonia lactiflora 'Festiva Maxima'	Peony	•	•					•		•								•				•						148
Papaver orientale 'Prince of Orange'	Oriental poppy	•						•					•					•						•				150
Penstemon digitalis 'Husker Red'	Foxglove penstemon	•	•	•				•		•								•							•			154
Phlox paniculata 'David'	Garden phlox	•	•	•				•		•									•	•	•	•			•	•		160
Polemonium reptans 'Blue Pearl'	Creeping Jacob's ladder	•	•	•			•									•	•	•										166
Primula auricula	Primula		•	•			•						•				•	•										180
Pulmonaria longifolia 'Bertram Anderson'	Longleaf pulmonaria		•	•			•									•	•						•		•			184
Pulsatilla vulgaris var. *rubra*	Red pasqueflower	•	•				•						•				•							•				186
Rudbeckia fulgida var. *sullivantii* 'Goldsturm'	Rudbeckia	•	•					•			•							•		•	•				•	•	•	192
Saxifraga x urbium 'Aureopunctata'	Saxifrage	•	•	•			•			•							•	•					•					198
Scabiosa columbaria 'Butterfly Blue'	Scabiosa	•	•				•									•		•								•	•	200
Scilla sibirica 'Spring Beauty'	Siberian squill	•	•	•		•										•	•										•	202
Sedum 'Autumn Joy'	Showy sedum	•	•				•							•						•	•			•		•	•	204
Thalictrum delavayi 'Hewitt's Double'	Yunnan meadow rue	•	•	•					•						•				•	•	•					•		216

Perennials – *continued*

Botanical name	Common name	Full sun	Part sun	Light shade	Full shade	<30 cm (<12 in.)	30-60 cm (12-24 in.)	60-90 cm (24-36 in.)	>90 cm (>36 in.)	White	Yellow	Orange	Red	Pink	Purple	Blue	Spring	Early Summer	Mid-Summer	Late Summer	Fall	Fragrant	Great foliage	Poisonous	Birds	Butterflies	Bees	Page number
Thymus serpyllum	Mother-of-thyme	•	•			•								•					•	•							•	220
Tradescantia x andersoniana 'Osprey'	Spiderwort	•	•	•			•								•			•	•	•								224
Tulipa tarda	Tarda tulip	•				•					•						•											226
Verbascum chaixii 'Album'	Nettle leaved mullein	•						•		•										•								228
Veronica x 'Sunny Border Blue'	Veronica	•	•				•									•		•	•	•	•				•			230

238

Trees

Botanical name	Common name	Evergreen	Deciduous	Full sun	Part sun	Light shade	Full shade	<1 m (<3.3 ft.)	1–3 m (3.3–10 ft.)	3–5 m (10–16 ft.)	>5 m (>16 ft.)	Green	Gold/Yellow/Orange	Purple/Red	Blue-green	Silver-gray	Ornamental bark	Ornamental flowers/catkins	Ornamental fruit/seeds/nuts	Fragrant	Shelter/food for wildlife	Page number
Acer tataricum var. *ginnala*	Amur maple		•	•	•						•	•	F	F			•		•		•	8
Aesculus glabra	Ohio buckeye		•	•	•						•	•	F					•	•		•	14
Betula papyrifera	Paper birch		•	•							•	•	F				•	•				38
Fraxinus nigra 'Fallgold'	Black ash		•	•							•	•	F									72
Larix sibirica	Siberian larch		•	•							•	•	F					•	•		•	114
Malus x *adstringens* 'Thunderchild'	Rosybloom crabapple		•	•	•					•				F				•	•		•	134
Picea pungens f. *glauca* 'Globosa'	Globe Colorado blue spruce	•		•					•						•						•	162
Pinus cembra	Swiss stone pine	•		•							•	•							•		•	164
Populus tremula 'Erecta'	Swedish columnar aspen		•	•							•	•	F									168
Quercus macrocarpa	Bur oak		•	•	•						•	•	F						•		•	188
Sorbus decora 'Grootendorst'	Showy mountain ash		•	•	•						•	•	F				•	•	•	•	•	208
Syringa reticulata	Japanese tree lilac		•	•	•						•	•		F			•	•		•		214
Thuja occidentalis 'Brandon'	Eastern white cedar	•		•	•					•		•	F								•	218
Tilia x *flavescens* 'Dropmore'	Linden		•	•	•						•	•	F					•		•	•	222

Shrubs

Botanical name	Common name	Evergreen	Deciduous	Full sun	Part sun	Light shade	Full shade	<1 m (<3.3 ft.)	1–3 m (3.3–10 ft.)	3–5 m (10–16 ft.)	>5 m (>16 ft.)	Green	Gold/Yellow/Orange	Purple/Red	Blue-green	Silver-gray	Ornamental bark	Ornamental flowers/catkins	Ornamental fruit/seeds/nuts	Fragrant	Shelter/food for wildlife	Page number
Amelanchier alnifolia 'Northline'	Saskatoon		•	•					•			•	F	F				•	•	•	•	22
Caragana arborescens 'Lorbergii'	Fern-leaved caragana		•	•						•		•	F					•	•		•	42
Cornus alba 'Sibirica'	Siberian coral dogwood		•	•	•	•			•			•		F			•	•	•		•	52
Hydrangea arborescens 'Annabelle'	Smooth hydrangea		•		•	•			•			•	F				•	•				102
Juniperus scopulorum 'Medora'	Rocky Mountain juniper	•		•						•		•			•						•	112
Philadelphus lewisii 'Blizzard'	Mock orange		•	•	•				•			•	F					•		•	•	158
Potentilla fruticosa 'Pink Beauty'	Potentilla		•	•	•			•				•	F					•				178
Prunus tomentosa	Nanking cherry		•	•	•				•			•	F					•	•	•	•	182
Rosa 'Winnipeg Parks'	Hardy shrub rose		•	•	•				•			•	F					•			•	190
Salix silicola 'Polar Bear'	Willow		•	•	•			•								•		•			•	194
Sambucus racemosa	European red elder		•	•	•				•			•	F					•	•		•	196
Shepherdia argentea	Silver buffaloberry		•	•	•					•						•			•		•	206
Spiraea japonica 'Little Princess'	Japanese spirea		•	•	•			•				•	F					•			•	210
Syringa meyeri 'Palibin'	Dwarf Korean lilac		•	•	•				•			•		F				•		•		212
Viburnum trilobum	American highbush cranberry		•	•	•				•			•	F	F				•	•	•	•	232

References

Books

Addison, Josephine, and Hillhouse, Cherry. *Treasury of Flower Lore*. London, Eng.: Bloomsbury Publishing, 1997.

Bennett, Jennifer, and Forsyth, Turid. *The Annual Garden*. Willowdale, ON: Firefly Books Ltd., 1998.

The Best of Fine Gardening: Perennials. Newtown, CT: Taunton Press, 1993.

The Best of Fine Gardening: Shrubs and Trees. Newtown, CT: Taunton Press, 1993.

Bird, Richard. *Hardy Perennials*. London, Eng.: Ward Lock, 1998.

Brickell, C., Cole, T., and Zuk, J., eds. *Reader's Digest A–Z Encyclopedia of Garden Plants*. Westmount, QC: The Reader's Digest Association, Inc., 1997.

Calgary Horticultural Society. *The Calgary Gardener*. Calgary, AB: Fifth House Publishers, 1996.

Casselman, Bill. *Canadian Garden Words*. Toronto, ON: Little, Brown and Company (Canada) Ltd., 1997.

Cavendish Books, *Cavendish Plant Guides: Bulbs*. Vancouver, BC: Cavendish Books Inc., 1997.

Cavendish Books, *Cavendish Plant Guides: Perennials*. Vancouver, BC: Cavendish Books Inc., 1996.

Cavendish Books, *Cavendish Plant Guides: Shrubs and Climbers*. Vancouver, BC: Cavendish Books Inc., 1996.

Cooke, Blaise. *Pelargoniums*. New York, NY: Lorenz Books, 1998.

Coombes, Allen, and Tripp, Kim. *The Complete Book of Shrubs*. Pleasantville, NY: The Reader's Digest Association, Inc., 1998.

Crockett, James. *Evergreens*. Alexandria, VA: Time–Life Books, 1971.

Crockett, James. *Trees*. Alexandria, VA: Time–Life Books, 1972.

Cutler, Karan D., ed. *Vines*. Charlotte, VT: Camden House Publishing, Inc., 1992.

Dobelis, Inge, ed. *Reader's Digest Magic and Medicine of Plants*. Westmount, QC: The Reader's Digest Association, Inc., 1986.

Ellis, Barbara W. *Taylor's Guide to Growing North America's Favorite Plants*. New York, NY: Houghton Miflin Company, 1998.

Galbally, John and Eileen. *Carnations and Pinks for Garden and Greenhouse*. Portland, OR: Timber Press, 1997.

Grimshaw, John. *The Gardener's Atlas*. Willowdale, ON: Firefly Books Ltd., 1998.

Harris, Marjorie. *The Canadian Gardener's Guide to Foliage and Garden Design*. Toronto, ON: Random House, 1993.

Heger, Mike, and Whitman, John. *Growing Perennials in Cold Climates*. Chicago, IL: Contemporary Books, 1998.

Hendrickson, Robert. *Ladybugs, Tiger Lilies &*

Wallflowers: A Gardener's Book of Words. New York, NY: Prentice Hall, 1993.

Hessayon, D. G. *The New Bedding Plant Expert*. London, Eng.: Expert Books, 1997.

Hill, Lewis and Nancy. *Successful Perennial Gardening*. Pownal, VT: Storey Communications, 1988.

Hogue, Marjorie M. *Amazing Annuals*. Willowdale, ON: Firefly Books Ltd., 1999.

Hole, Lois. *Bedding Plant Favorites*. Edmonton, AB: Lone Pine Publishing, 1994.

Hole, Lois. *Favorite Trees and Shrubs*. Edmonton, AB: Lone Pine Publishing, 1997.

Hole, Lois. *Perennial Favorites*. Edmonton, AB: Lone Pine Publishing, 1995.

Hole, Lois. *Rose Favorites*. Edmonton, AB: Lone Pine Publishing, 1997.

Jacobson, Arthur L. *North American Landscape Trees*. Berkeley, CA: Ten Speed Press, 1996.

Kelly, John, ed. *The Hillier Gardener's Guide to Trees and Shrubs*. Pleasantville, NY: The Reader's Digest Association, Inc., 1997.

Keville, Kathi. *Herbs: An Illustrated Encyclopedia*. New York, NY: Friedman/Fairfax Publishers, 1994.

Key, Hazel. *Pelargoniums*. London, Eng.: Cassell Educational Limited for the Royal Horticultural Society, 1993.

Knowles, Hugh. *Woody Ornamentals for the Prairies*. Rev. ed. Edmonton, AB: University of Alberta, Faculty of Extension, 1995.

Kremer, Bruno P. *Shrubs in the Wild and in Gardens*. Hauppauge, NY: Barron's Educational Series, Inc., 1995.

Lane, Clive. *Cottage Garden Annuals*. London, Eng.: David and Charles, 1997.

Leatherbarrow, Liesbeth, and Reynolds, Lesley. *The Calgary Gardener, Volume Two: Beyond the Basics*. Calgary, AB: Fifth House Publishers, 1998.

Lima, Patrick. *The Art of Perennial Gardening*. Willowdale, ON: Firefly Books Ltd., 1998.

Lunardi, Costanza. *Shrubs and Vines*. New York, NY: Simon and Schuster, 1987.

Martin, Laura. *Garden Flower Folklore*. Chester, CT: The Globe Pequot Press, 1987.

Martin, Tovah. *Heirloom Flowers*. New York, NY: Fireside, Simon and Schuster, 1999.

McDonald, Elvin. *The 100 Best Bulbs: A Practical Encyclopedia*. New York, NY: Random House, 1995.

The 1998 Prairie Garden. Winnipeg, MB: Winnipeg Horticultural Society, 1998.

The 1999 Prairie Garden. Winnipeg, MB: Winnipeg Horticultural Society, 1999.

Ortho Books. *All About Trees*. San Ramon, CA: Ortho Books, Chevron Chemical Company, 1982.

Osborne, Robert. *Hardy Trees and Shrubs*. Toronto, ON: Key Porter Books Ltd., 1996.

Page, Martin. *The Gardener's Guide to Growing Peonies*. Portland, OR: Timber Press, 1997.

Phillips, Roger, and Rix, Martyn. *The Random House Book of Perennials, Volume 1: Early Perennials*. New York, NY: Random House, 1991.

Phillips, Roger, and Rix, Martyn. *The Random House Book of Perennials, Volume 2: Late Perennials*. New York, NY: Random House, 1991.

Proctor, Rob. *Annuals and Bulbs*. Emmaus, PA: Rodale Press, 1995.

Proctor, Rob. *Perennials: Enduring Classics for the Contemporary Garden*. New York, NY: Running Heads Incorporated, 1990.

Rice, Graham. *The Complete Book of Perennials*. Pleasantville, NY: The Reader's Digest Association, Inc., 1996.

Sanders, Jack. *Hedgemaids and Fairy Candles: The Lives and Lore of North American Wildflowers*. Camden, ME: Ragged Mountain Press, 1995.

Simpson, Brenan. *Flowers at my Feet: Western Wildflowers in Legend, Literature and Lore*. Surrey, BC: Hancock House, 1996.

Smith, A. W. *A Gardener's Handbook of Plant Names*. Mineola, NY: Dover Publications, 1997.

Stearn, William. *Stearn's Dictionary of Plant Names for Gardeners*. London, Eng.: Cassell Publishers Ltd., 1992.

Sternberg, Guy, and Wilson, Jim. *Landscaping with Native Trees*. Shelburne, VT: Chapters Publishing Ltd., 1995.

Sunset Books, eds. *Bulbs*. Menlo Park, CA: Sunset Publishing Corporation, 1993.

Sunset Books, eds. *Trees and Shrubs*. Menlo Park, CA: Sunset Publishing Corporation, 1993.

Thomas, R. William, ed. *Trees and Shrubs*. New York, NY: William Morrow and Company, Inc., 1992.

Toop, Edgar. *Annuals for the Prairies*. Edmonton, AB: Lone Pine Publishing, 1993.

Toop, Edgar, and Williams, Sara. *Perennials for the Prairies*. Edmonton, AB: University of Alberta, Faculty of Extension, 1991.

University of Alberta, Department of Extension. *Home Gardening Course*. Edmonton, AB: University of Alberta, Faculty of Extension, 1986.

Wells, Diana. *100 Flowers and How They Got Their Names*. Chapel Hill, NC: Algonquin Books of Chapel Hill, 1997.

Williams, Sara. *Creating the Prairie Xeriscape*. Saskatoon, SK: University Extension Press, University of Saskatchewan, 1997.

Winterrowd, Wayne. *Annuals for Connoisseurs*. New York, NY: Prentice Hall, 1992.

Woods, Christopher. *Encyclopedia of Perennials: A Gardener's Guide*. New York, NY: Facts on File, Inc., 1992.

Zucker, Isabel. *Flowering Shrubs and Small Trees*. New York, NY: Michael Friedman Publishing Group, 1990.

Articles

Adam, Judith. "Scent and Sentiment." *Gardening Life* (Spring 1997): 50.

Alexander, Jack. "Take a New Look at Lilacs." *Fine Gardening*, No. 66 (April 1999): 32.

Baskerville, Joanne. "Hosta—Shady Aristocrats." *Gardens West*, Vol. 11, No. 6 (1997): 10.

Baskerville, Joanne. "The Old Crimson Clove." *Gardens West*, Vol. 12, No. 4 (1998): 25.

Butt, Donna. "Petunias." *The Gardener for the Prairies* (Spring 1999): 15.

Charest, Alain. "Wild and Woolly Mulleins." *Fine Gardening*, No. 55 (June 1997): 58.

"Discovery Elm." *The Gardener for the Prairies* (Summer 1998): 19.

Doyle, Judith. "Aconitum." *Calgary Gardening*, Vol. 12, No. 6 (July 1998): 12.

Doyle, Judith. "Campanula." *Calgary Gardening*, Vol. 8, No. 6 (July 1994): 8.

Doyle, Judith. "Echinops." *Calgary Gardening*, Vol. 8, No. 8 (October/December 1994): 8.

Doyle, Judith. "Geum." *Calgary Gardening*, Vol. 6, No. 3 (April 1992): 11.

Doyle, Judith. "Ligularia." *Calgary Gardening*, Vol. 9, No. 8 (October/November 1995): 8.

Doyle, Judith. "Picea." *Calgary Gardening*, Vol. 11, No. 1 (December 1996/January 1997): 10.

Doyle, Judith. "Primula." *Calgary Gardening*, Vol. 6, No. 2 (March 1992): 4.

Doyle, Judith. "Scilla." *Calgary Gardening*, Vol. 12, No. 2 (February/March 1998): 10.

Doyle, Judith. "Verbascum." *Calgary Gardening*, Vol. 9, No. 5 (June 1995): 8.

Doyle, Judith. "Veronica." *Calgary Gardening*, Vol. 7, No. 4 (May 1993): 6.

Driver, Margaret. "Sick Lilacs." *The Saskatchewan Gardener* (Summer 1997): 30.

du Toit, Angela. "Alchemilla." *Calgary Gardening*, Vol. 10, No. 6 (July 1996): 10.

Eddison, Sydney. "Desirable Daylilies." *Fine Gardening*, No. 56 (August 1997): 35.

Giles, Robert. "An Ode to the Lily." *Canadian Gardening* (October/November 1993): 43.

Girard, Ken. "Dwarf Conifers." *Calgary Gardening*, Vol. 11, No. 2 (February/March 1997): 8.

Girard, Ken. "Hostas." *Calgary Gardening*, Vol. 10, No. 6 (July 1996): 16.

Girard, Ken. "Penstemons—Beard Tongues." *Calgary Gardening*, Vol. 12, No. 7 (August/September 1998): 8.

Girard, Ken. "Peonies." *Calgary Gardening*, Vol. 7, No. 6 (July 1993): 8.

Girard, Ken. "Saxifrages." *Calgary Gardening*, Vol. 10, No. 3 (April 1996): 8.

Girard, Ken, and Doyle, J. "Stonecrops." *Calgary Gardening*, Vol. 12, No. 1 (December 1997/January 1998): 8.

Langston, Laura. "Poppy Power." *Canadian Gardening* (June/July 1998): 38.

Lanigan, Sharon. "Poppies for Pleasure." *The Gardener for the Prairies* (Fall 1998): 11.

Lima, Patrick. "A Yearning for Yarrow." *Canadian Gardening* (August/September 1993): 36.

Maddocks, Judy. "Columbine." *Canadian Gardening* (December 1997/January 1998): 90.

Matthews, Karen. "Hens & Chicks are Worth Crowing About." *Fine Gardening*, No. 52 (November/December 1996): 33.

Moro, Frank. "Extending the Season: Lilac Time Gets Longer." *The Gardener for the Prairies* (Winter 1998): 22.

Patry, Sandy. "Siberian Iris." *The Gardener for the Prairies* (Winter 1998): 18.

Peek, Elaine. "Lilac." *Gardening in Alberta*, Vol. III, No. II (March 1994): 25.

Peek, Elaine. "Penstemon Possibilities." *The Gardener for the Prairies* (Spring 1998): 34.

Peek, Elaine. "Primulas: The First Roses of Spring." *The Gardener for the Prairies* (Winter 1998): 11.

Pellett, Dorothy. "Designing with Hostas." *Fine Gardening*, No. 48 (March/April 1996): 70.

"Perennial Plant of the Year." *The Gardener for the Prairies* (Spring 1998): 39.

Sheldon, Elisabeth. "Alluring, Enduring Lysimachias." *Fine Gardening*, No. 51 (September/October 1996): 60.

Singer, Carolyn. "Artemisias Dress the Garden in Silver." *Fine Gardening*, No. 44 (August 1995): 48.

Spielberg, Sue. "Give Us Our Daily Blooms." *Practical Gardening* (August 1996): 34.

Troesch, Maureen. "Small Bulbs, Big Impact." *The Saskatchewan Gardener* (Spring 1997): 21.

Wilde, Ellen. "Splendid, Spunky Penstemons." *Fine Gardening*, No. 61 (June 1998): 28.

Index

In this index, numbers appearing in Roman bold type indicate main entries in the book; italic bold type indicates photographs.

Fern-leaved caragana (*Caragana arborescens*)
42–43, 77

Festuca glauca (blue fescue) 25, 137

Feverfew (see *Tanacetum*)

Filipendula (meadowsweet) 63, 133, 139, 217: *F. rubra*
(queen-of-the-prairie) 147, 217; *F. ulmaria*
(queen-of-the-meadow) 129, 217; *F. vulgaris*
(dropwort) 217

Flame willow (*Salix* 'Flame') 195

Flanders poppy (*Papaver commutatum*) 71

Flat sea holly (*Eryngium planum*) 69

Flax (see *Linum*)

Fleabane (*Erigeron*) 51

Flowering almond (*Prunus tenella*) 183

Flowering tobacco (*Nicotiana sylvestris*) *127*, **144–145**

Foamflower (see *Tiarella*)

Foamy bells (x *Heucherella*) 97

Forget-me-not (*Myosotis*) 65, 191

Forget-me-not, Chinese (*Cynoglossum amabile*) 71

Forsythia x 'Northern Gold' (forsythia) 53

Foxglove (see *Digitalis*)

Foxglove penstemon (*Penstemon digitalis* 'Husker
Red') 89, *128*, **154–155**, 163

Fragaria 'Pink Panda' (strawberry) 87

Fraxinus (ash): *F. americana* (white ash) 'Northern
Blaze' 81; *F. mandshurica* (Manchurian ash) 81; *F.
nigra* (black ash) 'Fallgold' **72**, *80*, **81**; *F.* x
'Northern Gem' 81; *F.* x 'Northern Treasure' 81;
F. pennsylvanica var. *subintegerrima* (green ash) 81

Fringed bleeding heart (*Dicentra eximia*) 62, 167

Fringed loosestrife (*Lysimachia ciliata*) 133

Fritillaria (fritillary): *F. meleagris* (checkered lily,
snake's head fritillary) 203; *F. pallidiflora* (Siberian
fritillary) 203; *F. pudica* (yellow fritillary) 203

Fritillary (see *Fritillaria*)

Fuchsia x *hybrida* 107

Fumitory (see *Corydalis*)

G

Gaillardia (blanket flower): *G. aristata* 82, 83; *G.* x
grandiflora 'Baby Cole' 82, 'Burgundy' 82,
'Goblin' ('Kobold') **82–83**, *121*, 'Golden Goblin'
82, 'Monarch' 82; *G. pulchella* 82, 83

Galanthus (snowdrop) 57, 202, 203: *G. elwesii* (giant
snowdrop) 57; *G. nivalis* (common snowdrop)
57, 183

Galium odoratum (sweet woodruff) 99

Garden monkshood (*Aconitum napellus*) 13

Garden mum (*Chrysanthemum* x *morifolium*,
Dendranthema x *grandiflora*) 45

Garden phlox (*Phlox paniculata*) 11, 41, 69, 119, 131,
160–161, 163, *169*, 179, 231

Garland spirea (*Spiraea* x *arguta*) 211

Gayfeather (see *Liatris*)

Gentian veronica (*Veronica gentianoides*) 231

Geranium (cranesbill) 21, 27, 29, 41, 47, 63, 97, 109,
111, 133, 139, 143, 151, 225, 231: *G.* x 'Ann
Folkard' 85; *G. cinereum* 'Ballerina' 25, 85; *G. dalmaticum* 85; *G. endressii* 85; *G.* x 'Johnson's Blue'
55, 65, 85, 133; *G. macrorrhizum* 85; *G.* x *magnificum* (showy cranesbill) **84–85**, *121*; *G. phaeum* 85,
'Mourning Widow' 17; *G. pratense* 85; *G. sanguineum prostratum* 85; *G. viscosissimum* (sticky
geranium) 84

Geranium (see *Geranium, Pelargonium*)

Geum (avens): *G. chiloense* 'Lady Stratheden' 87,

'Mrs. Bradshaw' 87, *G. coccineum* (*G.* x *borisii*) 87;
G. rivale (water avens) 87; *G. triflorum* (prairie
smoke, three-flowered avens) **86–87**, *121*; *G.
urbanum* var. *sibiricum* (Siberian avens) 87

Giant scabious (*Cephalaria gigantea*) 201

Giant snowdrop (*Galanthus elwesii*) 57

Giant tree lilac (*Syringa reticulata, S. reticulata* var.
amurensis) *174*, **214–215**

Ginnala maple (*Acer tataricum* var. *ginnala*) **8–9**,
73, 165

Gladiolus 89: *G. byzantinus* 89; *G. callianthus*
(*Acidanthera bicolor* var. *murielae, A. murieliae*,
peacock orchid, sweet scented gladiolus)
88–89, *121*

Globe caragana (*Caragana frutex* 'Globosa') 43

Globe Colorado blue spruce (*P. pungens* f. *glauca*
'Globosa') 9, **162–163**, *169*, 197, 215

Globe thistle (see *Echinops*)

Globeflower (*Trollius cultorum* hybrids) 65, 81, 167

Gloriosa daisy (*Rudbeckia hirta*) 193

Glory-of-the-snow (*Chionodoxa luciliae*) 57, 203

Goatsbeard (see *Aruncus*)

Golddust stonecrop (*Sedum acre*) 205

Golden bean (*Thermopsis rhombifolia*) 83

Golden bleeding heart (*Corydalis lutea*) **54–55**, *78*,
167, 199

Golden columbine (*Aquilegia chrysantha*) 29

Golden flowering currant (*Ribes aureum*) 23

Golden garlic (*Allium moly*) 21

Golden lemon thyme (*Thymus* x *citriodorus* 'Gold
Edge') 221

Golden London pride (*Saxifraga* x *urbium*
'Aureopunctata') *172*, **198–199**

Golden ninebark (*Physocarpus opulifolius* 'Dart's Gold')
9, 23, 53, 159, 197, 211

Golden oregano (*Oregano vulgare* 'Aureum') 25, 221

Goldenrod (see *Solidago*)

Goldmoss stonecrop (*Sedum acre*) 205

Goniolimon tataricum (German statice) 19, 119

Gooseberry (see *Ribes*)

Gooseneck loosestrife (*Lysimachia clethroides*) 129, 133

Grape hyacinth (see *Muscari*)

Grape, Manitoba (*Vitis riparia*) 101

Grape, riverbank (*Vitis riparia*) 101

Grass, ornamental (see *Arrhenatherum elatius* var. *bul-
bosum, Festuca glauca, Hakonechloa macra,
Helictotrichon sempervirens, Molinia caerulea,
Schizachyrium scoparium, Sisyrinchium montanum*)

Grass pink (*Dianthus plumarius*) 60, 61

Grecian windflower (*Anemone blanda*) 187

Greek oregano (*Oregano vulgare* subsp. *hirtum*) 221

Greek valerian (*Polemonium reptans*) 135, **166–167**,
169, 199

Green ash (*Fraxinus pennsylvanica* var.
subintegerrima) 81

Green-headed coneflower (*Rudbeckia laciniata*) 193

'Griffin' poplar (*Populus* 'Brooks No. 2') 177

Guelder rose (*Viburnum opulus*) 233

Gypsophila (annual baby's breath) 69, 151

H

Hakone grass (*Hakonechloa macra*) 99, 137

Hakonechloa macra (hakone grass) 99, 'Aureola' 137

Hakura Nishiki Japanese willow (*Salix integra* 'Alba
Maculata') 195